9 + 7

10

THE TEACHING OF THE
SOCIAL STUDIES
IN A CHANGING WORLD

THE TEACHING OF THE
SOCIAL STUDIES
IN A CHANGING WORLD

by

FREDERICK K. BRANOM, Ph.D.

Chairman, Department of Social Sciences
Chicago Teachers College

New York W·H·SADLIER·INC. *Chicago*

MANUFACTURED IN THE UNITED STATES OF AMERICA

TO

THE TEACHERS AND PUPILS
OF OUR GREAT LAND

PREFACE

ONE OF the great problems of modern times is the proper education of our boys and girls so that they will become good intelligent American citizens. The Social Studies have a leading role in helping to solve this problem by furnishing many of those experiences which pupils should have in citizenship training.

The Teaching of the Social Studies in a Changing World is written for prospective teachers and for those teachers in service in the elementary grades and high schools who are seeking better ways of teaching the social studies. Teaching never becomes monotonous to those individuals who really like to teach, because they are always trying to discover better methods of placing worthwhile experiences before their pupils. Problems are continually arising in the teaching of the social studies. Some of them are easy to solve, while others require much thinking and effort on the part of the teacher and pupils. The successful teacher is one who recognizes problems and who succeeds in wisely solving them.

It was in 1908 that the author began teaching in a one-room country school. Since that time he has had the priceless experience of teaching in every grade from the kindergarten through the high school. For many years he has been training teachers to understand and to teach the social studies. This book is based chiefly upon (1) first-hand experiences gained in more than thirty years of teaching, (2) conversations with teachers and pupils, (3) observations made in many social studies classrooms, and (4) extensive reading.

The Teaching of the Social Studies in a Changing World attempts to give some of the information which teachers want to know about the teaching of the social studies. The idea is stressed that teachers are teaching children, not subject matter, and that the schools exist for educating children. Such topics as the content of the social studies, the importance of the social studies teacher, the use of community resources, the teaching of current events, the use of audio-visual aids, various methods of teaching, the organization of the curriculum, and testing are discussed from various viewpoints. Questions for study and research and a well-selected bibliography of recent references follow each chapter.

The author believes that there is no one common method which should be used by all teachers. There are as many good plans as there are successful teachers. Each teacher makes his own plan after much thought and research. Even after the plan is made, the teacher must be continually revising it so that it will be attuned to changes which are taking place in our world. He who is content to employ the same plan which he used yesterday in teaching is not even standing still, but is going backwards. The teacher of the social studies occupies a responsible place in the lives of his pupils and he is ever seeking better methods of guiding them in living fuller and more useful lives. There will always be better methods of teaching for those who are willing to make the effort of discovering them. A teacher should feel free to experiment because progress can only be made by trying new plans.

The author has written this book with the thought of helping teachers to have more confidence in themselves and to perform their work more efficiently. He hopes that the reading of the different chapters will raise questions which will result in much constructive thinking and in better methods of teaching.

During the past few years much advance has been made in teaching the social studies, but many problems still remain to be solved satisfactorily. There will surely be problems as long as we keep on making progress. Improved methods of teaching await to be discovered by those teachers who are willing to work hard and who have visions of doing their work a little better tomorrow than they do it today.

The author wishes to acknowledge the suggestions and aid which he has received from his colleagues in the Department of Social Sciences in the Chicago Teachers College and from the many hundreds of students and teachers who have been in his classes. He also wishes to thank Dr. John A. Bartky, president of the Chicago Teachers College, for his cooperation and words of encouragement. Deep appreciation is due Opal Oneal and George Scott for their critical reading of the manuscript.

FREDERICK K. BRANOM

CONTENTS

THE TEACHING OF THE
SOCIAL STUDIES
IN A CHANGING WORLD

THE SOCIAL STUDIES AND THEIR CONTRIBUTIONS TO THE AMERICAN WAY OF LIFE

WHAT ARE THE SOCIAL STUDIES?

MANY PROBLEMS confront teachers in our schools, but the most important problem is to furnish those activities and experiences which pupils need in the preparation for good citizenship. Our schools must prepare children to be good citizens not only at the present time but also in the future. The children of today will be the adults of tomorrow, and they must receive good training in the schools if they are going to meet successfully the problems of life. The teacher should be a person of keen vision, much wisdom, and intelligent imagination. He somewhat resembles a man who climbs to the top of a high mountain peak to get a view of the surrounding country. In his imagination, the teacher often ascends to the top of some pinnacle and visualizes not only present-day society, but what he thinks the society of the future may be.

The people of the United States believe in democracy. They have faith in the American way of life and they are willing to make any necessary sacrifices in order to keep the torch of freedom burning in our country. Schools have been established all over our land where children may receive the right kind of training in the American way of living. In a democracy, there must be plenty of schools where all children have the opportunity of receiving the education which they need in living successful and happy lives.

Different subjects are taught in our schools. These subjects furnish many activities and experiences for the pupils. Every good activity contributes to citizenship. Therefore, every subject in the school aids in the training of useful citizens. If a subject does not aid in the training of useful citizens, it does not belong in the curriculum.

Since each subject in our schools (1) furnishes training in citizenship and in the American way of life, (2) gives children a deeper understanding of social life and develops in them the right kind of social living, and (3) deals with human affairs to a certain extent, some people think that all subjects should be included in the social studies. Sometimes such terms as social arithmetic, social English, and social art are used. Of course it is true that all subjects do have some connection with human beings. They have a social purpose or there would be no good reason for teaching them. However, just because any subject has a social purpose and treats of human affairs is no good reason why it should be called a social study. Only those subjects which give direct training in citizenship and which function very clearly in the development of American society should be called social studies. Such subjects treat chiefly of human affairs and of the interrelationships of men and of nations. They furnish much of the content which pupils should study for effective and intelligent citizenship.

The subjects which are generally considered as social studies in the grades and in the high schools are history, geography, civics, economics, and sociology. Some teachers have an incorrect idea about the social studies. They make the mistake of thinking that the social studies must be a combination of certain school subjects. For example, history, civics, and geography might be combined to form fused, integrated, or unified materials where subject boundaries do not exist or only faintly exist. Such materials are only parts of the social studies. They are some of the forms which the social studies may take in teaching. Even the term "social studies" suggests that there are several studies or subjects.

MEANING OF THE TERM "SOCIAL STUDIES"

What is there in a name? Some teachers and educators pay too much attention to the minor problems of life and not enough attention to the big problems. Too often they argue among themselves about the meanings of terms, while the actual teaching of a subject is slighted. So while we are striving to guide our boys and girls along the right paths of learning, let us keep from getting sidetracked over needless discussions of the meanings of terms. There have been too many educational meetings where most of the discussions centered around topics which showed the oratorical abilities of the speakers in place of their teaching abilities. Teachers usually go to educational meetings to get help and inspiration in solving their problems, but sometimes they are sadly disappointed in what they see and receive. Too much time is frequently taken up with the theoretical side and not enough time is usually given to the practical side. Now, we do not mean that we should not strive to understand the meanings of terms and the theories that are related to them; but we do mean that we should not let the little things of life so absorb our interests and thoughts that we fail to give the necessary considerations to the more important problems that are facing us. Successful teachers well know this to be true.

Should we use the term "social sciences" or the term "social studies" for the work which is being taught in the grades and in the high school? A few teachers think we should use the term "social sciences" while many others believe we should use the term "social studies." Since the ordinary teacher is more concerned with teaching children than with the name given to the work he is teaching, the question of what term to use is a minor one. The big question is how to teach successfully the children.

Those teachers who favor the term "social sciences" believe that this name is a more discriminating term than "social studies." They think that the term "social sciences" signifies that it includes only those subjects which deal mainly with the relations between people. On the other hand, they say that the term "social studies" is likely to give the idea that all subjects should be included in the term, since all of them have a social purpose and are related to human development.

Those teachers who prefer to use the term "social studies" think that the materials that are taught in the grades and in the high schools should not be classified as social sciences. They claim that the social sciences are materials which have been obtained by diligent research and experimentation by scholars, who carefully collected, observed, recorded, analyzed, and studied certain facts and drew conclusions from them. Our knowledge is increased by the social sciences. They are developed on the adult level, their materials are scholarly, and they are usually not in a form that can be easily understood by children. According to this view, the social sciences are for advanced students.

The social studies are parts of the social sciences which may be profitably studied by pupils. When these parts are studied by children we do not expect them to discover facts which are unknown to scholars in the social sciences. Of course the children will add to their own knowledge and discover facts which are unknown to them. However, they are not mature enough in experience to study the materials in such a way that our knowledge of the field will be increased.

Let us consider a fourth grade class which is studying about "Life in the Cold Deserts." The children read books which have been written for them on their reading level. They look at pictures, possibly visit a museum to see specimens from the Northland, and do many other activities in studying the unit. At the end of their study, they sum up what they have learned. However, their summaries do not add anything additional to our total knowledge of the cold deserts. The summaries which the children make this year will be similar to the summaries which the children in the fourth grade have made in past years. Naturally, some improvement will be shown because of using any new knowledge and methods which our scholars and teachers have developed during the past year. The children use the social studies materials which have been taken from the social sciences. These materials have been simplified so that they may be easily understood by the children.

Even in the upper grades and in the high school, the pupils are largely using social studies materials which are taken from the social sciences. Under the expert direction of teachers, pupils gradually learn how to depend upon themselves in studying. They search for facts in libraries and museums. They take excursions to obtain first-hand information. They carry on a certain amount of experimentation. Keeping all of these facts in mind, it is still probably true that the term "social studies" instead of "social sciences" better explains the work which is being studied in all grades.

WHAT IS AMERICAN DEMOCRACY?

Today, we hear much about American democracy. We hear or read that democracy is being challenged as never before and that it is on the defensive. We are told that too many of us have taken our democracy for granted and that it is time for us to wake up and help keep the torch of democracy burning. Otherwise, they say we are in danger of losing the blessings of liberty for which many of our ancestors fought and died. Just what do we mean by American democracy and what are the social studies doing to preserve and improve it?

We may say that American democracy is the American way of life. It is a loyal citizenship which believes that unity, justice, fairness, tolerance, honesty, personal integrity, human equality and brotherhood, freedom of discussion and inquiry, the nobility of labor, and the good of the community are worth any necessary sacrifices. A good citizen believes that the world owes him very little, but that he owes the world very much for the privileges which he enjoys. He realizes that his knowledge is very limited and he is willing to make an effort to learn more. He endeavors to understand the many elements and relationships that make up his environment.

The American way of life is one in which each person is given an opportunity of pursuing his own ambitions and interests, so long as he keeps in mind his social responsibilities and does not interfere with the general welfare of others. The true American is one who is willing to listen to his fellow men and to abide by the will of the majority, since he knows that his success and happiness are closely related to the success and happiness of others. He has an appreciation of the beautiful things of life, and he endeavors to spend his leisure time in a profitable way to himself and to his neighbors.

Probably all teachers would generally agree that a good citizen is one who, according to his ability, (1) takes part in public affairs, (2) cooperates and works in harmony with his neighbors, (3) tries to understand the local, state, national, and international problems of the day, (4) pays his just debts, (5) wisely supports and looks after his family, (6) supports all causes which are for the betterment of mankind and works against those which tend to degrade mankind, (7) practices the conservation of our human and natural resources, (8) is willing to assume his share of responsibility in our democratic society, and (9) tries in various ways to make this world a better place in which all people may live.

Of course there are many other qualities of a good citizen besides those which have been mentioned in this discussion. It would pay each person to make a list of the qualities which he thinks a good citizen should possess, and then compare his list with the lists made by others. By doing this he will have fixed more firmly in his mind the meaning of citizenship. He will likely realize that being a good citizen at all times and in all places is not so easy as it appears. Certain responsibilities, as well as certain pleasures, go with being a good citizen, and at times a good citizen may have to act contrary to the wishes of some of his friends.

It is no easy matter to furnish pupils with those life experiences which (1) teach them the meaning of good citizenship, (2) create within them the desire to form the right ideals, habits, and attitudes of good citizens and to take an active part in everyday affairs, (3) give them an intelligent understanding of our modern social institutions, (4) help them to find their places in society and to play their parts in the affairs of life, (5) cause them to use our resources efficiently and wisely, (6) impart to them an understanding of the more important problems of the people throughout the world, and (7) grant to them the most permanent and valuable things in life.

Teaching is no easy profession and when we think about the important part a teacher plays in the education of the youth of our land, we see that a teacher has a very responsible position. A teacher should be a guide and an inspiration to his pupils and he should be highly respected. He should have a good influence. Only those people should be teachers who actually love children and like to teach, who believe that the best educational opportunities should be given to the youth of our land, and who are willing to work hard in helping the children gain a better understanding of how to meet the problems of life. Teachers should realize that schools exist for pupils and not for the teachers who are employed to teach in them. The child is the most important part of any school.

A CHANGING WORLD

Many people talk about a changing world. Changes are continually occurring which give us new problems and which cause us to modify our ways of thinking and living. For example, one hundred years ago, the United States was chiefly a farming nation. There were no large factories or very large cities. There were no telephones, automobiles, electric lights, electric refrigeration, radios, or airplanes. There was enough land for all and the pioneer spirit was in the air. Women did not have the right to vote and they lacked many other rights which were enjoyed by men. Their place was supposed to be in the home. Families were generally large and the death rate, especially among infants, was high. Our knowledge of how to fight diseases was very limited and the average length of life was much less than it is at the present time.

Today, the pioneer spirit of settling new lands has largely passed, but the spirit of doing great deeds still remains. The United States is an industrial nation with large factories and cities. Telephones, radios, electric lights, electric refrigeration, airplanes, and automobiles are very common and inventions bring into daily use new objects. Great advance is being made in medicine and nursing. Women now have the right to vote and also the privilege of taking an active part in the affairs of the country. During the past one hundred years, great wars occurred which brought about many changes in our ways of living and thinking. The number of criminals has increased and the cost of crime annually is given in billions of dollars.

Even the home and the church have been greatly influenced by changing conditions. Great industrial problems, farm problems, social problems, political problems, moral problems, and spiritual problems confront the people as never before and these problems surely make life very complex. Today, an individual lives in a world of much broader horizons than did the people of the past. In fact, so many problems have risen to face us that we are having a difficult time of finding satisfactory solutions to all of them.

Some people speak and write as if a changing world is something new. However, since men have lived in groups upon the earth, things have always been changing. It is true that the changes taking place today are greater than the changes which took place one thousand years ago, one hundred years ago, or even fifty years ago. There are many more people today than at any other time in the history of the world. Our civilization is much more complex than it ever was in the past. Thus our problems are much more numerous and complicated.

Too many of us live in our own small world and know or care very little about the past. Since our knowledge is limited, some of us seem to forget that difficult problems have always confronted the people. If we read history intelligently, we will learn that all through the ages people have had just as much difficulty in solving problems as we have today.

The story of mankind is the history of the struggle that he has gone through in solving the problems of life. Our advance in civilization has not been gained without a struggle. Man has gained knowledge in order that he may have power to advance. Knowledge is power in that it enables man to accomplish certain aims. If a pupil is being educated, he should not only seek to obtain knowledge, but he should also seek the power of using his knowledge wisely. As long as we advance along the road of civilization, we will have difficult problems to solve. The successful solving of a problem means that we have taken a step forward. It is only when we fail to solve successfully our problems that we are going backward along the road of civilization.

GREAT PART PLAYED BY THE SOCIAL STUDIES

The social studies play a very important part in the transmission of our cultural heritage and in preparing pupils to meet unflinchingly the issues in this changing world. Anyone who cannot adapt himself to the changes which are taking place from time to time is at a great disadvantage. People pay taxes to support schools. Parents send their children to school in order that the children may receive experiences which they will likely not get at home or on the street. The program of the social studies must be flexible so that it can be adapted to the needs of the individual pupil.

The fate of democracy depends to a large extent upon the intelligence of its citizens. Washington, Adams, Jefferson, Madison, and other great Americans believed in free education so that our republic would have a supply of well-informed voters. Only by having well-trained and sensible citizens can we hope to preserve and improve democracy.

The social studies help pupils to gain an understanding of our institutions by studying problems connected with the home, the community, the state, the nation, and the countries of the world. They teach the interdependence of peoples. They not only give the pupils an opportunity of participating in social activities in and outside the school, but they help to give them the desire to do so. Such problems as (1) housing, (2) the work that different people do, (3) obtaining the necessities of life, (4) caring for the family, (5) guarding oneself against propaganda, (6) good government, (7) the resources of different countries, and (8) foreign trade are studied at certain levels. Children are taught how to collect and weigh evidence and how to think. Problems studied in social studies classes develop such qualities as initiative, open-mindedness, tolerance, unselfishness, social consciousness, responsibility, broad-mindedness, cooperation, a love for reading, and a desire to learn. If correctly taught, the social studies help the individual to adjust himself harmoniously to his group and to the community at large. They often awake in a person certain interests and hobbies which enable him to enjoy more fully his leisure time.

CLUBS FOR CITIZENSHIP TRAINING

One of the effective ways of training pupils in desirable citizenship activities is through clubs in the school. Pupils come together on equal ground where the spirit of comradeship prevails. Some of the clubs which have been formed by pupils in the social studies are history clubs, geography clubs, travel clubs, current events clubs, international-relations clubs, and student service clubs.

Clubs give pupils a more realistic view of contemporary life. Various sorts of interesting problems are discussed and conflicting views are often expressed. Active participation in the activities of clubs helps to give the training which pupils need in social living. They come to understand that the responsibility of having a successful club rests upon them. They learn how to select leaders after discussing the fitness of certain members.

The various committees give training in group work. The members learn how to work together in planning programs, in advertising the meetings, in getting members, and in considering many other problems which arise. Very aggressive pupils come to see that they must cooperate with all the other students. Even the timid pupils gradually grow in the power of taking part in the many activities of their club. Training in leadership is developed. The president must be impartial, he must be careful to see that no pupil monopolizes a discussion, he must know parliamentary procedure, and he must have the ability of leading the club to accomplish certain worthwhile objectives. Chairmen receive valuable training in presiding at committee meetings.

In organizing a club it is well to remember that it should be managed by the pupils with the teacher as an advisor. The members should be responsible for the programs and other activities. They should feel that it is their club. A good club in the social studies gives the pupils practice in worthy citizenship. They receive training in open-mindedness, fairness, and tolerance. Each member should have an equal opportunity of expressing himself and in helping to manage the club. No clique should be permitted to get control of it.

A club should have a regular time for meeting. The size of the room in which the club meets and the objectives of the club help to determine the number of members. Each meeting should have a well-planned program. Faculty members and outside speakers may be invited to appear on the programs. Pictures may be shown. Some of the most valuable programs are put on by members of the club. In many of the programs, discussions are held where the members have a chance of taking part in discussing the problems or in asking questions. In many cases, the programs of a club are related to the work which the pupils are doing in their classes. Hence, club work often motivates and stimulates classroom work.

The officers and the different committees should have regular periods for meeting to discuss the affairs of their club and to make plans. It is usually advisable for the faculty advisor to meet with them. However, he should let the pupils manage their club because they are the ones who should have the experience of engaging in desirable social activities. It is generally well to

plan some social event each term, such as a banquet, a picnic,
a trip to some well-known place, a party, or a ball game with
another club.

STUDENT GOVERNMENT ORGANIZATIONS FOR CITIZENSHIP TRAINING

Some schools have student councils which manage the affairs
in which all the students are interested. Other schools have a
form of student government which is similar to the government
of a city. The officers of a student government organization are
nominated and elected by the pupils in about the same way that
the officers of a city government are nominated and elected by
adults. Pupils receive actual practice in self-government which
resembles the actual practice which adults have outside the school
in governing themselves. By engaging in desirable social activities, pupils are preparing themselves for desirable social living.
Our modern schools are truly democratic institutions where
pupils are actually engaged in practicing the American way of
life.

PROBLEMS FOR DISCUSSION AND RESEARCH

1. Develop the statement that a teacher should be able to visualize
the society of the future.

2. What is the difference in meaning between the term "social
sciences" and "social studies"?

3. Explain your idea of the American way of life.

4. After much study and thought, make a list of the qualities of a
good citizen. Compare your list with the lists made by others.

5. Give examples showing that it is not easy to be a good citizen
at all times.

6. Make a list of ten of the chief problems which confront the
American people. Tell why you think each one of the problems is
important.

7. Discuss the statement that our problems today probably are not
more difficult for us to solve than were the problems of the past to
those people living in past times.

8. Explain and illustrate what is meant by adjusting oneself harmoniously to his environment.

9. Explain how our democracy should proceed to get an ample
supply of intelligent voters.

10. Discuss the part that the social studies play in the American way of life.

11. How do clubs teach students the principles of democratic living?

12. Discuss the importance of a school having some kind of student government organization.

REFERENCES

Alstyne, R. W., "Social Studies Versus Social Science," The Social Studies, XXVIII, 77-81, February, 1937.

Altschul, Helen, "The Citizenship Council as a Means of Character Building," Educational Method, XX, 191-195, January, 1941.

Barnes, Charles, "The Challenge to the Social Studies," Social Education, III, 77-82, February, 1939.

Bining, Arthur and Bining, David, Teaching the Social Studies in the Secondary Schools. New York: McGraw-Hill Book Co., 1941.
Chapter I. The Social Sciences and the Social Studies, 1-25.
Chapter II. Aims and Objectives, 26-48.
Chapter XVIII. Social and Civic Training, 338-356.

Clark, Harold, "What Makes a Good Environment?" Childhood Education, XVII, 108-111, November, 1940.

Committee on the Function of the Social Studies in General Education of the Commission on Secondary School Curriculum of the Progressive Education Association, The Social Studies in General Education. New York: D. Appleton-Century Co., 1940.

Cook, Lloyd Allen, "The Society in Which Children Live: The Impact of Social Agencies Other than the School on the Lives of Children," The Social Studies in the Elementary Schools, Twelfth Yearbook of the National Council for the Social Studies, 1941, 29-46.

Crary, Ryland, "The Democratic Spirit in the Social Studies Classroom," Social Education, IV, 456-461, November, 1940.

Dawson, Edgar, Teaching the Social Studies. New York: The Macmillan Co., 1928.

Deegan, Mary, "The Legion of Citizenship," The Elementary English Review, XVII, 274-275, November, 1940.

Dunn, Fannie, "How Democratic Is Your School?" The Instructor, L, 15, 65, September, 1941.

Frederick, Robert and Sheats, Paul, Citizenship Education Through the Social Studies. New York: Row, Peterson and Co., 1936.
Chapter I. Introduction, 1-16.
Chapter II. The Social Studies in Retrospect, 17-33.
Chapter III. How May Interest in the Welfare of Man be Aroused? 34-43.

Greenan, John, "Attitudes and Ideals in Social Studies Teaching," Social Education, IV, 44-51, January, 1940.

Hartford, Ellis, "Civic Leadership Through Clubs," Social Education, II, 91-93, February, 1938.

Hughes, R. O., "Social Sanity Through the Social Studies," Social Education, I, 3-10, January, 1937.

Hunt, Erling, "Twenty-five Years of Problems of Democracy," Social Education, V, 507-512, November, 1941.

———, "Educating Leaders for Democracy," Social Education, II, 541-544, November, 1938.

Improving Social Studies Instruction, Research Bulletin of the National Education Association, XV, November, 1937.
   Chapter I. Objectives of the Social Studies Curriculum, 193-198.

Irion, Theophil, "Social Studies From the Viewpoint of the Learner," Social Education, II, 103-107, February, 1938.

Jewett, Daisy, "Geography Clubs," The Journal of Geography, XXXIV, 335-337, November, 1935.

Kehoe, R. J., "High School Travel Clubs," The Journal of Geography, XXXVII, 109-111, March, 1938.

Knowlton, Daniel, "The Social Studies and Their Scope," Elements of the Social Studies Program, Sixth Yearbook of the National Council for the Social Studies, 1936, 7-28.

Kumpf, Carl, "Are Clubs Desirable in the Elementary School?" Educational Method, XVI, 142-147, December, 1936.

Macintosh, Helen, "Practical Citizenship Teaching in the Elementary School," School Life, XXVI, 16-19, October, 1940.

Marshall, James, "Teaching for Democracy," Social Education, III, 13-16, January, 1939.

Marshall, Leon, "Patterns Underlying the Details of Human Living," Social Education, 158-162, March, 1937.

McNutt, Russell, "Educating for World Citizenship," Social Education, IV, 33-39, January, 1940.

Moore, Clyde, "Building Social Foundations in the Elementary School," Social Education, V, 283-288, April, 1941.

Neuman, Basil, "The Role of the Social Science Teacher in a Troubled World," High Points, XXII, 5-8, September, 1940.

Rienow, Robert, "Scholastic Panic," Social Education, III, 315-317, May, 1939.

Roles, Nancy Evans, "What Social Studies Shall We Teach?" New Jersey Educational Review, XIV, 53-54, November, 1940.

Salisbury, W. Seward, "Positive Citizenship," Social Education, IV, 545-548, December, 1940.

Schleicher, Charles, "Can Democracy Be Efficient?" Social Education, IV, 231-234, April, 1940.

Schuker, Louis, "The History Club as Training for Citizenship," Social Education, IV, 13-16, January, 1940.

Schutte, T. H., *Teaching the Social Studies on the Secondary School Level*. New York: Prentice-Hall, 1938.

Chapter I. The Nature and Content of the Social Studies, 1-100.

Chapter IV. Aims, Functions, and Objectives of the Social Studies, 219-246.

Schwarz, John, *Social Study in the Elementary School*. New York: Prentice-Hall, 1938.

Chapters I, II, III, IV.

Stevens, Marion, "The History of Democracy," The Instructor, LI, 49-58, November, 1941.

Stowe, Lyman, "School Experience in Democracy," Social Education, III, 187-191, March, 1939.

The Social Studies Curriculum, Fourteenth Yearbook of the Department of Superintendence of the National Education Association, 1936.

Part One. Factors Conditioning the Social Studies, 19-50.

Swan, Augusta M., "Democracy in the Kindergarten," Childhood Education, XVII, 318-320, March, 1941.

Wesley, Edgar, *Teaching the Social Studies*. New York: D. C. Heath and Co., 1937.

Part One. The Foundations of the Social Studies, 3-58.

Part Two. The History and Status of the Social Studies, 59-144.

Whitney, Frank, "Citizenship Training," Social Education, II, 545-548, November, 1938.

Wilson, Howard E., "The Meaning of Citizenship," Harvard Educational Review, XI, 13-16, January, 1941.

———, "On the Making of Citizens," Social Education, III, 225-232, April, 1939.

Wirth, Fremont, "Objectives for the Social Studies," *Eighth Yearbook of the National Council for the Social Studies*, 1937, 21-43.

Wittke, Carl, "Freedom of Teaching in a Democracy," Social Education, II, 86-92, February, 1938.

Wrightstone, J. Wayne and Campbell, Doak S., *Social Studies and the American Way of Life*. Evanston: Row, Peterson and Co., 1942.

Chapter Two: HISTORY, THE STORY

THAT NEVER GROWS OLD

THE GROWTH OF HISTORY

DURING COLONIAL times, American children did not study much history. There were few schools, the teachers were usually poorly trained, books were scarce and expensive, children often had to work at home, and the people generally did not feel it to be their duty to make it possible for most of the children to receive much education. When children did attend school, they usually spent most of their time in studying only a few subjects such as reading, writing, spelling, and arithmetic. Sometimes a little history and geography were taught, but such subjects were not considered to be of great importance. It was not until after the close of the Revolutionary War that the first textbooks in geography and history were published in what is now our country.

After the United States became a nation, more schools were started. Children were given a better opportunity of receiving an education. Books on history were published in our country, and it slowly gained in importance as a subject to be studied. History finally came to be one of the chief subjects in the elementary grades and the high school. The belief gradually arose that no boy or girl could ever hope to develop the qualities of good citizenship without studying a certain amount of history.

WHAT PLACE SHOULD HISTORY OCCUPY
IN OUR SCHOOLS?

During recent years teachers have been considering, as never before, the reasons for teaching certain subjects. Just because a subject, such as history, has been in the curriculum for many years is no good reason why it should remain in the curriculum. Time changes, and so do our thoughts and ideas change about what we teach. Since the first World War, history has declined in importance in some schools. Some teachers and administrators have the mistaken idea that very little time should be spent by children in the study of history. To such teachers and educators, children would be just as well off, if not better off, if they spent less time upon the study of history and more time upon the study of some other subject. They say that people seem to learn very little from studying history. Wars still occur and groups of people still dislike one another. These teachers evidently do not know that the blame should not be placed upon history but upon the way it is taught.

Still other teachers believe that history should be combined with certain subjects, and that the children should study history only as it is needed to explain some topic or unit of work. Some teachers and principals think that a school cannot be progressive if history is taught as a separate subject. Therefore, if they are to be progressive, history must not be taught by itself. They look upon those elementary schools where history, civics, and geography are taught as separate subjects as being behind the times.

In some grades in certain schools, there are well-planned units on current problems. In discussing the problems and trying to understand them, much use is made of newspapers, magazines, motion pictures, and the radio. Various other sources of information are used. A certain amount of history is needed to understand the current problems, so books on history are consulted. Some teachers, who are following this plan, honestly believe they are teaching all the history that it is necessary for the pupils to know. They claim this is the best way of teaching history and that it is a progressive way. However, many experienced teachers question whether these teachers are altogether correct in thinking they are teaching enough history or teaching it in the best way.

One educator recently had about 1,500 seventh and eighth grade pupils list the subjects which they disliked. Seventy-two per cent of them said they disliked history. In fact, many of them listed history as the subject which they disliked the most. The chief reasons they gave for disliking history were that they had to memorize much of the material; the subject matter lacked continuity; and the material was dull, uninteresting, useless, and unimportant. Of course such investigations should not be taken too seriously, because pupils are likely to make statements without much thought. It is probably true that some pupils prefer the easy road of little study and light work because they are not old enough to know what is best for them. Again, just because certain pupils dislike a subject is not a good reason that the subject is to blame. The blame is due largely to the way the subject is organized and presented by teachers and to the books which children are encouraged to read. In fact, the reasons that the pupils gave for disliking history lead one to come to this conclusion.

Should history occupy a leading place in our schools? This question confronts many teachers. Some teachers are confused in their thinking because educators have not agreed among themselves about the place which history should occupy. Probably the principal reason why teachers and other educators are not agreed among themselves about the place which history should occupy in the curriculum is because some of them do not fully understand the nature of history and the contributions which it makes to our way of living. Many people still have the idea that history consists chiefly of dates, wars, political campaigns, and unrelated events. They do not realize that history is the story of the progress of man as he has struggled through the ages; that events are related, and that the details of wars and political campaigns are minor affairs in the evolution of civilization. Let us briefly make a study of this subject with the hope that we may come closer to knowing just how important it is for pupils to study history in the grades and in the high school.

WHAT IS HISTORY?

History may be said to be the story of past events. There are many different kinds of histories, such as the history of the sun, the history of the moon, the history of the earth, the history of plants, the history of animals, the history of religion, and the history of man. Anything that has happened belongs in the history of something.

The history that we teach in the school is chiefly the history of people. It is a study of human development upon our earth from as far back as we can trace man to the present time. In other words, it is a study of what man has thought, felt, said, and done throughout the ages. History tells us about the progress of man in society. As the fascinating story of man unrolls from the very dim beginning to the present time, we cannot help but feel that man is a very small being in this great world of ours, and that the greatest problem of all times has been that of obtaining the necessities of life in making a living. Just how well man has succeeded, only the records of history tell.

We do not know how long man has lived upon the earth because the earliest men left no traces of their existence. In fact, many of the acts of men today are not left in durable form to be read by people in future years. We learn about the history of man by examining the sources which are left behind. The signs of human activities upon the earth are called sources.

Men lived upon the earth for thousands of years before they learned to write. Indeed, some people think that this earth has been inhabited by man for at least 500,000 years. Since writing came into use only about 7,000 years ago, the unwritten period of mankind has been very long. The period before writing came into use is called the prehistoric period of history, while the historic period includes the years after written records were kept. Thus we see that the prehistoric period was very long while the historic period has been comparatively short.

Since man left no written traces of his activities during prehistoric times, it has been impossible to get very much accurate information about the people who lived on the earth in those years. A little information has been obtained from the bones of animals, the tools of stone and bone, products of clay, the skeletons of people, and a few other sources found in the earth at certain places. For example, we do know that the people made progress in obtaining the necessities of life as the years passed. They gradually improved their tools and their ways of doing things. Yet for all of our efforts, we have not been able to read very far into the life of man during prehistoric times. We do not know when or how man first obtained fire, tamed the dog, cow, and many other domestic animals, raised wheat and corn, made pottery, made the bow and arrow, invented the wheel, and made the boat. We can only guess how these and many other things might have come into use. Of course, during prehistoric times the people handed down certain information by word of mouth. The children were probably taught about certain events which their elders thought they should know. This was oral history.

When writing came into use, man had a way of recording his thoughts so that people might know some of the things he was doing. Many years passed before writing became very common. For a large part of the historic period, our sources of information are limited and it is often difficult to get accurate information about certain ages. As more documents were written and preserved, the sources of history increased, and for about the last thousand years they are rather abundant.

HERODOTUS, THE FATHER OF HISTORY

Herodotus was a Greek who lived during the fifth century B.C. He traveled over much of the world which was known to the Greeks. This known world included Persia, Babylonia, Egypt and northern Africa, Italy, Sicily, Greece, and other regions near the Mediterranean Sea. Herodotus inquired wherever he went and he was very keen to discover things. He wrote an interesting story on his travels. He said he included what he had seen with his own eyes, what he had learned from other people, and the conclusions that he had been able to make. He endeavored to write only about those things which were interesting and important. Even today, we try to select those topics in history which are interesting and important.

Herodotus proved to be a good story-teller. He told many marvelous tales, some of which were myths and legends. He wrote before any such subject as history had come into use. His method of getting information by inquiry proved to be sound. History comes from a Greek word which means inquiry or learning from inquiry. The history written by Herodotus was so good that in time all narratives of past events which resembled those written by him were called *historie* or *historia*. Thus we get the name of history. Herodotus came to be known as the "Father of History," even though he was not the first writer of history.

Another great Greek historian was Thucydides. His aim was to write history that would be useful in meeting events which might occur in the future. He believed that history repeats itself. He wrote chiefly about war and was careful to check the information which he got. He obtained most of his information by travel and by talking with people.

For many years historians wrote history for the sake of telling an interesting story or for the use which it might have in solving future problems. During recent years, some people have endeavored to write a scientific type of history. However, natural sciences deal with facts that can be directly observed and tested by experiment. History deals with facts and events that cannot be directly observed at the time of study. It is much more difficult to discover laws in history than it is in science. In fact, it is a question if we have made much of a beginning in writing scientific history.

The history of today still deals with inquiry. It is still a record of what man has done and thought. It endeavors to portray what has actually occurred. Historians still try to select and interpret events which are interesting and of importance. Yet, our interpretation of history today is not exactly the same as the interpretation that people made yesterday and it will not be the same as the interpretation that people will make tomorrow. New facts are being discovered and old facts are being revised and corrected. We look at things somewhat differently as the years pass. Our experiences change and so do our interpretation of events. Events which were once considered to be important may give way to those which were once thought of as being of minor concern. Our ideas of history change as we grow in knowledge.

DOES HISTORY REPEAT ITSELF?

You have probably heard it said that history repeats itself. Many people believe this statement and histories have been written with this thought in mind. It is an interesting expression and it may seem to some people that history does repeat itself. Through the course of time nations have risen and declined and it is only natural to believe that nations will keep on rising and declining as the years pass. The people of all ages have had certain big problems of obtaining the necessities of life, such as food, clothing, shelter, implements and tools, and recreational needs. Hence, the problems of one age resemble the problems of any other age to a greater or less degree. People must perform certain activities in solving their problems and it is undoubtedly true that the activities of one age have certain similarities to the activities of any other age. Since history is the story of what man has done, it might appear to some people that history does repeat itself at different times as the years roll by.

In the true sense of the word, history does not repeat itself. When an event or a condition occurs once, it can never occur again. It has passed forever. Other events or conditions will follow, but they will not be exactly the same as those which have already occurred. Events do not just happen without any connection to other events. They are related to certain events which have gone before and to those which are to follow. This is the development idea in history. History traces development and development takes place as events happen. History that is being made is like a mighty river which rolls on day by day. Sometimes the river has more water than at other times. So it is with the events of history. During some periods of history, far more events happen than during other periods.

One period of history differs from another period. People in one period do not have exactly the same experiences as the people of another period. They look at things somewhat differently. They have different feelings and thoughts. They react to many things in different ways. Changes are ever occurring. Therefore, it is impossible for history to repeat itself. However, the people of one period of history have some of the same general problems that the people had in other periods of history. Yet the feelings, thoughts, attitudes toward life, customs, and ideals of the people of one period of time are not the same as those of other periods of time. Looking at history in this way, we might say that it is a study of the actions and thoughts of people during various periods of time.

WHY TEACH HISTORY?

Why should pupils study history? This is an old question and it will always confront teachers. Throughout the ages much thought has been given to this question and it always will receive much consideration and thought. Since teachers are free to think and come to their own conclusions, there are bound to be many answers to this question. Some students have done considerable research on the objectives or reasons for teaching history, and they have listed their objectives in books, courses of study, and magazine articles on history. One student found more than one thousand objectives for teaching history. It seems as if almost every objective imaginable has been given, from learning to read books to being a good citizen. Of course many of the objectives mean practically the same thing. Again, in order to be as definite as possible, a person may list a number of objectives where he might have given only one general objective. It is also true that some of the objectives for teaching history may also be given for teaching other subjects.

Every teacher of history should consider carefully just what the objectives are in teaching history. Otherwise, teaching history would be something like the blind leading the blind. Without objectives, a teacher has no way of knowing whether the pupils are doing satisfactory work and are accomplishing the right results. A teacher has no way of judging the results of his work if he has no objectives. A teacher should realize that his main purpose in teaching history to children is to form good American citizens and not to form scholars or historians. Hence, the history that a historian studies includes much more than the history that a pupil studies.

A brief discussion of some of the reasons for teaching history and the contributions it makes for good citizenship follow:

1. To Learn the Historical Method of Studying History

The historical method is the natural way of studying history. A student of history would proceed somewhat as follows if he were using the historical method. First he searches in various places for materials to study. Such materials might include (1) objects such as tools, weapons, furniture, statues, pottery, and ruins, (2) pictorial materials, (3) oral materials such as legends, anecdotes, tales, songs, lectures, and conversations, and (4) written materials such as papers, magazines, books, diaries, journals, maps, memoirs, chronicles, and speeches.

The second thing he would do is to examine the materials very carefully and critically. He seeks to learn the answers to such questions as (1) are the materials authentic, (2) who are responsible for them, (3) are they representative of the age, (4) why were they produced, (5) are they copies or the originals, and (6) when were they produced. Many other questions would come to his mind which he would seek to answer while studying the materials.

The third step is to put the results of his work together in the form of a report or some other activity. He will look at the material in an objective manner and decide what parts he needs in order to do the work which he has in mind. If he is an author, he may write a book suitable for children, general adult readers, or scholars. If he is a teacher he may arrange his facts in such a way that they will be useful to him in teaching.

The pupil should receive a certain amount of training in historical method. In the lower grades the method will be on the level of the child. It will be very simple, yet the child will begin to learn methods of study. As he grows older, he will be able to comprehend better the meaning of the historical method of study, although he will probably not know it by this name. Of course the method should always be simple enough for a pupil of a given age to use. Children should never be expected to use methods which are beyond them. The historical method will gradually unfold to pupils as they grow in age and in the power to study.

Children should learn to seek the truth, to recognize the truth, and to value the truth. They should get into the habit of examining critically what they hear, see, and read so that they will not be misled by incorrect information. They should think before they make up their minds, but first they should strive to ascertain if the data which they have on hand are genuine and sufficiently adequate to enable them to reach some conclusion.

If a pupil uses the right method of study he will, among other things:

(1) Develop a sympathetic understanding for people and a critical and independent judgment.

(2) Develop tolerance and an open mind.

(3) Learn to collect and weigh evidence.

(4) Learn how to get accurate facts and develop skill in thinking and putting facts together.

(5) Get an insight into causal relations.

(6) Develop the imagination.
(7) Strive to improve the living conditions in his community.
(8) Learn to use books, pamphlets, newspapers, and magazines.
(9) Receive training in expressing himself both orally and in writing.

2. To Understand the Idea of Development

History should give the pupils the idea of development in a dynamic society. Human events are portrayed as they happened. They are shown to be related to what has gone before and to what will come. No events should be studied as isolated facts, but in relation to other events. In studying history, a person also traces the progress that man has made through the course of time. He also learns that nations have risen and fallen. It is not enough just to read about these things. A person should seek reasons for events occurring as they do. He should know not only what happened and where it happened, but he should seek to learn why it happened. The past should be made as real as possible to the pupil.

Present events are closely connected with what has gone before. Present events do not just happen, but there are reasons for their happening. These reasons are found in studying past events. For example, our present day automobile is not a product only of the thoughts of present day man, but it is the culmination of the thoughts of numerous men both in the present and the past who ever did anything connected with vehicular transportation. Thus one reason for studying history is to be able to interpret the present, because the present can be understood only in the light of the past.

In teaching history, some teachers prefer to begin with the past and move towards the present. If this is done correctly, the children should see how events have developed and they should get the idea of continuity. The story of history gradually unfolds as the pupils study and they come to see that certain events naturally follow other events. Where this method is used, the teacher should see that the pupils relate their work to the present, whenever they can do so. The great danger of teaching history by beginning with the past is that many teachers never reach the present. In some schools, the children never talk or study about current events or current problems because they spend too much time in studying about the past. There is no need of studying about the past just for the sake of keeping the pupils occupied. The past should be used to interpret the present and to prepare for the future. It may, even at times, aid a person in predicting certain events in the future.

Some teachers prefer to teach history by beginning with present day problems. The pupils study only those events in the past which play a part in interpreting current problems. This is called teaching history backwards. Whenever this plan is tried there is always danger that one unit may not have very close relation to another unit. Another danger of teaching history in this way is that too little time may be spent on the events which happened in remote times. The pupils may not get the idea of development, because the work may be too disconnected. We cannot get away from the past, even though we may wish to do so. Some people like to claim that they are self-made men. They are self-made men in the sense that they have succeeded in overcoming many difficulties through their own efforts and initiative. They have patiently struggled along, never admitting failure. In another sense, there are no self-made men. Every man is related to past events. And what he is, has been partly determined by past factors over which he has had little or no control. Thus we owe more to the past than many people are willing to admit.

3. To Develop International Understanding

If history is taught correctly, pupils should gradually come to have a friendly feeling for peoples in all parts of the world. The history of the United States is a part of the history of the world. People live in various countries somewhat as they are living in the United States. They struggle along to make a living and have numerous difficulties to overcome, just as we do in our country. Very often people of foreign countries do not look at things the way that we look at them, but there are reasons for this. History helps to explain these reasons. If we, in our imaginations, are able to put ourselves in the place of other people, we can see why they think and act as they do. We are better able to understand them and we have some of the information which will help us to interpret their actions. Very often we would act as they act, if we had their aims and desires. Hence, by understanding the causes for the actions of people, we come to understand them and have a friendly feeling for them.

A real study of history and geography tends to make us citizens of the world. However, many children and adults never reach this stage of citizenship because they have passed over too lightly the geography and history of other countries. They may have read briefly about what the people did in different parts of the world, but they never spent much time in thinking why they did it.

4. To Learn How to Spend Leisure Time Profitably

How to spend leisure time profitably is a major problem for many people. Today, all classes of people have a certain amount of leisure time. If the leisure time is spent wisely, people will be happier and they will be better and more useful citizens. A person who has more time on his hands than he knows how to use wisely is likely to be cross, pessimistic, and fault-finding. In all probability, he will not get along very well with his neighbors and he will be a poor citizen.

One way of spending leisure time is to read newspapers, magazines, and books and to listen to the radio. A study of history helps a pupil to read intelligently newspapers and magazines and to be interested in reading good books. It is difficult to think of a well informed person who does not do considerable reading. This period of time in which we are living might be called the reading age, because there is so very much printed material. Since a certain part of the printed material is of little value, children should be trained in the art of knowing what to read. This is a big job and should be given much thought by the teacher.

Likewise, our period of time might be called the radio age. Almost every home has a radio and some homes have two or more. Programs may be heard at almost any hour of the day or night. Many of the programs are highly worthwhile, but some are questionable from the standpoint of the child. A pupil who has learned to listen to the radio to get help in discussing current events and in solving problems should have learned to enjoy certain kinds of good radio programs during his leisure time.

There are historical museums in many parts of the country where objects of historical interest may be seen. These museums are visited by thousands of people daily. There are many places in the United States where events of great historical importance took place. Many of these places have been set aside by the government or by some organization so that they may be open to all people. Monuments, statues, markers, buildings, fortifications, and other objects often remind a person of the historical importance of certain places. For example, who has not heard of Bunker Hill, Plymouth Rock, the Statue of Liberty, Gettysburg National Park, Yorktown, the Mesa Verde National Park, Death Valley, and the Oregon Trail? Trains, automobiles, and airplanes furnish ample opportunity for people to move freely over the land. The American people are on the move. They spend much of their leisure time in travel. A study of history plays an important part in helping Americans to know what places to visit.

Millions of people spend some of their leisure time attending motion picture shows. Some of the pictures are based on history while others make use of certain events in history. Possibly the picture has something about pioneer life or is based upon some great episode in our history. Sometimes a picture is about the life of a famous person. Such historical pictures appeal to a great many people because they make history seem real and interesting.

5. To Develop Intelligent Patriotism

Some people seem to have the idea that patriotism is something which the schools should not teach. In some places a teacher is looked upon as being old-fashioned if he mentions the word patriotism. However, such people are incorrect in their thinking about patriotism.

Patriotism is a love for our country. It is a willingness on the part of an individual to support our country. Patriotism causes a person to believe in our country and to work to make it a better home for man. Patriotism causes a person to have national ideals and to respect the men and women who are operating our government for us. It also causes us to honor the great men of the past. Franklin, Washington, Jefferson, Jackson, Lincoln, Edison and many others were great Americans and their lives are worthy of study by American children. A patriotic citizen loves his country so much that he is willing to work hard to practise conservation of our resources so that the coming generations may have the means of living happily in our land.

If the history of the United States is taught correctly, a pupil cannot keep from having a love for our country. When he reads about the struggle which our country went through in becoming an independent nation, and when he learns that many people sacrificed everything that they had and even gave up their lives in order that our country might be free, he cannot but have a noble feeling for our great land. History shows that it is up to all of us to try to keep this land a home of free people who believe that government should be by the people for the benefit of all.

So far, we have been discussing true patriotism or intelligent patriotism. This is the kind of patriotism that every American citizen should have. It is natural for a child to think that his parents are the best people in the world. This does not mean that he dislikes other people or that he thinks that all other people are no good. It merely means that his parents come first in his mind. So why is it not possible for a person to think of the United States in somewhat the same way that a child thinks of his parents? Let us suppose that you recently traveled in many different countries, where you met fine people and admired them. Yet, you wanted to return to the United States. It was only natural for you to be glad to get back to your own country and to feel thankful that you are an American citizen. This does not mean that you look down upon the people in other lands or that you feel that they are inferior to Americans. Neither does it mean that you are finding fault with people in foreign countries or that you do not like them. It merely means that you appreciate the United States and all that it represents, and that you have a feeling of attachment for our country which all true patriotic citizens should have.

True patriotism for our country does not mean that a pupil must believe that all of our great American leaders never had any faults or that they never made mistakes. Neither should pupils be taught that the United States has always been right in all of its undertakings and that no mistakes have ever been made. Present true facts to pupils and let them decide for themselves. In a democracy a person has the right to give constructive criticism. It is only by correcting our mistakes and improving our ways of living that American democracy can advance.

6. *To Obtain Needed Information*

Is there a certain amount of information in history that every American citizen should know when he leaves school? If so, he should get such information while he attends school. On the other hand, if a person does not need to know any history, it does not matter whether a pupil gets any facts of history in school. Today, some educators talk and write as if facts are of little importance. Even those educators who say that facts should be taught claim that one fact should not be isolated from all other facts. They say that facts should be related to one another. They also say that the methods used in obtaining facts are just as important as the facts themselves. Amid all the conflicting opinions about teaching facts and not teaching facts, it is no wonder that many young and inexperienced teachers are confused.

A little serious thought will show any teacher that facts must be taught. No pupil can learn to reason accurately if he does not use facts. Probably one reason why so many inaccurate and careless statements are made by writers and others is because they lack facts. Pupils must be taught to search for the truth and not to make wild guesses. They must be taught to get accurate information and to use accurate information in their work. Facts in history are often used in talking with people, in interpreting the news, and in trying to understand the problems of the day.

There is no doubt but that pupils should know a certain amount of history when they leave school. Every American adult should know that Columbus first reached the New World in 1492, that there were thirteen American colonies, that the Declaration of Independence was signed on July 4th, 1776, that George Washington was our first president, that the Civil War was fought between the North and the South, that the United States was in the World War of 1914-1918 on the side of the Allies, and that the Tennessee Valley is that area drained by the Tennessee River. Many other facts worth knowing could be named. Facts should be learned while pupils are studying their problems and they should be related to other facts. Teachers are not agreed on just what information or how much information a child should get from year to year. There probably never will be complete agreement because the various experiences of teachers, their mental make-up, their attitude toward life, their knowledge of history, and their knowledge of children are not exactly the same. After much study and thought, a teacher should make a list of the important facts of history that he expects the pupils to learn during the study of a unit. Then he should teach in such a way that the pupils will learn these facts.

7. *To Develop Character and an Appreciation of Human Achievement*

If history is a study of everything that man has done, it is difficult to see how a pupil who studies history can keep from having his character influenced by it. As a pupil studies about the past achievements of man, he begins to understand what a great debt he owes to those who have gone before him. This will cause him to think of himself and he is likely to see that it is up to him to continue the work that has been started and to live in such a way that this world will be a better place for those who are to come after him.

Most pupils enjoy reading biography, especially when it is well written. A biography of a person also gives information about the period of history in which he lived. Children like to read about individuals who have contributed much to our history. They often think of the individual as their hero and they live and suffer with him. They often wish that they might be able to do some of the things which their heroes have done.

In reading about what our great men and women contributed to society and the part which they played in the development of our country, a person cannot keep from being thrilled and filled with a desire to live a worthwhile life. What person would not enjoy reading about the life of Franklin, Washington, Jefferson, Jackson, Lincoln, Roosevelt, Wilson, Boone, Fulton, Florence Nightingale, Edison, and many others?

One criticism that some people give about studying biography is that pupils may get an incorrect idea about the person being studied. They are afraid that pupils might get the idea that the person is perfect, that he never made any mistakes, and that everything he did always turned out for the best. Some people have even gone so far as to say that a biography should portray the bad side of a person just the same as the good side. It is well to remember if a biography is written for adults it should be written in a different way than for children. In a biography for children it is possible to give an accurate picture of a person without bringing in all his faults. We have had great leaders and the stories of their lives should be of much value to any true American. We should always be careful to see that their achievements are what interests children, not their faults.

PROBLEMS FOR DISCUSSION AND RESEARCH

1. Discuss the statement that people seem to learn very little from studying history. Do you believe this statement?
2. Give reasons for your liking or disliking history when you studied history in the grades and in the high school.
3. Have a group discussion on "What is History?"
4. Show how we obtain our knowledge of history.
5. What is your idea about the statement that history repeats itself?
6. Examine courses of study and talk to people. Make a list of the reasons for studying history. Check those reasons which may also be given for studying other subjects.
7. Explain what is meant by the term, "self-made men." Actually, are there any self-made men?
8. Explain the historical method of studying history.
9. What is meant by teaching history backward?
10. Show how history develops international understanding. What qualities should a citizen of the world possess?
11. State various ways that the study of history teaches a person to spend his leisure time profitably.
12. Give an example of some motion pictures and some radio programs which are especially good for teaching history.
13. Explain what patriotism means to you.
14. Make a list of some of the facts of history that a pupil in the eighth grade should know.
15. Make a list of the ten greatest men in American history. Compare your list with the lists made by others.
16. Why should children be encouraged to read biography?

REFERENCES

Bartlett, Ruhl, "Geographical Interpretation of History," The Social Studies, XXXIII, 250-252, October, 1941.

Beard, Charles, "A Memorandum for an Old Worker in the Vineyard," Social Education, II, 383-385, September, 1938.

Bining, Arthur, Mohr, Walter, and McFeely, Richard, *Organizing the Social Studies in Secondary Schools.* New York: McGraw-Hill Book Co., 1941.

Chapter IV. American History, 63-81.

Chapter V. European History, 82-97.

Chapter VI. World History, 98-117.

Chidsey, Alan, "Poor Old History," Social Education, I, 255-258, April, 1937.

Ellis, Elmer, Wirth, Fremont, Davey, John, and Wesley, Edgar, "American History in Junior and Senior High School," Social Education, III, 191-197, March, 1939.

Fahrney, R. R., "Teaching the Truth about History," Social Education, I, 98-104, February, 1937.

Hahn, H. H., "How History May be Made Real to Children in the Grades," Education, LVIII, 26-34, September, 1937.

Harper, Charles, "Why Do Children Dislike History?" Social Education, I, 492-494, October, 1937.

Hemleben, Sylvester, "Can We Teach Cultural History?" Social Education, III, 463-467, October, 1939.

International Understanding Through the Public School Curriculum, Thirty-Sixth Yearbook, Part II, The National Society for the Study of Education, 1938.

Chapter XI. History: Its General Function in the School, 95-104. By Guy Ford.

Chapter XII. History in the Elementary and the Junior High School, 101-108. By K. Sutton.

Chapter XIII. History in the Senior High School, 109-118. By Erling Hunt.

Johnson, Henry, *Teaching of History.* New York: The Macmillan Co., 1940. Chapters I, II, and III.

Kelty, Mary, *Learning and Teaching History in the Middle Grades.* Boston: Ginn and Co., 1936.

The Objectives to be Achieved, 4-10.

Kerider, J., "Why Study History?" The Social Studies, XXVIII, 243-244, October, 1937.

Klapper, Paul, *The Teaching of History.* New York: D. Appleton and Co., 1926. 3-24; 25-120.

McQueen, Donald, "The Spirit of History," The Chicago Schools Journal, XIV, 9-13, September, 1931.

Moon, Glenn, "For Sale: History," Social Education, V, 277-280, April, 1941.

Myer, Walter, "Social Wisdom from History," The Journal of the National Education Association, XXV, 299, December, 1936.

National Council for the Social Studies, First Yearbook, 1931. History and Patriotism, 7-14. By William Dodd.

Objectives in History, 15-23. By Avery Craven.

Roberts, Grace, "Is History a Dead Subject?" Texas Outlook, XXIV, 14, September, 1940.

Tuckman, William, "Music in Junior High School American History," Social Education, VI, 128-130, March, 1942.

Warren, Julius, "History in the New Social Studies Curriculum," Social Education, I, 251-254, April, 1937.

Chapter Three: GEOGRAPHY, THE STORY OF

MAN AND HIS NATURAL ENVIRONMENT

WHAT IS GEOGRAPHY?

THE ANCIENT Greeks were great geographers. They were the people who gave geography its name, which means "description of the earth." Some of the Greeks believed that the earth is spherical. Herodotus, Eratosthenes, Strabo, and other Greeks wrote books on geography. It was Eratosthenes who first determined the circumference of the earth. Since he gave his result in stadia we are not certain just how accurate his estimate was, but we believe that it was somewhat near the figure that we get today. The Greeks drew maps. They described the regions of the earth which were known to them. They also tried to explain such physical phenomena as storms, volcanoes, earthquakes, and tides.

As time passed, the science of geography grew. New regions on the earth were discovered and people learned more about them. Geography attempted to describe almost everything about the regions. Finally, it began to be seen that the field of geography included too much for any one science. So geography became the mother science to a number of other sciences which we study today. Some of these new sciences which separated from geography, are geology, zoology, botany, meteorology, and climatology.

Geography still remained an important science. For some years, the natural or physical features of the earth were chiefly studied, although man and other forms of life upon the earth did receive some attention. Gradually, the emphasis began to be shifted from the physical factors to life. Then for a number of years, much stress was put upon the influence of natural or physical factors upon life. Some geographers taught that the physical

34

factors largely or almost solely determined what man did in certain regions. For example, they taught that certain physical factors caused people to be farmers in some regions, while other physical factors caused people to be fishermen in other regions. By and by geographers came to see that they were putting too much stress upon the physical environment. They were not giving enough consideration to the other factors which help to influence what man does. For example, the United States has had the same physical environment for thousands of years, yet the Indians never advanced very far in using the land. They hunted, fished, and carried on primitive farming. They never developed the land such as it was developed after the coming of the white man. It must be remembered that customs, habits, laws, tariff, training, the outlook upon life, thoughts, and many other social factors help to determine what man does and the way he uses the land.

Gradually, geographers began to think of geography as being a study of the relationship of man to his natural environment. By natural environment are included such factors as location, shape, area, surface, soil, minerals, water bodies, climate, plant life, and animal life. In other words, geography came to be considered a study of the way man adjusts himself to his natural environment. Thus the activities of man are studied. We study why people work and play as they do and why they spend their leisure time in certain ways. We study the works of man. All of these things are studied in relation to the natural environment.

During the past few years, geographers have been thinking of geography as a study of the observable natural and man-made features of a region. The earth may be divided into many regions, each region having certain features which cause it to stand out from other regions. In a general way, the features in a geographic region are about the same in any part of the area. Usually the smaller the region, the more nearly similar are all parts of the area; while the larger the region, the more dissimilar are certain parts. By features we mean the factors of the natural environment and the works of man. Thus we may say that human geography seeks to explain the part that land, water, and air play in the development of any region by man. It helps to explain why the customs, habits, works, activities, and ideals of the people in various regions differ from one another.

In studying the geography of a region, we collect information about the things that can be seen in the region. We study about such natural features as location, shape, size, relief, soil, drainage, water bodies, climate, plant life, and animal life. We collect information about the works of man such as railroads, canals, airplane routes, roads, factories, mines, farms, buildings, churches, and schoolhouses. We try to explain the things which we see and to interpret the region as a home for man. We study (1) how the material needs of man, such as food, clothing, shelter, means of transportation, and tools; (2) how his occupations, such as hunting, fishing, herding, farming, mining, lumbering, manufacturing, transportation and shipping, professional activities, investment activities, and middlemen activities; and (3) how his higher needs, such as health, recreation, education, government, religion, and art are related to the natural environment.

BOTH A NATURAL AND A SOCIAL SCIENCE

The factors which go to make up geography include natural and social features. A person cannot make a detailed and well-rounded study of a region without studying both (1) the features of the natural environment and (2) man and what he has done. Hence, geography is both a natural science and a social science.

There are some geographers who put most of their time upon a study of the natural or physical features of a region. They are teaching physical geography and they think of the subject as a natural science. Even such geographers make some study of the works of man in the region, because of the close relation of the physical factors to the human factors. A study of physical geography shows the possibilities that the region offers to man. It furnishes a good foundation for a study of human or social geography.

Many geographers put much emphasis upon man and the way he uses the land. They study what man has done upon the surface of the earth. Of course they do not neglect studying the physical features, because in explaining the distribution and activities of people and the uses of the land, much attention must be given to the physical features. However, the main emphasis is upon man-made features and the distribution of people. They look upon geography as a social science. Some teachers call the geography which they are teaching social geography, while others call it human geography. These are good terms to use because they show that the emphasis is being placed upon the study of people.

The human element in geography helps to make it a very interesting subject. What is more fascinating than to try to learn why some regions have few people while other regions have many people? Social geography helps pupils to understand why some groups of people are more progressive than other groups. They come to see that the progress of people and the development of transportation go together. In studying the geography of different regions throughout the world, pupils are led to see that man does not build the same types of dwellings everywhere and they try to learn why this is so. They learn how groups of people depend upon agriculture, manufacturing, mining, logging, fishing, or hunting as they utilize the resources of the land.

GAINING GEOGRAPHIC KNOWLEDGE BY EXPLORING

Geography is as old as the human race. The earliest people learned their geography from experiences gained in obtaining food, clothing, shelter, and the other simple necessities of life. They gradually came to understand how temperature, rain, soil, hills, rivers, and other natural factors influenced their activities. They learned a few simple facts about their home region.

As time passed, people spread over much of the earth. Man has never been content to remain only in one place. Love for adventure, the desire to explore, the hope of bettering his condition, the longing for more land, the wish to trade, the search for food, and the delight of hunting are only a few of the reasons why man is always on the move. As people moved over the earth and settled here and there, their knowledge of geography increased. The Chinese, Chaldeans, Hebrews, Egyptians, Phoenicians, Greeks, Romans, Saracens, Norsemen, Crusaders, and other groups of people played important parts in adding to our geographic knowledge. Marco Polo, Vasco da Gama, Columbus,

Magellan, De Soto, the Cabots, Lewis and Clark, Peary, Amundsen, Byrd, and other brave men who faced unknown dangers to explore various parts of the world have done their part in adding to our geographic knowledge. The desire to make known all parts of the world still exists and explorers travel here and there in search of information. Man will never rest until all places have been thoroughly explored. Since this probably will never occur, the spirit of exploration will likely always be with us.

Since man likes to explore and to make discoveries, our geographic information is always increasing. We do not have to journey to far-away regions to make discoveries. There are plenty of things to learn in any community. Each one of us should be an explorer and a discoverer. There is always much joy in seeking and learning things for ourselves. Our lives are constantly changing as we learn how to adjust ourselves to the natural environment. As long as we are advancing along the road of civilization, we are learning more about our natural environment and the great influence which it has upon our lives.

ADJUSTING OURSELVES TO THE
NATURAL ENVIRONMENT

During the past years we have made much progress in adjusting ourselves to the natural environment. We have learned to overcome time and space by using rapid means of communication and transportation over land and sea and through the air. The telegraph, the telephone, and the radio enable us to send messages to almost any inhabited place in a very short time. Streamlined trains and automobiles on the land, fast moving ships on the sea, and swiftly moving airplanes through the air make places seem much closer to us than they seemed to people in the past. We have learned to turn night into day by discovering how to make electricity work for us. We know how to overcome heat and cold by heating our houses in winter and by cooling them in summer. We can even go farther than this by seeing that the air in our houses has the correct amount of moisture and that it is pure and free of dust and harmful germs. We have made some deserts yield an abundance of crops by bringing water to the land. Yes, we have even discovered how to grow new plants and to make the land grow more crops. Very great improvement has been made in raising animals. Today, from old mother earth we obtain coal, petroleum, natural gas, iron ore, lead, zinc, copper, tin, gold, silver, and many other useful minerals. Even the waters of the ocean are made to yield up their salt, bromine, and lime for the benefit of man. Day by day inventions are being made which not only produce new things for man, but which also permit him to have more time for leisure. This is certainly the machine age. Above all, such an advance has been made in medicine, hygiene, and health that the average person can look forward to spending many years upon the earth.

We have shown some of the ways in which man has learned to adjust himself to his natural environment. Man is the only living form that is able to do any thinking in meeting the problems of life. We have made so much progress that we are likely to forget that we cannot escape altogether from our natural environment. Everything which we have gained has been won at a cost and we must ever be on the alert to keep the gains we have made. It is when something goes wrong that we see our natural environment is still influencing our lives. A storm may cause much damage to life and property. Buildings may be blown down, telegraph, telephone, and electric lines may be broken, and railroads and public roads may be washed out or partly destroyed. Airplane transportation may also be interrupted. During some violent storms it is unsafe for men and animals to venture out upon the streets. Snow fences, snow sheds, and snow removal machinery silently indicate that man must struggle against natural forces to keep roads open throughout the winter. In some regions on the earth, earthquakes and volcanic eruptions have destroyed in a few minutes what it took man a lifetime to build.

Sometimes it costs us too much to change or modify our natural environment. In building roads we often go over hills and mountains or follow valleys, in place of building nearly level, straight routes. We may let low places remain wet, and arid places remain dry because of the energy and money which it would take to reclaim them. In some places, forests are left standing and minerals are left in the ground because the cost of getting them to a place where they may be used is too great. Even on the Great Lakes and on our northern rivers, water

transportation is stopped for a few months during the winter
on account of ice. Surely man is influenced by his natural
environment, and the more closely he comes to understanding
his environment the better he can adjust himself to it and
advance in the art of living.

SOME DISTINCT CONTRIBUTIONS OF GEOGRAPHY TO THE AMERICAN WAY OF LIFE

In teaching geography we should keep in mind not only the
facts which we teach, but also the attitudes toward life and
toward people which we expect the pupils to obtain. In the
past, many teachers paid too much attention to facts and not
enough attention to the attitudes of their pupils. They did not
realize that attitudes are just as important as facts. Attitudes
and facts should go together in geography.

Sometimes the author meets persons who think of geography
as consisting entirely of boundary lines, the drawing of maps,
the location of places, and facts about the places. Very often
some person says something like the following to the author,—
"So you teach geography. What a dry subject you teach. Let
me see. I remember drawing maps of the states and countries
and locating their capitals. How tired I got of drawing maps
and of memorizing facts about cities. I had to learn facts about
places which I soon forgot. I do not see how you ever got interested in such a dull subject." Or occasionally you meet someone
who is surprised to learn that geography is taught to students
in college. Such a person thinks of geography as being of little
importance and he has never realized the great role which geography plays in the affairs of the world. Geography is a subject
which should be studied, not only in the grades, but also in the
high school and in the college. It has a distinctive field of its
own. It makes specific contributions to the training of good citizens and to the American way of life. Briefly we will discuss
some of these contributions.

1. An Intelligent and Friendly Understanding of People

Geography contributes to an intelligent and friendly understanding of people. It is only by knowing people that we learn

to like and to respect them. Probably the lack of an intelligent and sympathetic feeling for other people is one of the chief causes why some countries make war on other countries. We gain much information about people by reading about them or talking to other people about them. We may also gain information by traveling among people and seeing how they actually live. However, it takes considerable reading, listening, conversing, and traveling to gather enough information to be really sympathetic with other people. By being sympathetic, we do not mean to be sorry for other people. We mean just the opposite of this. To have a true and sympathetic understanding of other people one must know the conditions they face and understand why they act as they do. A little reading and a few days of travel in a 'distant land may cause a person to obtain wrong ideas about a group of people. He may come away from the land thinking that the people are far different than they really are. He has not had time to know the people or to understand why they act as they do. Hence, he is not able to appreciate the people and to respect them in the right way.

The author once lived in a farming section where the soil was rolling and fertile and the farmers raised abundant crops. The farm buildings were painted and kept in good condition. The people were thrifty, they worked hard, and had many conveniences of life. There were excellent roads and each farm house had a telephone. Many of the houses had running water and electric lights. The people had plenty to eat and good, clothing to wear. These people were considered good citizens.

A few miles from this fertile farming section was a hilly region where much of the good soil had been carried away by erosion. The land was poor and it did not yield an abundance of crops. Most of the farm buildings were in a run-down condition and needed painting. The houses did not have running water or electric lights. The people had to work hard to get what little they had. They did not have much food to eat, neither did they have a large assortment of clothing. Many of the men and boys enjoyed hunting and fishing. The children went barefooted in the summer and their clothing was usually patched. These people were said to be lazy and shiftless by the people living in the more prosperous parts of the state. They were generally blamed because they could not make a better living from the land, and the more prosperous people usually felt sorry for them.

Now, why was there so great a difference between the people living in the two regions? Geography gives us the answer. The rolling, fertile land in one region made it much easier for the people to make a living than did the poor, hilly land in the other region. The people in the poor, hilly region were maladjusted to the soil. They were making a great struggle to get a living from land which should have been in forests or grass in place of cultivated farms. They were fighting against powerful natural odds. If the neighboring people on the better land had understood the geographical conditions which the poverty-stricken people were facing, they would not have looked down upon these people in pity and scorn. They would have realized that these poor people were making a great effort to win a living from the soil and they would have held them in higher esteem. Then they would have helped the people improve their land or they would have persuaded them to seek new homes in regions more suitable for farming.

Regions and countries throughout the world differ from one another. Since this is true, if we would merely think we would see that it is only natural for people in various parts of the world to have different customs and to look at things somewhat differently than we. For example, some people in our own country think of the Chinese as being queer people just because they do not do certain things as we do them. However, when we learn that the Chinese were the first people to use silk, tea, paper, gunpowder, the compass and many other common articles, we begin to realize that the Chinese are a wonderful people and our respect for them increases. As we learn more about them, we begin to understand that they are not queer people just because they do some things differently than we do them.

The more we learn about people the more we appreciate and respect them. Very often we learn that some people are more skilled in making objects than we are. Some Eskimos show great skill in making small tools out of bones and in making small boats. They are very skilled in hunting and fishing. Certain American Indians were skilled in making arrowheads, canoes, and in tracking animals. The Bushmen of Australia could make boomerangs which would return to them when thrown in the air. Many people in various places throughout the world are known for making certain objects which require much skill and thought. As we learn about such people, we cannot help but admire them, even though their customs are different from ours.

As we study about people in all parts of the world we come to see that they have many similar problems. They are occupied in making a living, in managing homes, in educating their children, in getting food and clothing, in making tools, in playing games, and in doing many other things. The farmer in the United States with his tractor and other modern farm machinery is doing about the same kind of work that the farmer of China or India is doing with his hoe and other hand tools. Thus we come to see that all of us are fellow-workers in this world and that certain common interests bind us more closely together.

As we study about the work which different groups of people do, we may think our ways of doing things are better than the ways they are done in other countries, yet we should not get the idea that our ways cannot be improved. It is only by recognizing our faults that we can make improvements and progress. When we realize that our methods of doing things can be improved, we are more likely to overlook some of the defects which we find in other countries. This tends to develop a more sympathetic feeling for other people.

Our sympathy and admiration for other people are increased by understanding the insight which they have had in facing the problems of life. People in some places irrigate the land, not only because there is a lack of rain but because they have the insight to do it. Thus the people on oases show a certain amount of intelligence when they bring water to their land. Likewise, the Eskimo shows insight when he builds a snow house or a house partly underground. The Chinese have shown insight by keeping their land in good condition for growing crops for more than forty centuries. In some mountainous regions of the world the roofs of houses are held down by stones. At first thought it may seem strange to us that heavy stones are used to hold down the roofs of houses so that the wind will not blow them away, but on second thought it does not seem so strange. Where nails are scarce, winds are strong, and stones are abundant, it is only natural to use stones to hold down the wooden roofs. Through years of experience, the people have learned how to build durable houses.

2. *An Appreciation of the Beauty in Nature*

A study of geography helps a person to discover, enjoy, and appreciate the beauties of nature. An active geographer never grows mentally tired of traveling. Some persons spend much of their time in playing cards or reading stories while taking a long journey by train during the day. A good geographer seldom does these things. He prefers to spend a part of his time during the day in looking out of the window at the scenery along the railroad. Many people travel to various places by automobile and they pay very little attention to the scenery along the road. The true geographer looks here and there as he travels. He is always thrilled by the things which he discovers along the road. Sometimes children surprise their parents on an automobile trip by pointing out things along the roadside about which they have studied in geography.

Great spectacles such as Niagara Falls, Boulder Dam, petrified forests, the Grand Canyon of the Colorado, and snow-covered peaks appeal to persons on account of their beauty and grandeur. Mountains with their ridges and peaks extending high into the air remind one of greatness, stability, and strength. One who has ever stood on a high mountain and observed the rising or setting sun in all of its beautiful colors will never forget such a scene. As one travels over the Great Plains of the United States and sees the vast expanse of rolling land stretching far into the distance, he is reminded of the Infinite and he begins to appreciate what a minute individual man really is in this vast world of ours. Even the forests have a beauty of their own and the wind rustling through the trees brings sweet music to the ear of the traveler. And who can ever forget the desert with its hills of sand, sparse vegetation, and great stretches of almost empty land? Yet, the desert makes a silent appeal to man. At night in the desert, the stars shine in all their glory and resemble jewels set in the great crown of the Universe. People who study about the natural environment cannot help but enjoy and appreciate the works of nature and to see the small part that man actually plays in this great world of ours.

A geographer learns to find beauty in almost every place. Many picturesque fishing villages are found along the coast of rocky countries. Even a city or a town far from the coast has certain things which attract the eye of the traveler. Bridges, highways, buildings, streamlined trains, airplanes, and other man-made features on the earth are often beautiful. The poet frequently sees beauty in places and objects which the ordinary individual cannot see. However, he who studies geography will likely catch some of the beauty of the places about which the poet dreams and writes.

3. Interdependence of People

Many people seem to think that one country can be entirely independent of all other countries. Have you ever thought what this would mean? For example, if the United States were entirely independent of other countries, we would have no trade with them. Then what would we do for tea, coffee, bananas, coconuts, palm nuts, quinine, tropical woods, cork, cacao, tin, asbestos, nickel, and other products which are not produced in large amounts in this country, but which we think we need? But you say, "Why not produce these products in the United States?" Many reasons may be given, but some of the chief ones are the following: (1) It is impossible to mine minerals in a region if they are not in the earth where they can be reached. Although the United States is rich in many minerals, it is very poor in tin, asbestos, nickel, and a few others. Hence, if we want to use the minerals which are lacking, they must be obtained from other countries. (2) The climate of the United States is not suited for growing bananas, coconuts, spices, mahogany, cacao, palm nuts, and other products which need a long, hot, moist growing season. If we are going to have such products, they must be imported from tropical regions.

Again, the United States produces a surplus of products which people in other countries need, such as cotton, corn, wheat, meats, apples, automobiles, machinery, and textiles. If we cannot sell our surplus to other people, the products will be left on our hands and we will have to stop producing so much. This will require fewer individuals to produce the products. It is the natural thing to trade our surplus products for the products which we need. Trade brings the peoples of one country into contact with those of other countries.

People living almost everywhere are affected directly or indirectly by the trade which is carried on between countries. This is as true of a rubber gatherer in the heart of the Amazon Region or of a miner in the tin mines of Bolivia, as it is of a farmer in Illinois or a city dweller in New York City.

Think what would be true if each country were entirely isolated from all the other countries. There would be no trade, no travel, and no communication between one country and another. We would not know about the events which are happening in other parts of the world. New inventions and new discoveries would remain in the countries where they were made and progress throughout the world would be very much slower than it is now. It is indeed very difficult to think of our world as being composed of isolated countries. The study of geography gives us a knowledge of regions and of countries throughout the world and it shows us that as long as progress is being made, all countries are bound to be related to one another by trade, travel, and communication. Geography teaches that it is unwise for any country to try to shut itself into a shell like a turtle and endeavor not to have any relation with other countries.

4. An Interest in Current Affairs and Their Interpretation

Radio programs, newspapers, and conversations with other people make it almost impossible for a pupil in school or for an adult not to know something about current affairs. Anything of importance that happens somewhere in the world is soon described on the radio and in the newspapers. People in the United States may listen to broadcasts from places widely distributed over the earth. An event means more to a person if he has some knowledge of the region in which it occurred. He will be able to interpret it more fully and to take more interest in it. Current events are always related to what has gone before and to what is to come.

It is easy to understand why we are concerned with events which occur in our own neighborhood, because we can see how directly they affect us. For example, let us suppose there is a dam in a large lake in our neighborhood. A break in the dam causes much land to be flooded. Houses are damaged, animals are drowned, and crops are destroyed. Transportation by road is stopped. Again, there may be factories in our community which give work to hundreds of people. If one of the factories closes, a certain number of people will be thrown out of work.

Some events which happen in other parts of the world have no influence upon our lives, but others do have considerable influence. For example, a country may put a high tariff on products which are imported from the.United States, thus cutting down our exports to that country. Wars between various countries affect people almost everywhere and there is always danger of wars spreading to other countries. Wars always affect trade and transportation in various regions.

In order to understand why present day events happen as they do, a person should have a knowledge of the geography and history of the regions where they occur. If people had a better understanding of current events, they would be able to solve more satisfactorily some of their own problems. Lack of accurate information in interpreting events is one reason why people are not better able to adjust themselves to conditions at home and abroad.

5. *An Appreciation of the Conservation of the Natural Resources*

When our forefathers landed on the eastern shores of North America, they found about two-fifths of what is now the United States forested. Tall trees reached high into the sky and there were trees as far as the eye could see. As the settlers gradually moved westward, they found the country to be rich in coal, petroleum, iron ore, copper, lead, zinc, salt, and many other minerals. Much of the land was covered with fertile soil. Wild animals roamed the forests and grasslands. The streams were abundantly supplied with fish.

If our forefathers could come back to the United States, what would they find? They would find that many of the resources were used unwisely while the country was growing into a great nation. They would see many places which should be reforested and much land upon which soil erosion should be prevented. They would see minerals being mined and used in a wasteful manner. Many of our streams and lakes would be found to be polluted with waste materials.

During the past one hundred and fifty years, the people of the United States have used their resources as if they were inexhaustible. Insects, diseases, storms, fires, and lumbering methods are destroying more wood than is being grown in the forests. Today only about one-fourth of the country has forests which could be cut for lumber. It is very difficult to imagine how much soil the land of the United States is losing annually on account of erosion. Think of it! We are losing from our farms every year enough soil to fill a train of freight cars stretching eighteen times around the earth at the equator. Millions of acres of land have been eroded so much that they are not now fit for farming. The waste of our minerals has been enormous. Millions of tons of coal and oil have been wasted during the past one hundred years. In some places, natural gas is permitted to escape into the air.

Due to careless methods of lumbering, mining, farming, manufacturing, and disposing of our waste materials, many streams and lakes have become filled with sediment. In some places the waste material has so polluted the streams that they are no longer suitable places for fish. We have given too little attention to the conservation of wild life and we have permitted too many birds and animals to be killed. If we are honest, we will admit that our record of wasting our resources has been one of which we should be ashamed.

What can teachers do concerning this great problem of conservation? We should strive to educate the public so that the people will cause this great waste to stop. In America we still believe in the people having a part in the solution of their problems. In a government where there is a dictator, all that is necessary to prevent waste is for the dictator to say the word. In a democracy such as we have in our country, public opinion must be the factor that decides what we will do about the matter.

The great task of educating the public about the necessity of conserving our resources falls largely upon the teachers of the social studies. The children must be told the truth about our resources, and they should fully realize the importance of conservation. It should be in the social studies classes that children learn how our great nation has been favored by nature with many resources. They should be led to see that if we expect our country to remain strong we must use our resources wisely and with as little waste as possible. So one of the main functions of geography is the teaching of conservation.

6. Aids in Making a Living

A certain amount of geography is useful in any occupation. It is true that people often make use of geographic knowledge without realizing that they are doing so. We shall give only a few examples to show how geography is used in some of the occupations.

A farmer needs to use geography in raising crops and animals. For example, he must test his soil to see if it has the right kinds and amounts of mineral matter which plants need. He must know if the growing season is long enough. Before he plants his crops he should strive to learn if there is a market for what he grows and whether he can easily ship his crops. If the climate is very dry and windy, the farmer must consider the possibility of the soil being blown away if he plows it. The farmer should not remove trees from steep hillsides and put the land in cultivated crops, because if he does this the soil will be washed from the slopes. The hilly land may be left for pasture and trees.

People who work for travel agencies need to know about the geography of the various regions on the earth. Travelers go to them for accurate information concerning the regions which they wish to visit. Railroad companies, steamship companies, and airplane companies employ people who know some geography.

Real estate men should know something about the geography of the region where they sell land. People thinking of buying real estate often ask questions about transportation facilities, the make-up of the population, and the location of schools, churches, and stores.

Let us suppose that a company is looking for a location for a factory. The geography of certain places where the factory may be located is carefully considered. Much attention will be given to such factors as the nearness of markets, the kind of power that may be easily obtained, the accessibility of raw materials, the ease of getting plenty of skilled and unskilled labor, the kinds of transportation, the water supply, the health conditions of the region, and the climate.

Salesmen for certain companies should have an understanding of geography. They should know how to reach the cities where they sell products. The weather often influences sales. A region with a rainy climate would be a better place for selling raincoats and umbrellas than a region having a dry climate. Likewise, a cold winter will cause a demand for blankets, overcoats, and other products which are commonly used during cold weather.

Reporters for newspapers can write better articles for their papers if they can use geography to help explain what they write. The same is often true for writers of magazines which give the news of the world. Lawyers often use facts of geography in pleading their cases. Ministers must know the geography of the Holy Land and of the neighboring regions in order to interpret fully the Bible. They often draw illustrations from geography in their sermons. Weather conditions play an important part in certain diseases. Some diseases are more common during the winter, such as colds and influenza. Dry weather is needed for curing some diseases. Aches and pains are likely to be more noticeable in damp, cool weather. Sometimes it is necessary for patients to be sent to a dry, sunny region; to a mountain resort; to the seashore; or to some other place where conditions are favorable for fighting certain diseases. Doctors should know enough geography so that they may advise their patients to visit the right regions.

Many of the workers in banks often use geographic information. Banks do not generally loan much money to companies or people in a region until they go over all the known conditions which might influence the paying of the loan at some future time. Some of the men in a large bank must be experts in foreign affairs, since its business may be influenced by events which are happening all over the world.

Many men who work for the government must use geographic knowledge rather frequently. Trained geographers are employed by the Bureau of Census, the Bureau of Foreign and Domestic Commerce, the Department of Agriculture, and many other government agencies. Many government publications on conditions at home and abroad are written by trained geographers.

Even people who have money to invest would probably make safer and better investments if they were acquainted with the geographic conditions of the regions where they invest their money. Many ·people have lost money in mines that never had any gold or other valuable minerals. People have bought supposedly good fruit-producing land in regions not adapted for raising fruits. Sometimes salesmen and advertising literature give people incorrect ideas of places, but a person who knows his geography is not likely to be misled.

PROBLEMS FOR DISCUSSION AND RESEARCH

1. Show how our idea of geography has developed through the ages.

2. Explain how geography is both a natural science and a social science. Which do you prefer to call it?

3. What part does exploration play in adding to our geographic knowledge? Make a list of some of the great explorers of the world and tell what each one did.

4. Explain and illustrate how man adjusts himself to his natural environment. Will man ever reach the point where it will not be necessary for him to consider his natural environment?

5. Discuss how geography helps to give a person a friendly understanding for peoples in all parts of the world.

6. Illustrate how a study of geography may cause a person to appreciate the beauties of nature. Of what importance is it for man to be able to appreciate the beauties of nature?

7. Show what it would mean if the United States were entirely isolated from all other countries. Even if it were possible for the United States to be entirely isolated from all other countries, would it be desirable?

8. What relation has geography to current events?

9. What is meant by the conservation of our natural resources? Give examples of waste and tell how it may be prevented.

10. Make a list of the chief occupations. Show how a knowledge of geography is helpful to a person in each occupation.

REFERENCES

Atwood, Wallace, "Geography and the Great Human Dramas," The Journal of Geography, XXXIX, 337-343, December, 1940.

Bagley, William, "The Element of Adventure in Teaching and Learning Geography," The Journal of Geography, XXVIII, 89-99, March, 1929.

Baldwin, J. W., "Geography and Latin American Good Will," Texas Outlook, XXIV, 6-8, June, 1940.

Barnes, Charles, "The Place of Social Geography in the High School," The Journal of Geography, XXXIII, 178-186, May, 1934.

Bining, Arthur, Mohr, Walter, and McFeely, Richard, Organizing the Social Studies in Secondary Schools. New York: McGraw-Hill Book Co., 1941.
  Chapter XIII. Geography, 234-249.

Bowman, Isaiah, Geography in Relation to the Social Sciences. New York: Charles Scribner's Sons, 1934.

Branom, M. E. and Branom, F. K., The Teaching of Geography. Boston: Ginn and Co., 1921.
  Part I. The Viewpoint, 3-74.

Browne, W. A., "A New Prospectus for Geography," The Journal of Geography, XXXIX, 17-25, January, 1940.

Curtis, Dwight, "Physical Geography Can Develop Social Understandings," Social Education, IV, 342-345, May, 1940.

Dodge, Richard, "The Aesthetic in Geography," The Journal of Geography, XXXVIII, 257-259, October, 1939.

Drill, Edna, "Nature Study and Geography," School Science and Mathematics, XLI, 442-447, May, 1941.

Fawley, Gladys, "The Social Value in Developing Readjustment Thinking in Geography," The Journal of Geography, XL, 192-196, May, 1941.

"Geography in the Elementary and Secondary Curricula," The Journal of Geography, XXXVI, 154-157, April, 1937.

Gluck, Harold, "Living with Geography," The Social Studies, XXIX, 310-318, November, 1938.

Hartshorne, Richard, The Nature of Geography. Lancaster: The Association of American Geographers, 1939.

Hudson, C. Donald, "Geography and Regional Planning," The Journal of Geography, XXXIV, 267-277, October, 1935.

International Understanding Through the Public School Curriculum, Thirty-Sixth Yearbook, Part II, of the National Society for the Study of Education, 1937.
  Chapter XIV. Geography, 119-126. By Derwent Whittlesey.
  Chapter XV. Geography in the Elementary and the Junior High School, 127-134. By Edith Parker.
  Chapter XVI. Geography in the Senior High School, 135-142. By R. H. Whitbeck.

James, Preston, "The Contribution of Geography to the Social Studies," Social Education, V, 334-338, May, 1941.

Lackey, Earl E., "New Geography for New Schools," The Journal of the National Education Association, 297-298, December, 1936.

Lawson, Douglas, "Geography Then and Now," The Elementary School Journal, XLI, 597-604, April, 1941.

Mason, Charles C., "Geography Made Meaningful," School Executive, LX, 18-19, November, 1940.

Merriam, Willis, "The Distinctive Contributions of the Geographic Point of View," Education, LVIII, 301-306, January, 1938.

Middlebrook, Pearl, "The Place of Geography in American Culture," Educational Method, XVII, 277-284, March, 1938.

Miles, O. K., "Some Evolutionary Factors in the Field of Geography," The Social Studies, XXVIII, October, 1937.

Miller, Geo. J., "Geography in Education," School and Society, XLIII, 1-6, April 18, 1936.

Mitchell, Lucy Sprague, *Young Geographers*. New York: The John Day Co., 1934.

Sletten, Cora, "Geography: A Promoter of Better Living," Educational Method, XVII, 259-261, March, 1938.

Switzer, J. E., "Geographic Interdependence," The Journal of Geography, XXXV, 99-105, March, 1936.

The Teaching of Geography, the Thirty-Second Yearbook of the National Society for the Study of Education, 1933.
Section I. The Development of Geography and Its General Contribution to Life, 3-72.

Thralls, Zoe and Reeder, Edwin, *Geography in the Elementary School.* Chicago: Rand McNally and Co., 1932. Chapters I, II.

Whipple, Gertrude, "Human Geography—From Slogan to Actuality," The Elementary School Journal, XLI, 337-346, January, 1941.

Chapter Four: THE TEACHER AND HIS
PLACE IN TEACHING THE SOCIAL STUDIES

AN IMPORTANT PLACE IN THE SCHOOL

MANY PEOPLE fail to realize the important place which the teacher occupies in the school. Too many people think of the school as being chiefly the school building and the grounds. In some places the people think they have done their duty if they have built an imposing structure. They point to it with pride, little realizing that it is what goes on within the building that really counts. They do not fully understand that the pupils and teachers are more important parts of a school than the mere buildings.

Many parents spend much time in thinking of the subjects which their children may take in school when they should be thinking of the teachers with whom their children will associate. The kind of teacher which children have is of much importance, because the teacher determines largely what goes on in the school. After all is said and done, it is the teacher that determines the kind of social studies that is taught. The teacher and pupils must respect and like one another. If the pupils dislike their teacher they will not do their best work. It is said that Socrates, one of the greatest educators of ancient times, once sent a boy home with this message, "I can teach him nothing, he does not love me."

The teacher should strive to make the school a pleasant place for the pupils. He should see to it that the pupils enjoy themselves while learning. The old fashioned school never gave much thought to the idea that learning should be made easy to the pupil. In fact many teachers believed that if the pupils had to work hard at disagreeable tasks, they would more likely re-

54

member what they were trying to learn. The children were told that what they were striving to learn would be needed by them in later years and that by working hard in school they would form the habit of being able to work hard when they left school. They were not supposed to question what they were told to do. It is no wonder that most children disliked school and that they came to look upon it as a place where pleasure was seldom enjoyed. Sometimes, the children were permitted to enjoy themselves when they had a spelling match on Friday afternoon or the teacher read them a story.

Time changes and it is a good thing for us that it does. Today, we believe that children should enjoy themselves at work as well as at play. Happy children in the schoolroom are more likely to become good useful citizens in later life, because the school is the place where children are living and learning those experiences which we think they should have. Pleasurable work done in the schoolroom is likely to be remembered with more profit than disagreeable work.

Today, we believe that the school must be a place where the pupils feel as if they are doing things. The spirit of victory must be in the air and each pupil must have confidence in himself. Very many failures in doing school work are not good for anyone, and a pupil who has failure after failure is likely to lose faith in himself. When a pupil loses faith or confidence in himself, he is no longer capable of doing good work. The teacher must try to make the school a place where busy pupils have many more victories than defeats. Hence, the teacher occupies a very important position in the school. He should strive to fill the responsible position which society has given him by doing his level best to be a great teacher.

QUALITIES OF A GOOD TEACHER

"What are the qualities of a good teacher?" and "Do I have these qualities?" are two questions which should always be in the mind of every good teacher. Two other questions which are just as important are "How can I get the qualities which I lack?" and "How can I improve the good qualities which I now possess?" With the hope of helping the teachers of the social studies to become better teachers, a brief discussion will be given of some of the qualities which teachers should have. This list has been prepared after consultation with hundreds of teachers and other people and after observing many teachers actually teach the social studies.

1. Pleasing and Vigorous Personality

The great men of history, such as Washington and Lincoln, were people of pleasing, vigorous, and inspiring personalities. Think of the teachers you have had who have inspired you to do your best so that you might get the most out of life. Then think of those who did not make an impression upon you and who did not inspire you to make much effort. Which teachers stand out the most prominently in your mind? With few exceptions, the teachers who had pleasing, vigorous, and inspiring personalities are those you remember with most pleasure. The teacher who is careful about his dress, who has a pleasing appearance, who is alive to what is happening around about him, who always has the welfare of the pupil at heart, who has boundless enthusiasm, and who brings sunshine, hope, and faith into the room, cannot help but be a leader and make lasting impressions upon his pupils. On the other hand, what pupil can receive inspiration and the desire to work from a teacher who feels and acts as if all is wrong with the world, who is careless in his appearance, and who appears lifeless and cold?

Ask any principal or superintendent what kind of teachers he prefers. Ask any parent what kind of teachers he wants his children to have in school. Ask any child what kind of teachers he likes the best. The answer in almost every case, possibly we would be safe to say in every case, will be "teachers of pleasing, vigorous, and inspiring personalities." This does not mean that personality is the only necessary quality that a successful teacher should have, but it does show the importance of it. Personality will not make a teacher truly successful who lacks knowledge of content and of methods. Like a clock which depends upon many moving wheels for keeping accurate time, so success in teaching depends upon a number of factors, each of which plays a leading part in making a great teacher.

2. *Sympathy*

Teachers are often asked if they do not get tired of teaching the same subjects year after year to their pupils. To an outsider who has never had the joy of teaching, it looks as if teaching the same subject again and again would become very monotonous. You may imagine how surprised people are when they hear teachers say that teaching the same subject over to boys and girls is not tiresome or monotonous. At first they think the teachers are only bluffing when they say that they enjoy teaching the same subjects year after year, but when a teacher gets through explaining that he is teaching children and not merely subjects, the idea begins to dawn upon them that teaching is not such a monotonous job after all. Each child has a mind of his own and he is capable of using it in thinking and reasoning. Teaching never grows wearisome because so many experiences are rising continually in the schoolroom. It is certainly an interesting task to lead boys and girls in reasoning and thinking so that they will develop the many different sides of their personalities.

In order to be a good teacher, a person must have sympathy for his pupils. A teacher must realize that learning is not merely an intellectual process. It is also an emotional process. Pupils in school need the sympathy of their teachers if they are going to enjoy their work and get the most out of it. The teacher should be a student of child psychology. He should understand the various stages through which the children pass as they grow from childhood to adulthood. He should strive to understand the interests of the children at the different periods in their growth. He should understand and appreciate the fact that all children do not have the same type of intelligence. Some children seem to be especially adapted for interpreting and understanding books, pictures, and similar materials. Other children are mechanically minded or enjoy working on concrete things. They like making objects with their hands, playing games, and doing other such activities. A third class of students have the ability of being leaders of students. They are what some people call "natural born leaders." Still another group of pupils are interested chiefly in art, music, literature, and other forms of aesthetic intelligence.

Since all pupils are not alike in their ability to think and to do school work, the teacher should try to understand each one of them. The teacher needs to be a student of human nature. He should be able to put himself in the place of the other person. An old successful teacher was once asked by a beginning teacher how he had been able over so many years to teach boys and girls to like not only their work but also to like him. He replied that he was interested in children and he tried to understand them. If the teacher and pupils really understand one another, school work will be a pleasure.

Some teachers with much knowledge of subject matter and of methods have failed because they did not know how to use tact and common sense; and without using tact and common sense, the right kind of sympathy between a teacher and his pupils, or between the teacher and his fellow workers will not be developed. A person who is tactful practices self-restraint, he does not lose his temper, and he is agreeable. He is careful about his remarks and he is not sarcastic. He encourages his pupils and tries to find good in what they are doing. He skilfully leads his pupils to change their methods whenever it is to their advantage. Such a teacher is surely a leader and not a taskmaster.

I am thinking of two teachers whom I once knew. Let us call one Mr. Untactful Teacher and the other one Mr. Tactful Teacher. Mr. Untactful Teacher said he believed in speaking his mind openly and freely. He wanted people to know where he stood. He said things without considering their effect upon his friends or any other person. He said he believed in freedom of speech, and that he was going to practice it. As a result of this, Mr. Untactful Teacher had few friends and even at times they were hurt by his remarks. His pupils did not like him and they did not get much joy from their work. They seldom started any work on their own initiative, but had to be told what to do.

Mr. Tactful Teacher always had a great many friends. His pupils liked him and they enjoyed their work. They started problems of their own and they were never afraid to approach him for help or encouragement. Mr. Tactful Teacher always considered his pupils before he spoke. When he saw that things were going wrong with the pupils, in place of finding fault, he encouraged them and skilfully led them to attack their work in a new way. He always appeared to be cheerful and happy. He even enjoyed laughing at humorous things with the children.

His schoolroom was a pleasant place in which efficient work was being done by the pupils.

Tactful teachers are liked by their fellow teachers and by the parents of the pupils. Generally, if the pupils like a teacher, the parents like him. Sometimes it is necessary for a parent to come to school to interview the teacher about his child who has had some difficulty with his work or with the other pupils. At such times, the teacher who understands human nature will greet the parent with a friendly smile and he will try to show him that he is really interested in the education of his child. Of course, the teacher may not always succeed in receiving the whole-hearted cooperation of a parent, but in most cases he will go away praising the teacher in place of disliking him. Tact is not a cheap or underhand method which successful teachers use in getting things done in the way which they think is right, but it is the common sense method where all factors are considered in a friendly atmosphere.

3. Sincerity

Teachers should have sincerity. They should be in earnest about their work. They should enter into it with devotion and should remember that anything worthwhile is worth a struggle. By having earnestness, devotion, and loyalty, a teacher gains the courage which he so much needs in being a successful teacher. He needs courage to stand for high ideals and to keep from following the road of least resistance. When things go wrong or move slowly in school, it is easy to become discouraged, but sincerity gives a teacher enough faith or optimism to enable him to overcome most obstacles. It gives him faith that the social studies he is teaching will tend to influence the lives of his pupils in the right way and that they will have a better understanding and appreciation of the American way of living. Any teacher who lacks this optimism will likely fail as a successful teacher.

Sincerity helps a teacher to be impartial. In this day and age of the world where people take sides on a question, it is somewhat difficult for a teacher to be impartial in a classroom, but impartial he must be. He must be broad-minded, fair-minded, open-minded, free from prejudice, and have tolerance for the views of others. He must guide the pupils in their thinking and reasoning without the least sign of prejudice or partiality. The school should be a place where pupils form their own opinions after hearing various sides of the question.

Pupils like a teacher better if he is impartial than if he is partial. If the word is spread around that the teacher has pets or favors certain classes of children, most pupils dislike being in his classes. A teacher must decide many issues, and he should decide them fairly and wisely. All classes of children should be treated with the same degree of fairness, whether they be from rich homes or from poor homes, whether they are clean or dirty, or whether their parents have some connection with the running of the school or are just ordinary people with no connection whatsoever with managing the school. When a child breaks some rule of the school or gets into trouble with some of his playmates, a teacher should look at all sides of the problem and consider it from various standpoints. He should try to put himself in the place of the child and imagine why it was that he acted the way he did. By doing this, the teacher will better understand the actions of the child and he will come to his conclusions impartially. Sometimes the teacher will see that it was only natural for the child to act as he did.

A sincere teacher will probably have a vivid imagination. He will think of ways of teaching and will imagine the results that may be obtained. In his imagination he will see places, scenes, and historical persons. He will imagine his pupils doing certain things and he will think of ways of aiding them. Imagination also gives a teacher a glimpse of some future time and of better methods of teaching pupils.

4. Progressiveness

By progressiveness we mean growth. Every teacher of the social studies must be continually growing in the knowledge of subject matter and in the power to teach, if he expects to be a superior teacher. We are living in a changing world where great events are occurring, where old methods are giving way to new, and where new problems must be faced and solved. The teacher who claims that the methods of today are the same as those of forty or fifty years ago, is so blind to what is happening in the world that he should not be a teacher. Progress is the watchword of every true teacher.

Just how do teachers go about making progress and keeping informed about the current problems and the latest methods of teaching? Some of the most common ways are as follows:

(1) They subscribe to one or more educational magazines which have helpful articles on the teaching of the social studies.

(2) They read newspapers and magazines.

(3) They read recent books on methods and on subject matter.

(4) They belong to organizations such as the National Council for the Social Studies, the National Council of Geography Teachers, and the National Education Association. They also join state or local organizations and take an active part in them.

(5) They spend a part of their vacation in traveling or in going to school.

(6) They attend lectures, visit places, listen to good radio programs, and talk with people.

(7) They experiment in new ways of teaching.

(8) Whenever the opportunity arises, they visit social studies classes in other schools.

(9) They take as much part as their time and circumstances permit in the various activities of their community.

5. *Knowledge of the Subject Matter*

A teacher of the social studies must have as thorough knowledge of the subject matter as possible. A successful teacher must have a knowledge of what he is teaching. If he lacks sufficient knowledge he will not be able to teach the pupils the things they should know. A person must have accurate information if he is going to think wisely. Much of our loose thinking is based upon inaccurate facts. Without question, one of the chief reasons why so many people are unable to think clearly on the events of today is because they lack accurate information. Of course some people have never formed the habit of doing much constructive thinking. It is important for the teacher of the social studies to have a broad knowledge of his field if he is going to be a good leader and a guide to his pupils.

Now, some teachers may claim that many teachers seem to get along without having much knowledge of what they are teaching. This is true, but the pupils would surely advance much more rapidly if these teachers were better informed. Again, think of the effect it will have upon the pupils in later years when they come to understand that they did not get the knowledge of the social studies they should have obtained in school. If the school is merely a place where children spend their time until they are old enough to get positions, it probably does not matter whether a teacher has much knowledge; but if the school is a place where children are truly trained to be intelligent citizens, it does matter. Of course it must be remembered that the teacher should have other qualities, besides knowledge of subject matter.

The social studies cover such a large field that it is impossible for a young teacher to obtain in a four-year college course all the knowledge that he should have. A teacher of the social studies in the grades and in the high school should know a reasonable amount of history, government, geography, sociology, economics, and anthropology. He may specialize in one or two of these subjects, if he so desires. He should also have a general knowledge of the other subjects which are taught in the school. In this way he can relate his work to the work which other teachers are doing. A teacher should be a well-rounded individual, because his main job is to teach pupils and not mere facts of subject matter.

The teacher is never satisfied with the little that he knows. He should strive to get more knowledge. He will gain his knowledge chiefly by reading books, newspapers, and magazines; by attending summer school classes; by conversing with people; by listening to lectures; and by traveling. Truly, it has been said that the search for information never ends until death.

6. Knowledge of Methods

It seems as if it is human nature for a person never to be entirely satisfied with what he has. He is always wanting more or something different. So it is with a progressive teacher. He is never satisfied with what he knows. He is always seeking knowledge because he realizes that knowledge is power. A knowledge of both subject matter and of method is very important. Many teachers who have much knowledge of subject matter and very little knowledge of methods wish that they knew more about the various methods used in teaching. On the other hand, many teachers who have been well trained in methods but lack subject matter often wish that they knew more subject matter. It is of very little importance to discuss which is of more value to the teacher, subject matter or method. The chief thing to remember is that both are important. Of course, there may be some teachers who are poorly trained in methods and yet are considered good teachers by their friends. Think how much better teachers they would be if they knew more about the methods of teaching.

Let us say that in a general way, we mean by methods the plans that a teacher uses in helping the pupils do their work in the social studies. Method is also concerned with the problem of how and when to do certain things. So it may easily be seen that no teacher can escape using some kind of method, even though he may give it little thought.

The teacher should strive to learn about the methods which are used by other teachers in teaching the social studies, so that he may determine whether he is using the best method. Even though a teacher is using a superior method, he will likely be able to improve his teaching by learning what other teachers are doing. There is no one best method that all teachers should use since teachers are not alike, since groups of pupils have different problems, and since conditions vary in different regions at various times. However, there is a method which is best for each teacher to use at any given time, and it is his job to find that method. As a teacher improves in teaching ability, his method of teaching will likewise improve, and therefore change. A teacher must be willing to experiment, because it is only by experimenting that progress can be made.

The teacher should strive to develop the art of asking questions and of telling and explaining. He should use a conversational tone in his classes. He should endeavor to get the pupils interested in their work and to keep them interested. Much use should be made of visual aids and illustrative material. Considerable thought should be given to the assignments so that they will be clear and meaningful. Likewise, tests should be given and they should be used wisely and intelligently. Supervised study should be employed and the lessons should be socialized. Pupils should always be encouraged to use their experiences and to depend upon themselves.

THE TEACHER AND DISCIPLINE

Poor discipline in the schoolroom has been the cause of the failure of many teachers. The chief reasons why some teachers of the social studies have poor discipline are (1) lack of preparation for teaching the social studies, (2) poor teaching personality, and (3) lack of teaching ability. So in order not to have poor discipline, the teacher should endeavor to see that none of these reasons exist. There is no good reason why a teacher should be allowed to teach the social studies who cannot have good discipline. Poor discipline is like a disease. It is caused by something which must be removed or overcome. If a teacher cannot remove or overcome this something, it is a very good sign that he is a failure as a teacher.

Young teachers sometimes have problems of discipline because they lack confidence which comes from experience. It is true that experience is a good teacher and that an experienced teacher should have better discipline than a beginning teacher. However, a young person with all the qualities of a good teacher will not have many serious discipline problems, if any.

Any child who is idle or is doing something that he does not want to do is likely to be mischievous. Hence, the teacher should try to see that the pupil is doing something worthwhile and that he enjoys his work. Encourage the pupils to do various kinds of activities in solving their problems. Let them see that you are really interested in them. Each pupil should be led to understand that he is only one of a group and that all must cooperate in having a good school. Put the responsibility of having good discipline upon the pupils by letting them take an active part in managing the schoolroom. Since we are preparing children to be good citizens, we should practice in our schoolrooms what we teach. If a pupil insists on doing things that he should not do, the displeasure of his fellow-pupils will usually be enough to make him fall in line. Only rarely does the good teacher have any serious discipline problem.

IMPROVING THE RELATIONSHIP OF TEACHERS
WITH ONE ANOTHER

All teachers of the social studies should have the same general aims, regardless of what grade or of what work they are teaching. All are working to give the children those experiences which will make them better citizens and will cause them to understand more clearly the meaning of American democracy. Everything should be done with the pupils in mind and one of the chief questions is, "How is what I am doing likely to affect the development of the children?" Still another question is, "Am I doing all that I can do for the proper development of the children?" Since every teacher of the social studies and of any other subject has dedicated himself to the cause of teaching, there should be cooperation between him and all other teachers. In union there is strength. Teachers should work harmoniously together, and each teacher should continually be working to improve his relations with the group.

Some of the definite ways of improving your relationship with other teachers are the following:

1. Consider the feelings of other teachers and never do anything to them that you would not want them do to you.

2. Treat all fellow teachers with respect and remember that any rivalry should be friendly, stimulating, and uplifting.

3. Freely exchange ideas and experiences about teaching with other teachers.

4. Take an active part in teachers' organizations and remember that you are but one in a group of teachers and that others have as much right as you in discussing questions, in offering suggestions, and in holding office.

5. Do not be jealous or distrustful of your fellow workers.

6. Cooperate freely and willingly with all your fellow teachers and let your motto be "teamwork."

7. Always stand ready to help a beginning teacher or someone who is in distress, but before doing so try to get their viewpoint so that you can offer your help in such a way that it will be gladly received.

8. Try to conduct yourself at all times so that your fellow teachers will not have any just cause to find fault with you.

9. Be careful about criticizing other teachers and do not take part in harmful gossip about them.

10. Try to find good in your fellow teachers and be friendly and sociable.

SELF ANALYSIS

Anyone who has an automobile or any other piece of machinery knows that occasionally it is a good idea to look over its different parts to see that all of them are in good order and are functioning efficiently. Time is saved, better results are obtained, and the operations costs are reduced by keeping machinery in good operating condition. Likewise, it is well for teachers to examine themselves occasionally to see that they are doing their work most efficiently. Teachers should not be satisfied merely to get along in teaching, but they should strive to improve their teaching. When a teacher becomes entirely satisfied with what he is doing, he is no longer making progress.

Teachers may discover many of their defects by self-analysis. They may take a scale that has been made for rating teachers and use it in rating themselves. Those qualities which are rated low show the teacher where he must make special effort to improve his teaching. When a teacher becomes perfect in his own mind, he should retire. No teacher ever reaches a place where it is no longer necessary for him to think about improving his teaching. A good teacher is always growing and discovering new ways of doing things.

The following scale contains some of the important factors that teachers should consider in self-analysis. It is put here with the hope that teachers will find it of value in analyzing themselves with a view of improving their teaching. Of course, the scale does not include every point which should be considered in rating a teacher, but it includes enough to cause a teacher to think. When a teacher begins to think along the right lines, he is on the road to improvement. The answer to each question in the scale should be yes, but the teacher in analyzing himself might use excellent, average, fair, or poor.

A SCALE FOR RATING TEACHERS OF
THE SOCIAL STUDIES

I. Knowledge of The Subject Matter.
   1. Have I a sufficient knowledge of the subject matter to teach the social studies?
   2. Have I made all possible effort and am I still making every possible effort to obtain more knowledge about the units I am teaching?
   3. Do I keep informed about current events and do I try to relate the work of the social studies to present-day happenings?
   4. Do I make use of the library, newspapers, and magazines in obtaining knowledge?
   5. Do I increase my knowledge by attending summer school or extension classes, by travel, by visiting places, by going to motion picture shows and the theater, by listening to good radio programs, and by associating with others?

II. Personal Traits.
   1. Do I give enough attention to my clothes and to cleanliness so that I will make a good personal appearance?
   2. Do I take care of my health?
   3. Have I sufficient self-control and patience that
      a. I do not lose my temper or "my head" in a trying situation?
      b. I listen to criticism without getting angry?
      c. I smile, even when things go wrong?
      d. I do not scold or answer children in a harsh tone?
      e. I do not get out of patience when I have to change my plans without much notice from my principal?
   4. Am I dependable and do I cooperate with my fellow teachers?
   5. Do I use tact and do the pupils accept me cheerfully as their leader?
   6. Am I loyal to my principal and my school?

7. Do I have a sense of humor?
8. Am I sympathetic and do I frequently praise the pupils for doing good work or trying to do good work?
9. Do I set an example for my pupils by being interested and by taking as active part as possible in the affairs of the community?

III. Methods of Teaching.

1. Do I have sufficient knowledge about the methods of teaching and the types of lessons so that I can use them efficiently in teaching the social studies?
2. Do I use questions skilfully and wisely?
3. Do I make the work in the social studies interesting and worthwhile to the pupils?
4. Do I lead the pupils to make their own decisions and to rely upon themselves?
5. Do I use original ideas in teaching and am I resourceful?
6. Am I genuinely interested in the pupils, do I encourage them, does the schoolroom have a friendly atmosphere, and do I always try to get the point of view of the pupils?
7. Do I use the right kinds of tests at the most opportune time and do I make good use of them?
8. Do I try to keep informed about the latest and most approved methods?
9. Do the pupils make efficient use of maps, pictures, charts, books, cartoons, pamphlets, newspapers, magazines, the radio, and the movies in studying their units of work?
10. Do I plan my work before I attempt to teach it?

IV. The Pupils.

1. Do the pupils enjoy their work and enter into it with enthusiasm?
2. Do the children help plan their work, do they develop initiative, and do they learn to depend upon themselves?
3. Do the pupils talk freely with the teacher?

4. Are the pupils courteous to one another and do they work well together?

5. Does each pupil seem to be making as rapid progress as possible?

PROBLEMS FOR RESEARCH AND DISCUSSION

1. Explain what is meant by saying that a teacher and a group of pupils constitute a school.

2. Give your idea of a good school.

3. After some reading, much thinking, and interviewing various types of people, make a list of the qualities of a good teacher.

4. What are some of the qualities which go to make a pleasing personality?

5. Give examples of tactfulness and untactfulness in some teachers which you have had.

6. Discuss the statement that a teacher should have faith, hope, and charity.

7. Give a good description of a progressive teacher.

8. What knowledge of subject matter should a teacher of the social studies have? What courses in college should he take? Name a few good books, other than textbooks, that a teacher in the social studies should read. Review an article in a recent magazine which should be read by a teacher of the social studies.

9. What magazines are especially helpful for getting ideas about the different ways of teaching? Review some article which you think is very good.

10. Give your idea about the kind of discipline a teacher should have in the classroom. How should a teacher go about getting discipline?

11. Think of the teachers you have had. What did you admire about them? What were some of the things you disliked about them?

12. Make a list of ways in which the relationships among teachers may be improved.

13. Examine several scales for rating teachers. Of what value are they? If you were a principal, how would you use such scales?

14. Think carefully and write a paragraph of not more than 250 words on "The Ideal Teacher."

REFERENCES

Association of Social Studies Teachers of New York City, *A Teaching Guide for the Social Studies*. New York: College Entrance Book Co., 1941.

III. The Personality of the Teacher, 30-34.

Bagley, William and Alexander, Thomas, *The Teacher of the Social Studies*. New York: Charles Scribner's Sons, 1937.

Bining, Arthur and Bining, David, *Teaching the Social Studies in the Secondary Schools*. New York: McGraw-Hill Book Co., 1941.
    Chapter XI. The Teacher of the Social Studies, 202-222.

Curti, Merle, "The Responsibility of the Teacher in Times of Crises," Social Education, V, 251-255, April, 1941.

Davis, W. R., "The Teacher of the Social Studies," The Social Studies, XXXI, 19-22, January, 1940.

Frederick, Robert and Sheats, Paul, *Citizenship Education Through the Social Studies*. New York: Row, Peterson and Co., 1936.
    Chapter X. The Education of Social Studies Teachers, 215-224.

Gruver, Harvey, "The In-Service Training of Teachers," Education, LVI, 227-230, December, 1935.

In-Service Growth of Social Studies Teachers, Tenth Yearbook, National Council for the Social Studies, 1939.

Jackson, W. C., "Devices for In-Service Education of Teachers," School Board Journal, CIII, 56, September, 1941.

Karlin, Jules and Steiner, George J., "Prospective Teachers Study and Serve Chicago," Social Education, V, 339-342, May, 1941.

Lind, John, "Travel as Teacher Education," Social Education, V, 196-198, March, 1941.

Mathews, Charles F., "Training of an Elementary Social Science Teacher," Texas Outlook, XXIV, 43-44, September, 1940.

Moore, H. K. and Benson, Bette, "How Teachers Annoy Pupils," Education, LXI, 51-55, September, 1940.

Roma, Gans, "The Teacher in the Community," Teachers College Record, XLIII, 100-107, November, 1941.

Sandison, Mildred, "The Growing Teacher," The Journal of the National Education Association, XXVIII, 183-184, September, 1939.

Sires, Ronald, "A Self Analysis Sheet for Social Studies Teachers," Social Education, IV, 569, December, 1940.

Skinner, Mabel, "The Problem of the Retarded Teacher," Social Education, I, 104-109, February, 1937.

Chapter Five: USING COMMUNITY

RESOURCES WISELY AND EFFICIENTLY

THE SCHOOLS ARE ON THE MOVE

DURING THE past few years, a growing number of schools have been making use of their community resources in teaching the boys and girls to be good citizens. It is being realized more and more that a good citizen must have an intelligent interest in his community and that the time to start to develop this interest is the very first day he enters school. Such an interest cannot be truly developed only by reading books, looking at pictures, or getting information about the community in a round-about way. Actual trips must be taken to various places in the community so that first-hand information may be obtained. Things about which we study in our books may often be studied first-hand in the community.

Various terms are used for trips taken by pupils from the schoolhouse. Some teachers call them excursions. Still other teachers call them field trips, journeys, or visits. Some teachers think that the term "field trip" implies more serious work than do any of the other terms. To some people an excursion, a journey, or a visit means pleasurable excitement and maybe no serious study. However, all school work should be pleasurable and should create a certain amount of excitement in the minds of the pupils. There is no good reason why an excursion, a journey, or a visit should not involve serious work if the teacher so desires. The name that we use is not so important. The big aim is to bring the pupils in direct contact with life in the community.

In our best schools, children in the kindergarten learn about their neighborhood by taking short trips. As they advance from

grade to grade they continue to take trips. In order to understand the simple facts of home geography, short excursions are
taken by third or fourth grade children. The best place to teach
about hills, valleys, streams, soil erosion, and many other natural
phenomena is not in the schoolroom, but outside the schoolroom.
To understand the problems of manufacturing, mining, farming,
fishing, and lumbering, visits to places where these industries are
carried on mean much more to pupils than merely reading books.
Whenever possible and practical, geography should be taught by
observing the actual conditions.

We try to make history seem real to pupils. We want each
child to relive the past in his imagination. In order to teach
history, we should get the pupils interested in the history of their
community. A little search in any community shows that there
are places of historic interest which should be visited by the
pupils. There may be monuments erected in honor of some great
men or events. A few old houses and churches may show the
types of buildings common to the neighborhood many years ago.
Furniture used in past periods of history may still be seen in
some houses. Possibly there is a museum in which relics and
models of historical articles may be studied.

To get a clear idea of the way a city is governed, classes often
attend meetings of the city council. To understand how our
courts function, visits are made to courtrooms where trials are
taking place. Social agencies, hospitals, the police department,
the fire department, the health department, and many other
places are visited. Today, our best schools are surely places where
pupils are on the move. Books are still used, but trips to actual
places are frequently taken to obtain first-hand knowledge.

NO FAD OR PASSING FRILL

When some teachers are asked if they take excursions with
their pupils, a common answer is somewhat as follows: "Oh, no,
I do not take excursions with my pupils. I have so much to teach
that I do not have time to go outside the building with my class."
Another common answer is: "We do not have time for play in
our school. My principal believes in work and he would never
think of giving me permission to take a class of pupils from the
school building." These same teachers often look somewhat mys-

tified when giving their answers for not taking excursions, and their actions seem to convey that an excursion is just another way of interesting children while not teaching them much of anything. Such teachers look upon school excursions as fads and passing frills, which will pass into oblivion in the near future; just as some other ideas of crack-brained teachers have been buried in the graveyard of impractical things. Of course such teachers are badly mistaken in their views.

Taking excursions to get first-hand information is nothing new. Man is a wandering person and he likes to travel over the earth in seeking knowledge about various things. From very early time until the present, he has been going here and there in search of information. Before man learned to write, the two chief ways that he had to get knowledge of distant places were either to visit them or to listen to people talk about them. We read about the Greeks and Romans visiting places to get information and new ideas. Some teachers in all ages have believed in having their pupils obtain a part of their knowledge by visiting places.

Those teachers who look upon excursions as a form of play do not understand the value of learning through concrete experiences. Neither do they realize that the community can furnish many of the experiences that children need in their school work. When they were children and went to school their work was based almost entirely upon books. Likewise, they still believe that almost all knowledge is obtained from books. They have the false idea that very little is learned from school excursions. In fact, they look upon school excursions as forms of delightful recreation where very little thinking or learning takes place. Those teachers who think that they have no time for excursions because they have so much work for their pupils to do, would be surprised to learn that well-planned excursions lighten the work in place of making the work heavier.

EXCURSIONS IN EUROPEAN COUNTRIES

Some European countries have made more use of excursions than has the United States. Before the last World War, it was a common sight in some European countries to see groups of children taking excursions to various places. Many of the excursions were taken to places in the local community and they lasted from a few minutes to a few hours in time. Some of the excursions were week-end trips and the children spent the night away from home. Still other excursions occupied several days and were taken to places considerable distances from the regions where the children lived. Occasionally a group of children from one country visited a neighboring country. Most of the excursions were grouped into the following four classes:

(1) Those for physical development.
(2) Those for recreation or pleasure.
(3) Those for instruction.
(4) Those for a combination of reasons.

The children on overnight excursions in European countries usually spent their nights in youth hostels. The hostels were established especially for young travelers. The rates were low and everything was clean. There were large rooms where the young folks could gather and meet one another or read. There were rooms for boys and other rooms for girls. There were stoves for cooking. Various modes of travel were used by the children, such as hiking, riding bicycles, and riding on trains.

YOUTH HOSTELS

During recent years youth hostels have been opened in certain sections of the United States. The hostels have beds, blankets, cooking utensils, and other needed materials. The hostels are open to members who pay a small sum for the privilege of spending the night in them. The hostels help to make traveling inexpensive and are likely to increase in the future. Since most school excursions in the United States are seldom more than a few hours long, very little use has been made of the hostels by our schools. However, the time may come when it will be a common occurrence for children in the high school and in the seventh and eighth grades to spend more than one day on an excursion away from home.

WHY TAKE EXCURSIONS?

Many schools have come to recognize excursions as a regular part of their program. They have learned from experience that many of the important objectives of school work may be obtained better and more easily by taking field trips than by trying to have the pupils do all their work in the schoolroom. Field trips add interest to the school work, they arouse the curiosity of the pupils, and much joy results from the discoveries which are made. They make the work seem more nearly real and meaningful because actual experiences are likely to be understood better than the mere reading about them. The noise of waterfalls or of machinery, the odor of certain places, the actual work on a farm or in a factory, and a real trial in a courtroom are likely to make deep impressions on pupils which will be remembered a long time. Pupils are taught to observe accurately and keenly on field trips. They learn how to think by evaluating and organizing various kinds of materials. Under expert guidance, pupils learn to see much where many people see very little. Their interests are broadened and they come to have a higher regard for their community.

Those teachers who take field trips with their classes believe that the work of the school should be related to the activities of the community and that the community should be a laboratory for the school. The people of a community take more interest in their schools when they understand that their children are actually interested in problems that concern everyone. Pupils visit places in the community to get new problems and to supplement and explain the work which they are doing in the school. Sometimes the material which they read in books would be much more meaningful if certain trips were made.

While visiting places in the community, pupils gradually come to understand the interdependence of people. They learn something about occupations and they appreciate more fully the value of work. They see that it is necessary for various kinds of work to be done and that the man in work clothes should be respected just the same as the man in finer clothing. Field trips also develop a better understanding between teachers and pupils. On such trips, pupils and teachers get to know one another better. Timid pupils are no longer likely to be afraid of the teacher, and the observing teacher sees things that helps him to understand better his pupils.

Properly conducted field trips give pupils experience in planning and working together. Self-initiative, responsibility, and

leadership are developed. At the same time, pupils learn to follow directions and to listen to others.

Teachers may learn if field trips are valuable to pupils by
observing what they do after returning from the trips. If a pupil
repeats some of the trips by himself or with some of his relatives
or friends; if he is stimulated to start a school museum, to keep
the alley behind his house clean, or to do some other worthwhile
community activity; if he becomes interested in taking other trips
during his leisure time; or if he takes a more active interest in
the problems of his community, a teacher feels sure that the
school excursions have been of much value to him.

TEACHER PREPARATION

The teacher should know thoroughly the region in which the
school is located, if he is going to make use of its resources in his
teaching. This often means that the teacher should spend some
of his spare time in visiting places in the region. He should
study the community and learn what the possibilities are of using
its various resources. Sometimes groups of teachers join together
to study their community. Many teachers never fully realize the
problems of their community and its resources until they begin
to study it.

The principal often aids his teachers in preparing to take
excursions with their classes. He may issue a bulletin stating
much of the necessary information that teachers should have
concerning excursions. Sometimes it is necessary for the principal to get permission for a teacher to visit a particular place
with a class. If a teacher knows this ahead of time, it will likely
save him much annoyance and trouble.

ARRANGEMENTS BY THE TEACHER

The teacher should make arrangements for an excursion several
days before it is to be taken. He may have a committee of pupils
to assist him whenever it is possible, because children should
be given as much responsibility as possible.

One of the first things a teacher should do when he is thinking about taking an excursion is to discuss the proposed excursion with the principal or some other administrative official

to whom he is directly responsible. He should obtain permission to take his pupils on the excursion. Of course if a teacher does not have some administrative official over him, he decides for himself whether to take the class on an excursion, providing his school board does not object. If there is a principal he may do much in making an excursion a success. (1) He may encourage the teacher by letting him see that he realizes the value of the excursion. (2) He may give the teacher the benefit of his experience in taking excursions. (3) He may help the teacher make the arrangements for the excursion. Sometimes the principal can get results more easily than the teacher, since he is the one in charge of the whole school. (4) He may let some of the older pupils go along to help care for the children. (5) He should arrange to care for any pupil who cannot go on the journey. (6) He may discuss the value of excursions with the parents.

After selecting a place to which an excursion may be taken, the teacher should visit it with the idea of learning what the pupils may see on their trip. The teacher may find that the pupils would not see or hear enough to pay them to go on the trip, although the chances are that he will find the place to offer splendid opportunities for an excursion. By visiting the place in advance of the class, the teacher learns what things to point out to the pupils. He may also explain to the guide the purpose of taking the trip and give certain suggestions which will tend to make the work of the guide more valuable. Before making up his mind to take the excursion with his class, the teacher should make certain that it is safe for the pupils to visit the place. It is unwise to take undue risks with pupils. The teacher must always remember not to take the pupils to any place where there is danger of some child being injured.

The teacher should obtain permission to take his class to visit a certain place on a given date from the manager or the person who is in charge. Proper arrangements should be made so that everything will be ready for the class when it arrives. It is very unwise to make a surprise visit with a class to a factory, a museum, or any other place. Some factories never admit pupils to observe what is going on within their walls. Sometimes there are only certain days when visitors are admitted. If too many people go to a certain place at any one time, all of them cannot be accommodated. Hence, the wise teacher always makes arrangements for visiting a given place a few days ahead of time.

Some other things that the teacher should determine are (1) the time of leaving the school building and of returning to it with the class, (2) the cost of the excursion to the pupils, (3) what will be done about lunch if the children are on the excursion during their lunch period, (4) the kind of transportation that will be used, (5) the route to take, (6) what stops are to be made on the route and how much time to spend at each stop, (7) what the pupils are expected to learn on the excursion, and (8) how to prepare the pupils for the excursion. If the place to be visited is near the school building, the pupils will walk to it. If the place cannot be easily reached by walking, some other method of transportation must be used, such as the street railway, private automobiles, and busses. Teachers should always make sure that responsible people are in charge of automobiles and busses and that the cars are adequately insured for accidents. In some places, school busses are used.

Most teachers do not think it is necessary to get permission from the parents to take a class on a short walk near the school, providing there is no danger of the children getting hurt and the children are gone only a short time from the building. The parents take for granted that short trips near the school are a part of the regular school work. For example, a first grade teacher might take his class for a short walk near the school to observe the buildings and streets. He may visit a nearby store. A short walk in a small park to observe the plants, animals, and playgrounds might be taken without the permission of the parents, providing the park is very near the school and the walk is not dangerous. Of course, if there is a principal or some other person in charge of the school, he must always be consulted before taking a class out of the building.

Generally speaking, whenever the teacher takes a class from the school on an excursion, he should get permission of the parents. This is very important for the teacher to remember. Parents have a right to know where their children are at all times. Hence if the children go on an excursion, the parents should know it. Since there is always some element of danger involved in any excursion, the consent of the parents must be obtained. Then if there should be an accident, the parents should not hold the teacher responsible. The teacher must remember that the parents have trusted the care of their children to him and he must keep the idea of safety in mind at all times.

Most teachers believe that it is the wisest plan to get the written consent of the parents for their children to go on an excursion. Some schools have printed forms which are filled in with the necessary data by the teacher. The pupils take the form home to be signed by their parents.

In some schools the teacher and pupils compose a letter which each pupil copies and takes home to his parents. The letter contains all necessary details such as the place to be visited, the date, the time when the class is to leave the building, the time when the class will return to the building, the method of transportation to be used, and possibly something about what is to be studied. At the close of the letter something like the following is added: I give my permission for (*name of pupil*) ....
to go on the excursion.

(*name of parent*) ....

PUPIL PREPARATION

Whenever practical, the pupils should aid the teacher in planning and making arrangements for an excursion. Excursions mean more to pupils if they really feel that they have had an active part in planning them. Leadership and responsibility are developed as well as many other good traits. Committees are frequently appointed by the pupils to work with the teacher in making arrangements for an excursion. There are many details which may be looked after by the committees.

The interest of all the pupils should be aroused before they start on the trip. There are various ways of doing this. Sometimes pictures, posters, and other materials of interest are put on the bulletin board. The teacher and some of the pupils often give short talks on what may be seen. Some one who has already visited the place may give a vivid description of what he saw.

The pupils should be given the necessary instructions such as (1) the location of the place to be visited, (2) the date of the excursion and the time of leaving the school building and returning to it, (3) the kind of transportation to be used and the cost, and (4) what to do about lunch. They should get the written permission of their parents. The teacher and pupils should discuss the importance of observing all safety precautions such as (1) being careful in crossing the streets and in getting on and off the cars and busses, (2) keeping hands off movable machinery and obeying any signs, and (3) staying near the teacher or guide. Each pupil should understand that a certain amount of responsibility rests upon his shoulders.

It is always a wise idea to discuss the matter of discipline with the children. They should understand that they should obey certain rules of conduct and not bring disgrace to the school. A teacher who has good discipline in the schoolroom need have no fear of not having good discipline on an excursion. However, if a teacher has poor discipline in a schoolroom, he will probably have poor discipline on a field trip. It is too much to expect children to conduct themselves properly on an excursion when they are unruly in the schoolroom. A teacher who cannot have good discipline in the inside of a building should never venture out in the open world with a class of children. Such a teacher brings disgrace to the profession of teaching.

The teacher and pupils may make a list of things which they would like to observe on the excursion. There may be certain questions which they wish to have answered. Sometimes the questions are written on paper. Usually the questions require short answers. If the children are visiting a museum, they may write their answers as they go from one exhibit to another. If there is no opportunity for writing the answers to questions while on the excursion, the pupils may write them on their return to school, providing written answers are thought to be necessary. Many teachers think that the children on an excursion should do very little writing, since it is difficult to observe and write at the same time. For this reason they instruct their pupils to see and to remember as much as they can. The children should stay near the guide so that they can hear what he says. Guides should be instructed to talk loud enough to be heard and to use language which the children can understand.

FOLLOW-UP WORK

After the pupils return from an excursion, there is a certain amount of work to do. There should be a discussion of what they saw or learned. In the discussion, the pupils will have an opportunity of asking questions about anything that was not clear to them. Sometimes a pupil comes to an incorrect conclusion about something he has seen, and in the discussion he is able to change his views. It is always a good idea to have the pupils summarize what they learned.

The excursion may call for various reports. There may be group reports or individual reports. They may be written or given orally. Sometimes a pupil wishes to obtain more information about something he observed on the excursion. Possibly, some questions are raised which require the reading of special references. One important function of an excursion is to raise questions for further study. On some excursions, the pupils have papers on which they answer questions. The answers to the questions may be corrected by the pupils in class or by the teacher. The pupils should use the knowledge which they have gained in studying new problems. Sometimes the work in other classes may be motivated by the knowledge obtained on an excursion.

Tests may be given after the pupils return from an excursion to check some of the chief points which the pupils should have learned. These may include both the essay type and the new type test. Pupils enjoy answering the true-false test, the completion test, the matching test, the multiple choice test, and other forms of the new type test when the results are used wisely by their teachers.

TYPES OF EXCURSIONS

Local Trips Near the School. The children in the kindergarten or first grade may visit some of the different rooms in the buildings and take a walk over the schoolgrounds. Later, they may take short walks over the neighborhood to observe buildings, plants, animals, the ways the streets run, the work that people are doing, and many other things. Many short trips within walking distance of the school may be taken by pupils in various grades. Usually, such a trip occupies only one or two regular class periods. Local trips may be taken to a neighborhood park, a stream, a hill, a farm, a garden, the police station, the fire station, the library, a store, the postoffice, and a building in the process of being erected. The wide-awake teacher will have. no difficulty in finding places to visit with his class.

Community Trips. Many school trips occupy a half day or a whole day. Such trips may be taken to a farm, a mine, a museum, a factory, a railroad station, a wharf, the waterworks, and a court-room. The class may visit places to study erosion, the kinds of soil, the uses of the land, the work of rivers, and many other topics. Community trips are usually meant when mention is made of field trips in the upper grades and the high school.

Community Surveys. Classes in high schools and in the eighth grade frequently make community surveys. Sometimes the survey is of the entire community. At other times the survey may be of a certain section of the community. A certain school in Wadsworth, Ohio, reports that the pupils in one of their graduating classes wrote a book on their town. The pupils made many trips to various places to get information. They interviewed people, read old newspapers, magazines, histories, books, diaries, and letters, and examined old photographs. They visited factories, the library, newspaper offices, the city hall, the court house, and neighboring towns in search of information. High school pupils in Chicago and in many other places make community surveys which are a credit to their schools.

Sometimes the surveys which pupils make are very useful in improving conditions in the community. In Greeley, Colorado, a junior high school group of students made an accident survey of their city. The pupils collected such data as the number of accidents, where the accidents occurred, and where bicycle accidents occurred. They put their data in written and graphic form and presented the results of their research to the city council and the police. The pupils made definite recommendations about the placing of stop signs and the stationing of officers at certain places during specified hours of the day. Since the survey appeared to be sound, the police authorities were able to use it and they made several changes in line with the recommendations.

Travel Tours. Groups of high school students sometimes spend several days or a few weeks on trips to distant places. They visit such places as state capitals, the national capital, large cities, or some region in which natural features and man-made features are to be studied. The trips are carefully supervised and everything is well planned before starting out. Schools that offer such trips generally report favorably concerning them. During recent years, the number of schools offering travel tours has increased. More schools will likely offer travel tours, because the American people are gradually learning that one of the best ways of obtaining knowledge is to get it first hand.

PROBLEMS FOR RESEARCH AND DISCUSSION

1. Examine two or more courses of study in the social studies with a view of seeing what use is made of community resources. Report on what you learn.
2. Discuss the value of field trips or excursions.
3. Make a list of trips which children, studying the social studies in the grades, might take in your region. Make another list which high school pupils might take.
4. Make a study of youth hostels in this country and report on what you learn.
5. Examine the literature on excursions or field trips and learn what certain schools are doing. Prepare a report on your research.
6. What should the teacher do in preparing for a school excursion?
7. Suppose you are a teacher and are going to take your class on an excursion to some definite place. Write a letter which you and your pupils might compose for the parents of each child, asking permission for the child to go on the excursion.
8. Discuss the topic, "preparing pupils for an excursion."
9. Do you believe in note taking by the pupils on an excursion?
10. Describe how you would go about having the pupils in the upper grades make a community survey.

REFERENCES

Blouch, Adelaide, "Field Activities in the Middle Grades," The Journal of Geography, XXXIX, 246-248, September, 1940.
Brown, Inga, "Use of Community Resources in Rural Schools," Social Education, V, 520-524, November, 1941.
Carley, Verna, "Teacher Education in the Study of a Region," Educational Method, XX, 226-236, February, 1941.
Clarke, Katherine, "Making Community Study Effective in the Grades," Social Education, IV, 111-114, February, 1940.
Cline, Justin, "Youth Hosteling: Social Travel Toward Democracy," Educational Method, XX, 251-257, February, 1941.

Committee on the Function of the Social Studies in General Education of the Commission on Secondary School Curriculum, Progressive Education Association, *The Social Studies in General Education.* New York: D. Appleton-Century Co., 1940.
Chapter VIII. Social Education and Community Living, 281-311.
Crewson, Walter, "Field Work in Secondary School Geography," The Journal of Geography, XL, 153-156, April, 1941.
Crewson, Walter, "The Local Community as a Resource for Teaching High School Geography," The Journal of Geography, XXXIX, 105-109, March, 1940.
Davis, L. C., "Field Work in Geography," Educational Method, XVII, 293-296, March, 1938.
Dornblut, Julius, "Administering Elementary School Excursions," Educational Method, XVII, 70-73, November, 1937.
Eisen, Edna, "Field Work in Junior and Senior High School," The Journal of Geography, XXXVII, 75-77, February, 1938.
Goodwin, A. N., "Community Resources and the Social Studies," Social Education, IV, 414-416, October, 1940.
Gregg, F. M., "An Important Principle in Teaching Primary Grade Geography," Elementary School Journal, XLI, 665-670, May, 1941.
Harden, Mary, "The Community as a Laboratory for Elementary School Social Science," Social Education, I, 266-270, April, 1937.
Hensley, Eugene, "Reliving History Through School Trips," School Activities, XII, 346-350, May, 1941.
Hoban, Charles, Hoban, Charles, Jr., and Zisman, Samuel, *Visualizing the Curriculum.* New York: The Cordon Co., 1937.
Chapter I. Why Visual Aids in Teaching, 1-28.
Chapter II. The School Journey, 26-62.
Horn, Ernest, *Methods of Instruction in the Social Studies.* New York: Charles Scribner's Sons, 1937.
Chapter X. Sources of Concrete Experience, 393-440.
Johnson, William, "The Use of Community Resources in Education," Social Education, XXXI, 147-154, April, 1940.
Kindred, L. W. and Stephenson, O. W., "The Technique of the Field Trip," Social Education, V, 21-26, January, 1941.
Kruglak, Haym, "The Specialized Field Trip," The Educational Screen, XX, 341-355, October, 1941.
McKown, Harry, and Roberts, Alvin, *Audio-Visual Aids to Instruction.* New York: McGraw-Hill Book Co., 1940.
Chapter IX. School Trips and Tours, 181-210.
Merriam, Willis, "Field Work as a Factor in Dynamic Geography," The Journal of Geography, XXXIV, 157-160, April, 1935.
Northwest Regional Council, "Seattle Children Study Their Region," Curriculum Journal, XII, 114-117, March, 1941.

Olsen, E., "Community Study in Realistic Education," Educational Screen, XX, 224-261, June, 1941.

——, "A High School Uses the Community," Educational Method, XX, 236-244, February, 1941.

Parker, Edith, "Geography and the Community," The Journal of Geography, XL, 98-108, March, 1941.

Raleigh Public Schools, "Field Trips and Excursions," American Childhood, XXII, 8-10, 52, April, 1937.

Remmlein, Madaline, "Excursions Are Often Hazardous," The Nation's Schools, XXVII, 55-56, May, 1941.

Research Bulletin of the National Education Association, XV, November, 1937, Improving Social Studies Instruction.
Chapter VI. The Local Community As An Area of Study, 227-231.

Ridgley, Douglas, "Some Possibilities for Field Work in Elementary Geography," The Journal of Geography, XXXIV, 161-168, April, 1935.

Rife, Marvin, "Tours in Dynamic Education," Educational Method, XX, 223-226, February, 1941.

Riggs, Margaret, "Geography Field Work in the Small City," The Journal of Geography, XXXVII, 28-31, January, 1938.

Snedaker, Mabel, "Using Community Resources in the Primary Grades," Social Education, IV, 180-182, March, 1940.

Utilization of Community Resources in the Social Studies, Ninth Yearbook, National Council for the Social Studies, 1938.

Ward, Douglas, "Community Surveys for Junior High Schools," Social Education, IV, 553-556, December, 1940.

Wesley, Edgar, Teaching the Social Studies. New York: D. C. Heath and Co., 1937.
Chapter XXII, Utilizing Community Resources, 432-447.

Wood, Dora, "Planned Field Trips," School Science and Mathematics, XLI, 28-35, 1941.

Woolston, Loren, "Experimenting with Community Study," Social Education, II, 614-616, December, 1938.

Chapter Six: CURRENT EVENTS—KEEPING

ABREAST OF THE TIMES

IMPORTANCE

AN EVENT is something that takes place, so a current event is something that has happened recently. Now, two questions arise: "What is meant by recently?" and "How old can an event be before it stops being current?" These questions cannot be answered so definitely as one might wish. The answer depends upon many factors, such as the person who is thinking of the event, the time when the event occurred, the time when the person first heard of the event, and its importance.

Some people think of current events as things which are going on at the present time. Newspapers contain many current events which happened only a few minutes or hours before they were published. Weekly magazines discuss current events which occurred during the previous week. Monthly magazines often discuss problems which are still called current. Even some yearbooks claim to tell about current events which happened during the year.

Let us suppose that an event happens and that the world does not learn about it for several months or possibly for several years after it happened. For example, news of a discovery in a far away place may not reach us until several months after the discovery was made. Or maybe something happens to a far distant star about which astronomers do not learn for many years. When we first learn about such discoveries, we classify them as current events although the events happened long ago. Probably in such cases it would be more nearly correct to talk about current news instead of current events.

Teachers always have given some attention to current events, but it has been only during the present century that the teaching of current events has assumed great importance. The first World War of 1914-1918 gave a great incentive to the teaching of current events. Teachers and pupils began to take more interest in the events which were occurring. People became interested as never before in what was going on in the world. In order to be an intelligent citizen it was necessary for a person to be informed about current events. Teachers began to stress current events in teaching geography, history, civics, and other subjects. Children were interested in studying current events because they could see how many of the events were related to their lives.

After the first World War, the teaching of current events grew steadily in the schools. Teachers and pupils began to realize more and more that they are living in a dynamic society where many changes are taking place. Events are occurring daily which affect the lives of all of us. It is unwise for the schools to remain ignorant of current problems and to assume an ostrich-like attitude in regard to them. When pupils see how their lives are related to the various events which are happening in the world, they take an interest in studying them. They gradually learn to develop critical thinking and to understand the meaning of American democracy. They come to understand better the place which they occupy in this world and they are able to make better adjustments to their environment. Where current events are carefully taught, they vitalize the whole life of the school.

The pupils in our schools cannot help but know that important events are occurring throughout the world. They hear people on the street, in the homes, and in other places talk about certain events. They hear about them over the radio and read about them in the papers. They even see some of them happen. Since children are bound to have some knowledge of current events, and since their thinking and attitude toward life will be somewhat influenced by them, it is well that children study current events under expert guidance. Without forming the habit of intelligently learning about current events, people are just as likely to be misinformed as well as correctly informed. Many people believe that our present-day civilization cannot long survive if people are ignorant of the political, social, economic, moral, and spiritual problems which confront us. If this is true, we must not wait until people are adults before we expect them to become interested in current events. If we wait too long, many people will never become interested. Neither should we wait for pupils to reach college before they study current problems, because many children never reach college. All children go to school, and it is the business of the school to train people to think for themselves. Hence, the school must not only pass on the cultural heritage of the past but it must also deal with the happenings of present and recent times. In fact, it should probably go further and let the pupils in the higher grades occasionally speculate about the future.

WHERE SHOULD CURRENT EVENTS BE TAUGHT?

Many schools make it a part of their work to teach current events. Some courses of study state that current events are to be taught in certain grades. They give instructions in teaching current events. Many high schools have courses which are called modern problems.

In what grade should we begin to teach current events? The answer will depend upon the teacher and what the teacher thinks and teaches. Even before children learn to read about current events, they are likely to hear about them through news commentators over the radio. Likewise, they hear their parents and others discuss current happenings. Very often, the teacher tells a simple story in which current events are mentioned. For example, in the lower grades in studying about people of the cold deserts, the teacher may tell about some explorer who has recently returned from the Northland.

There are papers containing current events which are especially written for children of different ages. As a child advances in his ability to read and to listen to programs over the radio, his ability to study and interpret current events increases. Thus the extent to which current events can be taught depends largely upon the ability of the pupils to understand them.

REASONS FOR NOT TEACHING CURRENT EVENTS

1. Lack of Time. Many teachers of the social studies claim that they do not have enough time to teach current events and to teach all the work that is given in the course of study. It is true that teachers usually find that the course of study has enough work to keep the pupils busy without teaching current events. In fact, some of the courses of study contain more work than the pupils can find time to do. Therefore, if teachers are to teach current events, some of the work that is given in many courses of study must be omitted. Many teachers think that their course of study should come first, so they do not spend time in teaching current events.

If a course of study omits the teaching of current events, it should be revised. Many schools have already made over their courses of study so that current events may be taught. However, a certain amount of current events may be taught with any course of study, because the work of the social studies should always be related to current happenings.

2. *Lack of Interest by the Teacher.* One of the chief reasons for not teaching current events is that many teachers are not interested in teaching them. Some teachers do not realize the important place that current events should occupy in the school. They do not understand that a good citizen must have some knowledge of what is happening in the community, state, nation, and world at large. Those teachers who fail to realize the value of teaching current events are unlikely to spend much time in teaching them. They are likely to be poorly informed about events which are taking place in the world. It takes considerable time and work for a person to have an intelligent knowledge of the events which are happening and why they are happening. Some teachers are not willing to spend the necessary time to obtain this knowledge. Fortunately, the number of such teachers is growing smaller as the years pass.

3. *Lack of Training of the Teacher to Teach Current Events.* Many teachers have never received any or very much training in teaching current events. Such teachers may think that they do not have the knowledge or skill that is needed to teach current events successfully. Probably the lack of training is the chief reason why some teachers find it very difficult (1) to get the pupils interested in studying current events, (2) to get all the pupils to do their proper share of the work and to take an active part in the discussions, (3) to create a permanent desire in the pupils to read newspapers and magazines and to listen to good radio programs, (4) to teach the pupils to interpret the news, (5) to

know what problems or events to select for study, and (6) to teach controversial subjects.

4. Lack of Suitable Material for Study. Some teachers of the social studies claim that their pupils find it difficult to get suitable materials for studying current events. This problem is common to most teachers, and it is one that involves much thought and attention. Material that is suited for the high school and possibly for the seventh and eighth grades is often unsuited for the lower grades. Some of the material in newspapers and magazines is not always free of propaganda. When children become old enough they should be encouraged to read wisely and widely and to listen to various programs on the air. They should become interested in attending lectures and forums where current events are discussed. The newsreel should give a certain amount of information. Children should be encouraged to visit exhibits and to take excursions with the hope of gaining information. The older pupils might be urged to carry on certain investigations.

5. Lack of Skill in Handling Controversial Subjects. Many teachers have never learned how to teach controversial subjects. They lack skill in presenting all sides of a question to pupils. Knowing their weakness, they are afraid that the community will find fault with them if they attempt to teach problems about which people disagree. Again, the pupils may come to the wrong conclusions. Since most teachers need the money which they get in teaching, they feel as if they cannot afford to take the chance of losing their positions by teaching controversial issues.

Now, what should a teacher do who is afraid that if he teaches current events he will get into trouble? He should keep in mind the following points: (1) He should try to develop the necessary qualities that a teacher should possess to teach current events as mentioned a little later in this chapter. (2) He should understand that many current events are free from controversy. (3) He should realize that it is poor teaching to expect children to study about controversial subjects before they are old enough to understand the issues. This means that children in a given grade are not expected to study every current problem. (4) He should realize that the teaching of some current problems are more likely to cause a disturbance in the community than others. Since it is impossible to teach every current problem, the teacher will endeavor to use wisdom in helping the pupils select those problems which they wish to study. Many teachers prefer to omit those topics which they think are likely to cause ill feeling in the community, since there are others just as valuable which the pupils may discuss.

6. *Lack of Background by the Pupil for Understanding Current Events.* Some teachers feel that pupils do not have sufficient background to make much of a study of current events. It is true that pupils in the lower grades do not have much background, but their background expands as they progress in their work. By the time students have reached the last year of the senior high school, they should have a rather large background. Pupils in their senior year in high school should get far more out of the study of current events than the pupils below them. This is only natural.

There are many current problems which even adults do not have the background to understand so fully as they might wish. Many adults are confused over numerous problems which are now before us, such as the money problem, the tariff problem, the tax problem, and the rights of labor and capital. Even though most adults confess that they are not able to understand fully these problems, this fact does not keep them from being studied. There are many problems that most adults would never tackle if they had to wait until their background was large enough to explain satisfactorily everything about them. So adults try to understand current problems, even with a limited background. Likewise, current problems should not be omitted from the school just because the background of the pupils is limited. Of course the pupils should study problems on their own level, and those which are too difficult should not be studied.

7. *Lack of the Relation of Current Events to the Work Which the Pupils Are Doing.* Very often it is difficult for teachers of the social studies to relate the work which the pupils are doing to current events. Events happen regardless of what topics the pupils are studying. Sometimes the events are related to the work of the school, and at other times there is very little relation or the relation is not so evident. Those teachers who think that the only current events which can be discussed by pupils are those which are directly related to the work being done by the pupils, may find there is a lack of current events suitable for

discussion at certain times. Hence, there may be days when no current events are mentioned by the pupils.

REASONS FOR TEACHING CURRENT EVENTS

Talk to almost any educator and he will say that our schools must not be concerned so much with things that have happened in the far-distant past, that they neglect the things that have recently happened or are happening at the present time. Our schools are preparing children to live in the present and the future, not in the past. Therefore, it is necessary that we make children aware of present-day events as well as the events of yesterday. Modern events or problems belong to the environment of the pupils. Many high school teachers are teaching modern problems in their schools. Let us give briefly some of the reasons why current events should be taught:

1. Current events help to get the pupils interested in all parts of the world. Events occur in various places and people play an important part in them. Hence, through a study of recent happenings, pupils become interested not only in their own region but in many other lands.

2. Current events give pupils a knowledge of significant happenings. Pupils come to have a desire to learn why events occur as they do, and they often enter into the study of them with vim and enthusiasm. The knowledge gained in studying current events will have some influence in determining the acts of the students as citizens.

3. Current events make school work more worthwhile and interesting, by showing that the work done in the schoolroom is related to events which are happening and which have happened in the world outside the schoolroom.

4. A study of current events gives pupils a better understanding of their surroundings, thereby aiding them to adjust themselves to their environment.

5. A knowledge of current events helps pupils to understand more fully the interdependence of people. For example, some current events about Brazil might lead the pupils to see how the United States depends upon Brazil for coffee, while Brazil depends upon the United States for manufactured products. A recent event about farming might cause the pupils to understand

how city people and country people depend upon one another.

6. The teaching of current events helps the pupil to learn to read newspapers and magazines intelligently. It is estimated that 40,000,000 newspapers are in daily circulation in the United States. Almost every adult, as well as many children, reads one or more papers daily. Children read the newspapers which their parents take at home. They should be taught to think when they read and not to accept everything as true.

7. A study of current events furnishes the pupils with an opportunity of discussing recent happenings. It is only in a democracy that people can come together to discuss freely modern problems. By intelligently studying modern problems, pupils learn the art of suspending judgment until they have plenty of facts on all sides of the question. Critical thinking and an appreciation of our democratic methods are developed through discussions. By studying and discussing certain aspects of recent problems, pupils become more civic minded. For example, a study of housing often gets children interested in their own homes, and certain improvements result.

8. By studying current events, pupils develop a very useful technique for interpreting them.

SOURCES FOR CURRENT EVENTS

Where can pupils find material on current events which they may study? This is a question which confronts teachers and pupils. If pupils do not have sufficient material for study, their discussions will be based on inadequate information which may cause incorrect opinions to be formed. It is a wise plan for teachers and pupils to discuss places where information may be obtained about current events. Such a discussion should take place at the beginning of the term and at any other time when pupils seem to be having difficulty in finding current events.

Some of the common sources for current events are as follows:

1. Newspapers. Both community papers and daily papers should be used. In small places, the daily newspaper of a large city should be read.

2. Magazines. Weekly and monthly magazines or periodicals should be used. Some magazines make an effort to be of special service to pupils.

3. Current Events Magazines and Papers for Children. There are magazines and papers containing current events which are published especially for children. The articles have been written by experts and contain recent material which can be easily understood. Some teachers make the mistake of letting the pupils get most of their material on current events from these sources. Teachers should remember that pupils should be encouraged to get material on current events from many sources if they are going to receive the most good from the study.

4. Yearbooks. There are a number of yearbooks which are published annually. Some of them contain recent statistics and summaries of events which happened during the year.

5. Various Kinds of Bulletins. Some societies, organizations, and companies issue bulletins from time to time on current events.

6. The Radio. The radio is one of the chief sources for news and for obtaining information about many events. A summary of the news of the world may be obtained at various times during the day. There are also discussions of current topics by noted men and women. Consult the daily newspapers for the different radio programs.

7. Motion Pictures. Many motion picture theaters show pictures of recent happenings as a part of their program. Sometimes the school may obtain films from some government agency or from some other source which are very valuable in teaching current events. Possibly, a pupil has a friend who takes motion pictures for pleasure. The friend may have taken pictures lately which would be of interest in teaching current events.

8. Listening to Lectures and Discussions. Almost every community has meetings where current problems are discussed. There are many organizations that are interested in current problems. In some schools, the classes that are interested in current events send some of their members to the meetings to listen to the discussions. The pupils make reports to their classes on what they learn.

9. Talking with Parents, Relatives, Friends, Business Men, Government Officials, and Others. Much information concerning current problems may be obtained by talking with people and by listening to their conversations. Trips may also be taken to obtain interviews with people who are supposed to have certain information. The mayor, the aldermen, the ward committeemen, the chief of police, the fire chief, and other city officials may be visited when studying recent problems dealing with the city. In discussing such problems as housing, social security, and insurance, numerous government agents, employers and employees are interviewed.

10. Actual Information Through Travel. In some cases, pupils have obtained information by actually traveling to the places under discussion. For example, in one city there was much discussion over enlarging and improving the airport. Besides reading and talking to people, the students actually took several trips to the airport in order to make their own observations. In another school, the children were discussing the Tennessee Valley Project. One child got so interested that he persuaded his parents to take him on a trip during his vacation to the Tennessee Valley. When he returned to school he gave his classmates some of the first-hand information which he had gained.

NECESSARY QUALITIES FOR A TEACHER OF CURRENT EVENTS

What are the qualities that a teacher of current events should have? Are they any different from those which any good teacher of the social studies possesses? The answer to this last question is no. Every good teacher of the social studies teaches current events and he has certain qualities which make him an excellent teacher.

Some qualities that a teacher of current events should possess are (1) knowledge of current events, (2) skill in teaching, (3) tact and common sense, and (4) respect for the opinions and ideas of the pupils and of the people of the community. It is difficult to give a simple explanation of what is meant by common sense. One person humorously said that "common sense is that which all of us think we have, but which most of us lack at times." Common sense is something that we should strive to have, and it is developed through experience. It is sound, practical judgment.

A teacher should always respect the opinions of his pupils just the same as he expects his pupils to respect his opinions. He should also respect the opinions of the people in the community. The teacher has no monopoly over the opinions of the people in the community. Just because the teacher has different opinions than some of the leading people in the community is not necessarily a proof that the teacher is right and that the others are wrong. It has happened more than once that a teacher was wrong in his view. No person is perfect, not even a teacher.

A teacher should be careful not to indoctrinate the pupils. Many teachers have pet ideas which they unconsciously force on their pupils. Pupils should be taught to think and to reason and to formulate their own ideas after getting the facts. The teacher should be careful not to do the thinking for the pupils. Always remember that the schools exist for preparing pupils to be more useful citizens in our democracy. Of course, a teacher should be free to express his ideas, because his training and experience make him better able to understand a problem than his pupils. No one wants to be under a teacher who is never sure of himself and who is always saying that he does not know the answers to certain questions. A teacher should have opinions about many subjects and he should try to learn what people are thinking and saying. A teacher should be a leader and an inspiration to his pupils, but true and great leaders are never developed in an atmosphere where thinking, reasoning, tolerance, truth, justice, and honesty are lacking.

WHEN TO TEACH CURRENT EVENTS

When to teach current events and how to teach current events are two very important questions. In a school where the curriculum is already crowded with material to be taught, it is a problem to find the time or the place to teach current events. It stands to reason that if current events are taught, some other material must be omitted. A course of study should never remain fixed, but it should be subject to continual revision and improvement.

Since a school should relate its work to present-day happenings, a certain amount of current events may be taught at any time. In fact, one of the best times to teach current events is when the pupils can easily see the connection between what they are studying and what is actually happening in the world.

Some teachers of the social studies take a few minutes every day for teaching current events. The pupils have brief discussions. They also put clippings of current events on the bulletin board or in their clipping books.

In some schools, a class period or a certain amount of time once a week is given to the discussion of current events. Where this is done the teacher must be careful to see that the pupils do not form the habit of looking for current events only on the day before the class discusses them. If the pupils do this, it is a very good sign that they are studying current events just to please the teacher and not because they are interested in learning about them.

In many high schools a course is given in modern problems. Pupils receive credit for this course just the same as they receive credit for any other course. The course is usually given for juniors and seniors, because it is better suited to the older pupils who have had more experience in looking up materials. In some high schools, the course in current events is combined with a history course or a course in government.

HOW TO TEACH CURRENT EVENTS

Various methods are used in teaching current events, but many teachers still feel as if they have not yet found the best method. New methods are being introduced from time to time. The method that is used is determined partly by the age of the pupils.

In some schools, current events are taught incidentally as pupils find recent happenings that are related to the work which they are doing. The drawback to this method is that incidental teaching often turns out to be poor teaching. The chances are that very few current events are taught incidentally, because incidental methods very often fail to cause pupils to do their best work.

It is a good plan to relate the school work to current events whenever it is possible to do so. The pupil should be encouraged to be on the lookout for recent events. In planning his daily work, the teacher should carefully consider if there are any recent happenings at home or abroad that are related to the work. If such current events are found, they should be discussed by the pupils.

Pupils read newspapers and magazines and listen to radio programs in their search for current events. During the period set aside for current events the pupils present the results of their work in various ways. There may be class discussions. Sometimes the pupils have a debate on certain current problems. Occasionally, they write on one or more topics. Now and then the pupils may dramatize current problems. In some schools, sessions of Congress and of the state legislatures have been dramatized with success.

During election time, the pupils in many high schools and the older pupils in some elementary schools make a study of the problems that are before the voters. Different pupils present the platforms of the various parties and of the principal candidates for office. The pupils make an attempt to understand the issues. Finally, they vote by secret ballot, making their election as much like a real election as possible. The pupils in some high schools try to understand more fully how people are nominated for president and for vice-president by holding their own conventions. In the conventions held by the pupils, they endeavor to make them resemble the conventions held by the two major political parties. Most pupils enjoy taking part in a spirited discussion. Pupils get ideas about the way of holding their convention by listening to the radio and by reading newspapers and magazines, providing it is about the time for the major political parties to hold their conventions.

There are various radio programs which pupils like to imitate in studying current events. One such program is where people are chosen to answer questions. Pupils get much enjoyment by sometimes conducting their lesson on current events as if it were a radio program. The pupils write questions on current events, along with the answers, and place them in a box. One of the pupils is appointed to conduct the questioning period. The questions are answered by certain pupils as they are drawn from the box. Since children like to listen to such programs on the radio, the teacher has no trouble in getting the pupils interested in putting on a radio program of their own.

In some schools, much success has been had by using the technique of the Town Hall Meeting of the Air. This method is frequently used by pupils above the sixth grade. Some very interesting and instructive assembly programs have used the plan of the Town Hall Meeting of the Air. A description showing how an eighth grade conducted such an assembly follows:

After consultation with the teacher, the children selected a current problem for their assembly program. The pupils looked up materials in newspapers, magazines, pamphlets, and books. They consulted maps and textbooks. They talked to people and listened for news about the problem over the radio. They studied the history and the geography of the problem. The teacher told them to get all the facts they could before making up their minds on the question. Then they would be able to defend the stand they took. The pupils met a number of times to discuss the problem. When time came for the assembly program, the pupils selected one of their number to be the chairman. Then six pupils were selected to talk on the question, three on one side and three on the other side. Each pupil was to talk for three or four minutes. The remainder of the program was to be given over to the answering of questions from the floor.

The program was carried out as planned. The six pupils got all the children in the audience interested in the problem. At first, only a few children asked questions, but before the end of the program many children were asking them. The children became very enthusiastic and sometimes there were several pupils on their feet at one time wanting to ask questions.

In teaching current events, pupils are encouraged to bring in clippings. There are different ways of using the clippings. One way is to have them shown when reports are given. If a pupil thinks it will add to the report, he may read a part or all of a clipping to the class. At the end of the discussion, some of the clippings are put on a bulletin board. Each pupil may have a book in which clippings are pasted. One room had this title for its chief bulletin board, "News from Here and There and Everywhere."

Committee work is often used in teaching current events. There are different ways of appointing the committee. One way is to have all the pupils meet together with the teacher several days before reports are to be given. Several topics are chosen for study. The pupils studying the same topic form a committee. A chairman for each committee is appointed. He endeavors to see that each pupil does his share of the work and that the group makes a good report.

Another plan is to divide the class into a number of groups, with a chairman for each group. Each group is responsible for reporting on current events which happen in a certain part of the world. For example, one class divided the world into four divisions. They were (1) the United States and Canada, (2) Latin America, (3) Europe, and (4) the rest of the world. Four groups were formed and a division was given to each group. The pupils in each group studied the current events that took place in their division of the world. Before a report was given, the chairman called his group together to go over its work. Sometimes all the pupils in a group made the report. At other times, one or two pupils prepared reports from the material which the members of the group gave them. At stated times, the class met as a whole when the different groups reported. About once a month the groups exchanged among themselves the divisions of the world about which they were studying.

PANEL DISCUSSIONS AND CLUBS

The panel discussion method, sometimes called the panel forum method, is frequently used by some teachers in the high school and in the seventh and eighth grades. Since high school pupils are older than pupils in the seventh and eighth grades, much better results are obtained by using the panel discussion with high school pupils.

The panel discussion method should be clearly explained to a class that is starting to use it for the first time. They should be told that the panel method provides for discussion so that all sides of a problem may be clearly understood. First, a problem of current interest is chosen and is given to the group of pupils on the panel. One of the pupils in the group is made chairman. After the group has had time to study the problem, the panel discussion is held. The chairman keeps the discussion moving by asking questions, summing up what has been said, and in other ways. The pupils on the panel raise questions, answer questions, and discuss various sides of the problems. However, no long speeches are to be made by anyone. The chairman throws the problem open for discussion by all members of the class near the end of the hour. The discussion must not be permitted to turn into a debate, because arguments between a few pupils are likely to confuse the class. The last two or three minutes are spent by the chairman in summing up what has been said.

Sometimes a club in a school is formed for the express purpose of studying current problems. The amount of work that is done by the club is determined by the interest and enthusiasm of its members. Faculty members and outside speakers are frequently invited to discuss current problems. Very often the students put on their own programs. Some student programs are very good. A club sometimes is invited to put on an assembly program for the entire school. Frequently a club is invited to put on a program for some civic organization outside the school. In sponsoring a club, a teacher should keep in mind that the members should take an active part in it.

LEARNING TO READ NEWSPAPERS INTELLIGENTLY

The newspaper is one of the chief sources for current events. Since this is true, an effort should be made to teach pupils to read newspapers intelligently. This is a difficult job because most people have prejudices and pet ideas that are hard for them to forget. It is easy for us to believe those things which we want to believe and to disbelieve those things which we do not want to believe. Again, it is impossible for a person always to know what statements are correct and what statements are incorrect in a newspaper. It is also often difficult to detect articles which have been written for propaganda purposes. Learning to read a newspaper intelligently is something that cannot be done in a few weeks or months. It is only by much critical thinking that a person gradually grows in the power of reading a paper.

An early step in teaching advance pupils to read a newspaper is to have them learn how the school paper is made, providing there is one. The pupils find out who wrote the articles. They make a check to learn if the articles have been correctly written. It may be that the description of some article in the paper is not exactly correct according to their own version of what happened. It is a fact that some people cannot accurately report what takes place. The teacher may prove this to the pupils by having them visit a certain place. On returning to the schoolroom each pupil is required to write a description of what he saw. The descriptions of all the pupils will not agree. The pupils are told to visit the place a second time to see who is correct. They now begin to understand how easy it is for a person to make a mistake in reporting what he saw.

Another step in teaching the pupils to read a newspaper is to take a trip with the class to the office of a local newspaper, if there is one. The pupils learn how news is obtained for the paper. Likewise, if the school is in a large city, the pupils visit the building where a daily paper is published. The work involved in collecting and printing news is explained to the pupils. The pupils try to learn what efforts are made to get reliable news. Many questions are asked and answered. The pupils learn that many people are employed to get news for a large newspaper and they begin to understand why the news in one newspaper might not always agree exactly with the news in another newspaper. However, since the reporters try to report the truth, much of the news in newspapers is in common agreement.

All pupils cannot read a daily newspaper at home because some parents do not get a daily newspaper. Pupils cannot be expected to read what they do not have or what they cannot obtain easily. A daily newspaper should be taken by the school, so that the pupils not having access to a paper at home may be able to read a paper. The pupils should learn something about the sources of the news.

Some articles are written by special correspondents whose names are given at the beginning of the articles. Other news articles have at the beginning such letters as (AP) or (UP) which mean the Associated Press and the United Press, respectively. Sometimes the articles tell how they came to the paper, such as by special cable or by special radio. Some articles begin with such expressions as "It was reported," "It is believed," "From best government sources it was learned," or "It is asserted." These terms lead one to think that the persons who wrote such articles were uncertain about their authenticity.

Sometimes pupils read articles where the headlines do not agree with the facts as given. High school pupils should be encouraged to read the editorials and to know where to look for them. They should be able to distinguish editorials from news. Likewise, pupils should learn where to look for the weather report, news about sports, news about markets, and other special features in the paper. It is often a good idea for a pupil to read more than one newspaper, so that he can compare the news in one paper with the news in another paper. He must learn to read newspapers critically. As pupils advance in power to read a newspaper, they should learn the art of skimming through its pages to see what interests them. People generally do not care to read everything that is printed in a paper. A good reader can tell at a glance whether he thinks an article is of enough value and interest for him to read.

STEPS IN TEACHING PUPILS HOW TO READ NEWSPAPERS

The following simple outline has been used in teaching pupils in the eighth grade to read newspapers. Two or more daily papers were used. The outline may also be used with high school pupils.

I. Objectives
1. To teach pupils to read intelligently the right kind of material in newspapers.
2. To give the pupils an interest in reading newspapers.
3. To have the pupils learn that newspapers furnish worthwhile material on many questions and problems which confront people daily.

II. Ways of Raising the Problem
1. Teacher refers to some interesting article that he read in the paper. Let the pupils tell anything of interest they have read. Clippings may be put on the bulletin board.
2. Ask the pupils what they like to read in the newspapers. Many will mention comics, pictures, and news about various sports. The teacher leads the pupils to see that a newspaper has material about many subjects.

III. What a Daily Newspaper Contains
1. Local news
2. Domestic news

3. Foreign news
4. Cartoons
5. Comics
6. Editorials
7. Articles on health, physical culture, and beauty
8. Letters from readers
9. Syndicated features
10. Radio programs
11. News about sports
12. Financial news, market reports, stock reports
13. News about amusements
14. Articles about home economics, recipes
15. Birth and death notices
16. Pictures
17. Advertisements
18. Weather reports
19. Society news
20. Stories

IV. The Front Page
1. What news and other material is on the front page?
2. Read the headlines and the material underneath one or two of the headlines. How do you think the headlines were determined? Compare two or more newspapers for the same day. Do they have the same news on their front pages?
3. Is the weather report on the front page of a daily newspaper? See if the weather report reads about the same in two or more papers for the same day.
4. Is there a cartoon on the front page? If so, tell what it shows.

V. Local and Domestic News
1. What is local news?
2. Where is local news printed in a paper?
3. How is the local news obtained?
4. Do all the daily papers have the same local news? Do they generally agree on what is said?
5. What is domestic news?

6. Where is the domestic news printed? How is it obtained by the paper?
7. Do all the papers carry about the same domestic news? Do they agree on what is said?

VI. Foreign News
   1. What is foreign news?
   2. Where is foreign news placed in the newspapers?
   3. How is foreign news collected? Are the names of any of the foreign correspondents given? What do (AP), (UP), and any other such letters mean?
   4. Compare the foreign news in one paper with the foreign news in other papers. Do the newspapers generally agree on their foreign news?
   5. About what fraction of the news is foreign news?

VII. Editorials
   1. Where are the editorials usually printed in a newspaper. By whom are the editorials written?
   2. Read the editorials in more than one newspaper. Which do you think has the best editorials?
   3. By whom are the syndicated columns written? Read some of the articles.

VIII. Other questions
   1. Why do most newspapers have advertisements?
   2. Why do many people read the advertisements?
   3. What type of pictures are found in the papers?
   4. About how much of a daily newspaper is taken up with sports?
   5. Why are the radio programs printed in a paper?
   6. Read some of the letters from the readers, if there are any. Why does a newspaper print such letters?
   7. Read some of the health articles, if there are any. Do you think they are of interest?
   8. What kind of financial news is in the paper?
   9. What do the stock reports and market reports include?

IX. Some Activities Not Already Mentioned
>   1. Make a collection of different kinds of newspapers.
>   2. Put clippings of interesting events on the bulletin board. Paste clippings in a blank book.
>   3. Form a committee and make a room newspaper.

PROBLEMS FOR DISCUSSION AND RESEARCH

1. Make a list of reasons for teaching current events.

2. Make a list of reasons which teachers sometimes give for not teaching current events.

3. Read a daily newspaper and one or two recent magazines. Make a list of current events or problems which might be discussed in social studies classes.

4. Give a good discussion on "Teaching Controversial Subjects in the School."

5. What is propaganda? How can propaganda be recognized? What should the teacher do about propaganda?

6. List the chief sources from which pupils may get material on current events.

7. What are the necessary qualities that a teacher should have who teaches current events?

8. Explain when and how current events are taught in different schools? What plans seem best to you?

9. What use did you make of current events when you attended the elementary grades and the high school?

10. Is it good teaching to allow pupils to get most of their material on current events from one source, such as a paper which is especially written for them? Explain your answer.

11. Make a study of some publications containing current material which have been written especially for children. Describe in detail one such paper, telling why it is especially good. What changes in the paper would you suggest?

12. When should we begin to teach a child to read a newspaper? How would you go about teaching an eighth grade pupil to read a newspaper?

13. Take any daily newspaper, explain how you think it could be improved.

REFERENCES

Adriance, Robert, "History and Contemporary Problems," Education, LVIII, 5-12, September, 1937.

Bernard, Kenneth, "Some Guiding Principles in Teaching Current Events," Social Education, IV, 325-326, May, 1940.

Berwald, Rose, "Learning to Use the Newspaper," The Elementary English Review, XVII, 257-262, November, 1940.

Bining, Arthur, Mohr, Walter, and McFeely, Richard, Organizing the Social Studies in Secondary Schools. New York: McGraw-Hill Book Co., 1941.
Chapter XII. Current Events, 216-233.

Cuber, John, "Social Education and the Newspaper," Social Education, III, 177-180, March, 1939.

Education Against Propaganda, Seventh Yearbook, National Council for the Social Studies, 1937.

Ellwood, Robert, "Current Events by Panel Discussion," Social Education, III, 381-384, September, 1939.

Gathany, J. and Fraser, R., The Consideration of Current Events and Current Questions, Elements of the Social Studies Program, Sixth Yearbook, National Council for the Social Studies, 1936, 144-157.

Helmreich, E. C., "Current Events and the Reading Program," Social Education, IV, 557-558, December, 1940.

Improving Social Studies Instruction, Research Bulletin of the National Education Association, XV, 1937.
Chapter V. Dealing with Controversial Subjects, 218-226.

Johnson, Henry, Teaching of History. New York: The Macmillan Co., 1940. Chapter XVI. The Treatment of Current Events, 323-345.

Lawrence, Herman, "Methods of Teaching Current Events," Social Studies, XXIX, 245-250, October, 1938.

Leggit, Dorothy, "Reading Newspapers and Magazines," The Social Studies, XXIX, 296-301, November, 1938.

Mason, Marcella, "Current Events in the Middle Grades," Social Education, VI, 18-20, January, 1942.

McCrory, Mae, "Children and the News," Education, LVIII, 89-93, October, 1937.

Meyer, Frank, "Current Events in the Junior High Schools of Michigan," The Social Studies, XXXI, 363-365, December, 1940.

——, "What Bothers Current Events Teachers," Social Education, IV, 324, May, 1940.

——, "Parliamentary Current Events," Social Education, V, 194-195, March, 1941.

Miller, Willis, "Modern Geography and Current Events," The Journal of Geography, XXXV, 279-284, October, 1936.

Murra, Wilbur, Contributions of Research to the Teaching of Current Events, The Contribution of Research to the Teaching of the Social Studies, Eighth Yearbook, National Council for the Social Studies, 1937, 188-206.

Myer, W. E., "The Use of Current Events Magazines," The Social Studies, XXVIII, 24-27, January, 1937.

Palm, Reuben, "Teacher, Society, and Current Events," Social Education, III, 97-98, February, 1939.

Pierson, Anna, "Teaching Current Events," Social Education, I, 113-116, February, 1937.

Repass, Frances, "An Experiment in Teaching Current Geography," The Journal of Geography, XXXVI, 321-324, 1937.

Scanlan, C. G., "A Unit in Current Events," The Social Studies, XXVIII, 259-261, October, 1937.

Schutte, T. H., *Teaching the Social Studies on the Secondary School Level.* New York: Prentice-Hall, 1938.
  Chapter VIII. Current Events, 444-465.

Terkel, Meyer, "A Town Hall Meeting of the Air Auditorium Program in an Elementary School," Education, LXI, 38-42, September, 1940.

———, "Current Events in Elementary School," Social Education, III, 313-314, May, 1939.

Thralls, Zoe, "Geography and Current Events," The Journal of Geography, XXXIX, 200-202, May, 1940.

Tyler, I. Keith, "Radio's Function in Education," Educational Method, XVIII, 147-154, January, 1939.

Ungashick, Jane, "The Use of Current Events in Geography Teaching," The Journal of Geography, XXXIX, 315-319, November, 1940.

Wesley, Edgar, *Teaching the Social Studies.* New York: D. C. Heath and Co., 1937.
  Chapter XXIII. Utilizing Current Events, 448-466.

Chapter Seven: THE PLACE OF TEXTBOOKS,

WORKBOOKS, AND COLLATERAL READING

IN THE SOCIAL STUDIES

1. TEXTBOOKS

AN IMPORTANT PLACE

THE TEXTBOOK has occupied a very high place in teaching the
social studies for a great many years. In many schools it has
even had more influence than the teacher, although this is not
true in many of our best schools today. Whenever teachers meet
to discuss teaching problems, one of the topics that generally
comes in for discussion is the textbook. It has been both highly
condemned and highly praised. Some teachers seem never to get
tired of finding fault with the textbooks they use. They do not
realize that in many cases it is their poor teaching methods which
should be condemned and not the textbooks. Far too many
teachers try to cover up their poor teaching by putting the blame
on the textbook, when the blame should rest on themselves. No
textbook for pupils is self-teaching. Teachers are always needed
to see that it is used correctly and with the greatest efficiency.
Hence, the blame of poor teaching cannot be entirely placed
upon a textbook, even though it may be a poor one.

Some teachers believe it is a good plan for the pupils to study
a number of textbooks in a given subject. They think that the
children will get a better idea of what they are studying, since
all books do not develop a given topic in the same way. One
book may clear up questions which the other books failed to do.
On the other hand, there are other teachers who say that it is
usually a waste of time for the pupils to use more than one or

two good textbooks in studying a given subject. They claim that all good modern textbooks in a given subject cover about the same ground and that the pupils gain very little that is new in reading books that are so much alike. They think it would be better for pupils to study one or two good textbooks and to spend their remaining time in doing collateral reading.

There are some teachers who say they do not believe in using textbooks, yet they base their work on two or three books. The pupils are required to study these books. Even though these teachers are not using the name "textbooks," they are actually using textbooks if they require the pupils to base most of their work on two or three books. Changing the name does not necessarily bring about any other changes.

The textbook has occupied a very important place in the social studies because it has filled a felt need. Otherwise, it could not have remained so important for such a long period of time. One reason why textbooks have been used so much in our schools is because so many teachers feel that they do not have a sufficient knowledge of what they are trying to teach. Such teachers would feel lost without a textbook, and the pupils certainly would be lost.

A second reason often given for the use of textbooks is that many schools do not have enough reference books for the pupils to read. Indeed, many schools would find it very difficult to get along if they had to rely only on reference books. Most schools do not have the money to purchase all the reference books which they need.

BOOKS ARE STOREHOUSES OF KNOWLEDGE

Some people may wonder why it is that pupils should get so much of their information from books. They ask why pupils cannot take trips to various places and obtain information. Again, they also say that the teacher should use more oral instruction and not rely so much upon printed material. Of course, pupils should take trips to various places, but it is impossible for pupils to obtain the greater part of their information about distant places by taking trips. Likewise, it is impossible for many teachers to present most of the material pupils should know by oral instruction, since their knowledge is limited.

Even if all teachers had sufficient knowledge of the subject matter, it would still be a matter of wisdom to have the pupils get some of their knowledge from books, because one of the chief ways of obtaining knowledge is through the printed page. Most of the knowledge of past ages is stored up in books, and an intelligent person surely would feel lost in this world if he did not know how to read books. One of the chief ways that man has of communicating his thoughts to others is by putting them into print.

Books are very common in the United States. No other country begins to compare with our country in the quantity and the quality of its textbooks. Many of the textbooks in the social studies are highly illustrated with pictures, maps, and graphs. This is especially true of the geographies and the histories. Our country believes in free education for its children. The aim has been to furnish the schools with the necessary tools that they need in doing a good job in educating children. Hence, much encouragement has been given to the production of good textbooks. The United States is very fortunate in having the resources which help to furnish our people with a high standard of living and the means with which to purchase books.

THREE KINDS OF TEXTBOOKS

Let us think of a textbook as a book which the students are required to study or to read rather frequently and which contains material on many of the units which a class generally studies in a given grade. Broadly speaking, textbooks may be divided into three groups.

The first group of textbooks contains those books which merely outline the topics or units which they contain. Any discussion is very brief. Such books are used chiefly to present the work and to raise questions and problems. Pupils must use other source material to get help in solving their problems. Very few books in the social studies have been written along these lines for use in American schools. They have never made much of an appeal to American teachers and pupils.

The second group of textbooks consists of those books which give some discussion of the topics or problems which they present. For a few of the topics and problems, there may be enough discussion so that the pupils need use no other sources of material unless they wish; but for most of them additional sources of material should be consulted by the pupils, if they are going to understand fully the problems which are to be solved. The authors of such textbooks advise the pupils to read additional references and to consult other sources of information. Most of the textbooks in the social studies belong to this group.

The third group of textbooks are those in which the authors have endeavored to give full treatments of the problems and topics discussed in the books. A pupil finds all the material he needs to read in such a textbook.

It may readily be seen why this third group of textbooks is not very large. In the first place, to attempt to write all that the pupils need to read on certain problems and topics would require many pages of material. Such books would likely be too bulky for pupils to handle. Of course, such books might be broken up into smaller books but this would add to the expense of the books. Although most people want their children to have the best books from which to study, many of them would object to the expense of buying so many books for one subject. Some parents are never able to understand why good books should cost more than poor ones.

In the second place, many questions are continually being raised in class which cannot be answered by consulting any one book. If a pupil is going to be trained to think and to use materials, he must be encouraged to go beyond his textbook for aid. It is too much to expect any one book to contain everything which is needed to solve problems.

HISTORY OF AMERICAN TEXTBOOKS

Jedidiah Morse published a textbook in geography in 1784, which he called "Geography Made Easy." It is thought that this was the first geography textbook to be published in our country. Since this date, many geography textbooks and atlases have been published, and authors are still trying to improve their books so that geography will be easy to understand.

Probably the first textbook in history to be published in our country was by John McCulloch, in 1787, who called his book "Introduction to the History of America." As the years passed, many other textbooks in history were written, and publishing companies are still adding new textbooks to the list.

The early textbooks in geography and history were small and poorly printed. They would be considered unattractive by our standards of today. They had few maps and pictures. As might be expected, the pictures were usually poorly selected and were often dim, while the maps were generally poorly drawn. Some of the sentences were difficult to read and many of the authors apparently did not give much thought to the words which they used. The books were filled with information which the pupils were expected to memorize. Naturally, a pupil with a poor memory was considered a weak student. The geographies had much description, while the histories had many dates. Many of the authors were not teachers, so it can easily be understood why the books were often unadapted to the needs of the pupils.

As would be expected, textbooks gradually improved as time passed. The books became more attractive. More maps, pictures, and graphs were added. They were better selected and were more closely related to the printed material. Sentences became less difficult to read and the authors gave increased attention to the vocabulary which they used. There were more pages and the printing was more carefully done. Questions were added at the end of each chapter and at other places to help the children understand better the printed page. Suggestions were given for study and the reader was often helped to organize the work he was doing.

Today, improvements are still going on in our textbooks. Most of our modern textbooks follow the ideas of our leaders, while a few stand out in front and help to determine new educational trends. However, it is well to remember that textbooks cannot be too far ahead of the educational ideas of today if they are going to be used in our schools. Authors and publishers must pay some attention to the various courses of study and to what teachers think the pupils should study.

ARE TEXTBOOKS STILL NEEDED?

If the American schools do not have good textbooks to use, the blame cannot be placed entirely upon the shoulders of authors and publishers. No publisher can afford to publish a textbook if it stands little chance of being used in a number of classrooms. Some teachers believe that there is not enough general agreement among school systems about what work to teach in the different grades. A school system often makes a course of study in the social studies with the idea that it must be different from all other courses if it is going to be considered modern and progressive. Hence, even though many courses of study are consulted and much material is obtained from them, the prevailing idea of some writers of a new course seems to be that their school system cannot dare to have practically the same course which is used in any other place. The likely result is that the course is not so good as it might be. It is time that the writers of our courses of study learn that to make a course of study different from all other courses of study just for the sake of being different is not a sign of progressiveness, but a sign of retrogression and ignorance. The only good reason why one school system has a course of study that differs from other courses of study is that the teachers of that school system truly believe that their course fits the needs of their pupils better than any other course.

Today, our textbooks in geography, history, and the other social studies have made great advance in respect to those published about one hundred and fifty years ago. Many of the authors of present-day textbooks are teachers of children or are connected with teachers' training colleges. The authors are experts in their field and they know children. They have made a study of the science of education. Likewise, publishers have worked hard to make their books attractive. Competition is so keen among publishers of textbooks, that a poor textbook stands very little show of being used in many classrooms.

Committees from time to time have made studies of the use of textbooks in the schools. Even though they may not have approved of the way in which many teachers use textbooks, yet nearly all of them have come to the conclusion that textbooks are needed in most schools. We are still living in a textbook age, and it seems as if this age is going to be with us for some years to come, even though there are a few teachers who do not believe in using textbooks.

It is said that teachers in Europe often think of the textbook method as the American way of teaching, since they use chiefly the oral method. Probably one reason why textbooks are not so common in European schools as in American schools is that European teachers actually believe that the oral method is superior to the textbook method of teaching. Possibly, another reason is that the people in Europe are not so able financially to purchase textbooks as are the people in the United States. Just because the teachers in the United States do not follow the methods used in Europe is no good reason why their methods are poorer than those used by European teachers. After all, the results are what count. When we think of the great upheavals that have taken place in Europe during the past one hundred years, one sometimes wonders if the schools of Europe have not failed somewhere along the line. Of course, we should profit by what others do, but we should try to avoid their mistakes. Pure imitation is not progress, providing we can get better results by doing things in a different way.

REASONS FOR USING TEXTBOOKS

Mention has already been made that two reasons why textbooks play so important a part in the teaching of the social studies are (1) many teachers do not have sufficient knowledge of the social studies to teach without textbooks and (2) most schools are so poorly equipped with reference books that the pupils would not have enough material to study if they had no textbooks. A few educators apparently think that these are about the only reasons why teachers wish to use textbooks, but they are mistaken in their views. Some other reasons for using good textbooks are the following:

(1) A textbook is a fine source for securing accurate information on many problems, since it covers a definite field. If a pupil consulted only reference books, he would very likely be unable to find information on many of his problems, since his time is limited for study. On the other hand, each member of the class is able to get some information on most of his problems from a textbook.

(2) Where textbooks are used, the teacher may make definite assignments with the knowledge that pupils will have at least one specific source of information. However, this does not mean that other sources are not used. A good textbook often gives

suggestions for reading various references and for doing different kinds of activity work. Busy teachers generally find the questions and suggestions in a textbook very helpful.

(3) A textbook is very useful in making summaries and reviews of certain units of work. It also furnishes materials for drills.

(4) The topics and problems in a textbook are developed according to the material that has gone before and to what will come after. Where textbooks are used, pupils are likely to see the relation of the various problems to one another. Textbooks also help the teacher and pupils to see the importance of different topics and to determine how much time to spend on each one.

(5) Good textbooks in the social studies are highly illustrated with maps, pictures, graphs, charts, and various kinds of tables. It is rare to find a schoolroom which has all the pictures and wall maps which might be used profitably. In fact, most rooms are poorly equipped with such materials. If for no other reason, good textbooks should be used for the visual material which they contain. Pupils should make much use of the maps and pictures in their books. During the class discussion, it is often wise to let the pupils have their books open so that they may consult the maps and pictures in their books. Some teachers frequently say that they do not make much use of maps in their teaching because they have few or no wall maps. If the pupils are using a good textbook in geography, the lack of wall maps is indeed a very poor excuse for not using maps in the classroom.

(6) A good textbook in the social studies often has near the end of the book certain materials which are not easily obtained elsewhere. For example, a geography may have tables of statistics showing the chief imports and exports, the population of the chief countries and cities, and the areas of countries. The Constitution of the United States and the chief events in history, with their dates, are found near the end of some school histories.

SOME LIMITATIONS OF TEXTBOOKS

All textbooks have certain limitations. No matter how well a textbook has been written, it should not be expected to do the impossible. A wise teacher knows that there are certain limitations in using any good book. He tries to keep these in mind so that his pupils may use efficiently the textbook in gaining information and in solving problems. Some of the chief limitations of textbooks in the social studies are the following:

1. A textbook is likely to lack sufficient material on some units which the pupils study, since courses of study usually differ from place to place. A textbook cannot be expected to have a wealth of detail on every problem. Questions are frequently raised which can only be answered satisfactorily by consulting other sources of information.

2. Whenever possible and practical, the progressive teacher tries to relate the work in the schoolroom to events outside the schoolroom. The authors of textbooks in the social studies do not possess the power of knowing what is going to happen in the future, but must write about events that have already happened. No textbook can describe current events as they occur, no matter how recently the book has been written. So in studying current events, additional sources must be used. However, a good textbook in the social studies should help the pupils interpret and understand current events.

3. Although a textbook in the social studies may contain many pictures and maps, it cannot be expected to have all the maps and pictures that the pupils might desire to use. It is often advisable to consult maps and pictures which are not found in the textbook. During the year, the teacher and pupils will come across many maps and pictures.

4. Many textbooks in the social studies have graphs and tables of statistics. If the books are old, the pupils and the teacher may desire to use more recent statistics than those which are found in the textbooks. Again, pupils may need to use other statistics than those in their textbooks.

5. No textbook is self-teaching in the sense that teachers are not needed. A textbook can never take the place of a good teacher. Both are needed. The teacher is needed to give suggestions, to guide the pupil in his thinking, to give aid when it is needed, and to make sure that the textbook is used wisely and efficiently. Frequently the teacher and pupils think of other questions, problems, and activities than those listed in the textbook.

6. Some textbooks are difficult for the pupils to read. This is sometimes due to the poor reading ability of the pupils. It may also be due to the inability of the authors to write on the reading level of the pupils. Sometimes the topics are too difficult and abstract. In some cases, so many facts are given on one page that the reading matter is dull and uninteresting.

DANGERS TO AVOID IN USING TEXTBOOKS

One of the chief dangers in using a textbook is that the pupils are likely to memorize the ideas of the book without doing any appreciable thinking. Pupils must be taught how to think in solving their problems. They must learn to observe, to search for explanations, and to reason. The part that the teacher plays has an important bearing upon whether the pupil merely memorizes the ideas in his book or whether he learns to think. If a pupil is required to answer questions which depend upon memorizing the text, he naturally does little thinking. On the other hand, if the questions require thought, a pupil will undoubtedly do some thinking.

Another danger that should be avoided in the use of textbooks is that a pupil should not come to depend too much upon any one book. A pupil should not regard a textbook as containing all the printed material which he needs to consult. There are some problems that never can be solved satisfactorily no matter how much a person reads and thinks; but the more intelligent reading he does the more likely he is to come to some well thought out conclusion about them.

Due to limited space, a textbook cannot be expected to give all the information that is available on any large problem. Pupils must gradually get into the habit of consulting various references, even though they may be using the best textbook in the world. The number of references a pupil consults will be largely determined by the time at his disposal, the ease of getting references, and the interest which he has in the problem.

TEACHING PUPILS TO USE TEXTBOOKS

It is true that some teachers and pupils misuse textbooks, but this is no good reason for saying that textbooks should not be used by the pupils. The same teachers and pupils who incorrectly use textbooks would misuse any other material if they made no greater effort to use it than they do textbooks. A poor teacher will probably never teach his pupils to study any kind of material very successfully. A good textbook, if used wisely by the pupils, is a useful tool in any school. Pupils should learn to turn to the textbook as one of their sources of aid, but not the only source. It is the business of the teacher to teach pupils to use textbooks wisely. He must not leave it to chance.

It is often a good plan for the teacher to show the pupils how to use a textbook so that thinking will take place. He may proceed as follows: He discusses with the pupils the problem that they are studying. He shows the pupils how to read certain pages in the book to get information which will aid in the solving of the problem. He reads certain paragraphs aloud. He stops now and then to recall things that he already knows which are related to what he is reading. He frequently turns back to reread some statement. Certain questions come to his mind which cause him to consult other sources of information. If a paragraph is not clear after the first reading, he reads it again. The teacher spends as much of the period as he thinks is necessary in showing the pupils how to study. But he should not stop here. Throughout the term he should always be on the alert to show the pupils better methods of study.

Another plan is to show the pupils how to analyze their textbooks briefly to see what a certain unit includes, so that they may know some of the chief problems to study. A good textbook helps pupils raise problems and questions which can be answered by consulting various sources of material.

In studying a textbook under the direction of the teacher, the pupils should get training in learning the following:

(1) How to get help from the book in answering questions and in solving problems.

(2) How to use maps, graphs, charts, pictures, and statistics.

(3) How to read the printed matter with understanding.

(4) How to raise questions and problems.

(5) How to follow any good suggestions which the book gives.

(6) How to make the best use of any questions and problems which are listed in the book.

(7) How to use the table of contents efficiently.

(8) How to use the appendix, if one is given.
(9) How to use the index efficiently.
(10) How to pronounce the names of people and places.
(11) How to use other sources of information along with that in the book.

SELECTING TEXTBOOKS

There are a number of good textbooks in geography, history, and the other social studies from which school systems may choose their texts. Teachers should be consulted when textbooks are adopted, because the teachers are the ones who are going to see that the books are used efficiently. The adoption of uniform textbooks is practiced in some states. Those who believe in state adoptions say that (1) the prices of books are lower, (2) pupils moving from one part of the state to another do not have to buy new textbooks, (3) teachers do not spend any time with book-agents and in deciding what books to use, (4) state agencies are better able to select good textbooks than the teachers in most school systems, and (5) it is possible to have the same course of study throughout the state since uniform textbooks are used.

Many educators do not believe in state adoptions. Some of the arguments against state adoptions are (1) textbooks should not be forced upon the teachers in a school system, (2) teachers and others in a school system are better able to select their textbooks than some state agency, (3) a state agency is likely to be partly political and it may not always have the best interests of the pupils at heart, (4) since the adoption of a textbook in a state will mean considerable business for a company, there may be a tendency for some companies to use unfair methods in trying to get the business, and (5) state adoptions often do not encourage the frequent improvement of textbooks. One thing that should always be kept in mind is that nothing should be allowed to stand in the way of permitting any school to use the best textbooks that have been published.

A GUIDE FOR SELECTING TEXTBOOKS

In some schools, textbooks are selected in a haphazard manner; while in other schools an attempt is made to select books according to some well thought out plan. Many teachers do not know what criteria to use in selecting a textbook, and the result is that they do not consider many important items when they make their decisions. Some groups of teachers, publishers, and others have made score cards for judging textbooks, but they generally have not proven to be very effective. In many cases, the items on the score cards are based on the opinions of those who made them; and the opinions of teachers do not always agree on the importance of certain items and the value which is to be given to each one. Naturally, the items on the score cards made by publishers are likely to favor the selection of their own books.

Willis O. Underwood has published a rather comprehensive guide for textbook analysis on pages 23-24, in the School Board Journal for March, 1941. He based his guide on (1) questionnaires sent out to a number of teachers to learn what items they considered in judging textbooks, (2) personal interviews with many textbook committees, and (3) seven score cards for textbooks that had been published in educational journals. His guide for textbook analysis has seven main headings with items under each head to be considered. The main headings are (1) authorship, (2) content and organization, (3) vocabulary and readability, (4) method and motivation, (5) teaching and studying aids, (6) mechanical make-up, and (7) miscellaneous.

For a good many years the author has advised many teachers concerning the selection of books. He has also made selections of books for use in his classes. Here are some of the questions which should be asked and answered satisfactorily about every book before it is selected for use in the social studies:

1. Has the author the training, knowledge, and experience which are needed for the writing of a good book?

2. Is the book accurate? Does it cover the field satisfactorily? Is the material unbiased?

3. Does the book follow modern educational ideas in its organization and content? Are the topics covered in enough detail? Are the topics well selected and do they meet the needs of the pupils?

4. Is the material suited to the age of the pupils who are going to study it? Does it appeal to the pupils? Will the pupils likely enjoy reading the book?

5. Are the vocabulary and the sentence structure adapted to the age of the pupils who will use the book? Is the style clear? Will the pupils likely understand what they read?

6. Are the titles in the book well selected?

7. Are there sufficient maps and graphs? Are they accurately drawn and well selected? Can they be read easily by the pupils? Are they of the right size?

8. Are there enough pictures? Have they been well selected and do they fit in with the reading material? Are they large enough?

9. Does the book contain any aids or suggestions for study and for activity work? Will they help the children think and reason? Do they seem to belong in the book?

10. Do the table of contents, the index, the appendix, the table of statistics, and the glossary give valuable information which the pupils may readily use?

11. Is the book the correct size? It should neither be too large nor too small.

12. Is the book well bound and attractive? Does the book use the right size and kind of type? Is the paper of a high grade? Are the pictures, maps, and other visual materials clear?

13. Can the book be used with the course of study which is being followed?

14. Is the book of recent date and does it sell at a reasonable price?

2. WORKBOOKS

IMPORTANCE

During the past twenty or thirty years the use of workbooks has increased rapidly. Many textbooks in the social studies have workbooks. There are also workbooks which do not follow the organization of any particular book, but have been written with the idea of using them with any one of a group of textbooks. Generally, the teacher and pupils prefer to use a workbook which follows the organization of the textbook which they are using. If a workbook is used which follows a different organization than their textbook, the pupils frequently have difficulty in answering many of the questions. A workbook is written with the idea of helping the pupils do better work in studying their textbooks and in solving problems.

WHY USE WORKBOOKS?

Like the textbook, the workbook has been condemned by some educators who believe they should not be used by the pupils. They claim that the use of workbooks is likely to develop poor habits of study. It is undoubtedly true that some workbooks do not aid in learning or they contribute very little to it. However, this is no more of a reason for doing away with all workbooks than it is for banishing all teachers from the classroom just because there are a few poor or mediocre ones in our midst. If a workbook aids the pupils better than anything else which the pupils and the teachers have at their disposal, it should be used. A workbook should make a valuable contribution to the work of the pupils, and it never should be used just for keeping the pupils busy.

If workbooks are used, the teacher should be on the watch for certain dangers. There is always danger that the work may become mechanical and that the pupil may do little thinking. Again, useless drill must not be carried on. Some workbooks do not seem to develop the resourcefulness of pupils. Sometimes the questions and problems are of such a nature that they are not worth the time it takes in answering them. Some workbooks are too much like the busy-work type of material which modern schools claim they no longer use. Teachers should also be careful that they do not rely too much on the workbook for teaching. It is very easy for lazy teachers to fall into the habit of thinking that the workbook relieves them of the responsibility of asking questions, raising problems, and evaluating the work of the pupils. A workbook, no matter how fine it is, can never take the place of a good teacher.

If good workbooks are used intelligently by pupils, they aid the pupils in studying. Workbooks tend to make the work more definite, they guide the pupil in his study, and they are often useful for drill, review, and testing. They aid in individual instruction and help to make a pupil more independent in his study. Many of the exercises in a workbook are similar to those which the teacher would have his pupils naturally do The questions, problems, and exercises are in printed form so that the pupils may use them whenever there is a need. If workbooks are not used it is often necessary to give many questions and problems orally to the pupils or write them on the blackboard. Workbooks save time for the teachers and pupils.

3. COLLATERAL READING

THE IMPORTANCE

Various terms are often used which mean the same as collateral reading. They are supplementary reading, library reading, reference reading, and the reading program in the social studies. All of these terms mean the reading of references other than textbooks. The value of collateral reading has been recognized by teachers for a good many years. Although various committees have made reports recommending that collateral reading should be done along with the study of textbooks, there are still schools in which pupils do very little reading outside their textbooks. On the other hand, there are many schools where much collateral reading is done by the pupils.

At first thought it may seem strange that so little collateral reading is done in some schools, since it is so important. Probably the two chief reasons given by teachers for not having their pupils do much collateral reading are (1) the time is so short for studying the textbooks that the pupils do not have time to do collateral reading, and (2) the scarcity of reference books in the school library and the neighborhood library. Three other reasons which are commonly given are (1) pupils are likely to become confused if they read many books while studying a unit, (2) some teachers do not wish to have their scheme of organization broken up by having the pupils get facts and ideas by reading a number of reference books, and (3) some teachers believe that all the information that pupils need to know on a given subject is in their textbooks.

Scarcity of books is the only good reason for the pupils doing little collateral reading. Many schools are gradually adding books to their library, and public libraries always try to work with the school. Teachers who believe in collateral reading usually find some way of getting a few books for their pupils to read, even though their schools are in poor districts where funds are scarce.

There are certain dangers which should be avoided where much collateral reading is done. In those schools where no one textbook is used and where pupils are encouraged to read a few pages in many different reference books, there is always danger of pupils becoming confused and of not concentrating long enough on any one problem. Poor habits of study are likely to be formed and much time may be wasted. Aimless reading and skipping around in book after book just for the sake of using many references are to be condemned. Browsing in books may be practiced occasionally by pupils, but it takes much more than browsing to solve problems and to accumulate information which will be useful in meeting new situations.

Collateral reading must be done under careful guidance by the teacher and it should aid pupils in forming correct habits of study. Some books are difficult to read while others are rather easy. It takes more time to read difficult material than easy material. In some cases, a pupil may consult a reasonable number of references, but in other cases it may be best for a pupil to read only one reference. If the material which a pupil needs to know is found in one book, it is usually advisable for him to read this one book rather than to read a few paragraphs in many books. Again, there is usually no need of reading the same thing over and over in several different books.

WHY READ REFERENCES?

It is true that textbooks usually occupy an important place in good teaching. If textbooks are used correctly, they are useful tools in helping pupils do their work. However, to understand clearly the unit that is being studied, a pupil often needs more information than he can get in his textbook. This means that the teacher must give the additional information to the pupils or they must get it from some other sources. Teachers do give much information to their pupils, but they should be taught to get information for themselves. Pupils should read reference books, take excursions, listen to the radio, read newspapers, and do many other activities in obtaining information.

In encouraging pupils to do collateral reading, some of the questions a teacher should keep in mind are the following: (1)

What are the reasons for collateral reading? (2) What books should the pupils read? (3) How many pages should be read by the pupils? (4) Should each pupil do the same amount of reading? (5) When should the pupils do their reading? (6) Should the pupils spend time in taking notes when reading? (7) What should pupils be expected to remember from their reading? (8) Are all references of equal importance?

Some of the reasons for collateral reading are (1) to make things about which the pupils read seem more nearly real and meaningful, (2) to obtain information, (3) to give pupils more of an interest in what they are studying, (4) to give a new point of view, (5) to stimulate pupils to take more of an interest in reading, and (6) to get acquainted with some of the good books which have been especially written for them.

All books should not be read with the same degree of care. When pupils read certain books chiefly for information, they should try to remember much of what they read. Notes may be taken or an outline of what is read may be made. When pupils read books chiefly for some other reason than information, it is usually best for the teacher not to place too much emphasis upon facts. A large part of the outside reading of pupils should be for pleasure, to gain a liking for the subject, and to form habits of good reading. Probably the chief reason for encouraging pupils in the high school to read historical fiction is to arouse an interest in history. It is not necessary nor usually advisable for pupils to make long reports on books. In fact, many children have had their desire for reading killed on account of the long reports which they had to make. If reports on readings are to be made, it is generally advisable for the teacher and pupils to determine together the nature of the report.

SELECTING BOOKS FOR COLLATERAL READING

During recent years, many books have been written for pupils of different ages. How is the teacher going to be able to know which of these books to advise pupils to read, or if he has any school funds, which books to buy? Many textbooks suggest books for the pupils to read. Such magazines as the Journal of Geography, Social Education, the Social Studies, the Grade Teacher, and the Instructor make many suggestions. Advertisements of books and the book reviews in educational magazines and papers are very helpful. Lists of books are published from time to time by certain libraries. To be helpful, a list should contain a short description of each book and the age of the pupils for which it is written. The United States Office of Education publishes a list of books for children and a list of inexpensive books for school libraries. Every teacher interested in selecting books for the social studies library should be sure to read the very valuable and practical article by Kennedy and Painter, in the Twelfth Yearbook of the National Council for the Social Studies, 1941, pages 101-153.

Since all children in a given grade are unlikely to have the same reading ability, a list of books should contain some books which are more difficult to read than others. A pupil should not be expected to read a book which is too easy for him. Neither should he read a book that is too difficult. This does not mean that a pupil will never read a book that has been written for more advanced pupils. For example, some eighth grade pupils may frequently wish to read certain pages in a book that has been written for high school students or even for college students.

Just how many pages of collateral reading should be read by each pupil cannot be answered definitely. Pupils above the sixth grade should be expected to read far more pages than those below the sixth grade. Again, some pupils read more rapidly than other pupils. Some books are more easily read than other books. In some schools, more time is given to the social studies than in other schools. The idea is that each pupil should be working efficiently at his own rate of speed, whether he reads a few pages or many pages a month. After all, the important thing is not the exact number of pages that a pupil reads, but whether he is doing his proper share of reading and is gaining those experiences which are thought best for him to have.

Most school systems do not have a superabundance of money with which to purchase books for collateral reading. They must be very careful about the books they select. By adding a few books every year, their libraries are gradually built up. Since new books are being published from time to time, it is a good idea to add books to a library whenever the opportunity arises. Whether to have only one copy of a book or several copies is a question upon which all teachers are not agreed. If the book is a very good one which it would pay all pupils to read, most teachers would agree that there should be at least two copies. What the teacher should keep in mind is that quality, not variety, should be the deciding factor.

4. SOURCE MATERIALS

By source materials we mean such printed or written materials as documents, letters, diaries, and descriptions which were written by eyewitnesses or those who actually took part in the affairs. In the seventh and eighth grades of the elementary school, the pupils occasionally read source materials for illustrations and atmosphere, and for stimulating the interest in certain topics. In the high school, pupils may frequently read source materials not only for these reasons, but to learn that people in past times did not always agree among themselves on what was happening. Most pupils enjoy reading original accounts. History or geography becomes more vital and interesting to a pupil when he is able to read an account of a journey written by an explorer or traveler, or a description of an event written by a person who actually saw it take place.

Source materials should be used with reason. Some teachers do not use enough source materials. However, teachers should not attempt to base all their work on source materials. In the first place, there are not enough source materials available for pupils to use. In the second place, pupils in the grades and high schools do not have the necessary background and experience to come to certain conclusions about events. Even historians and geographers often differ among themselves about the right conclusion to draw from a mass of conflicting material. Pupils should not read source materials which are too difficult for them to understand.

PROBLEMS FOR DISCUSSION AND RESEARCH

1. Make a list of reasons why the textbook occupies an important place in most schools.
2. If you were writing a textbook in the social studies for the seventh and eighth grades, what would it include?
3. Into what groups may you put textbooks? Explain each group.
4. Describe the history of American textbooks in the social studies.

5. Why are textbooks needed?

6. Discuss the limitations of textbooks.

7. What are some of the dangers which should be avoided in using textbooks?

8. Explain how pupils should be taught to use a textbook?

9. How should textbooks be selected? What are the chief topics which should be included in a rating scale for the selection of textbooks?

10. Examine a few textbooks in the social studies for the grades. Give your opinion of them.

11. What are the advantages and disadvantages of using workbooks? Do pupils generally like to use workbooks?

12. Examine several workbooks in the social studies. Do these workbooks cause a child to think? Give your impression of them.

13. Discuss the importance of collateral reading.

14. Why is not more collateral reading done by the pupils in many schools?

15. How may the teacher go about selecting books for collateral reading?

16. Discuss the value of source material.

REFERENCES

Bining, Arthur and Bining, David, *Teaching the Social Studies in the Secondary Schools.* New York: McGraw-Hill Book Co., 1941.
  Chapter IV. The Lecture and Textbook Methods, 68-87.
  Chapter XIII. The School Library and the Social Studies, 240-257.
  Chapter XIV. Written Work and Outside Reading, 258-274.
Canty, Mary, "More About Reading," Social Education, III, 83-88, February, 1939.
Children's Catalog: A Dictionary Catalog of 4000 Books. New York: H. W. Wilson Co., 1941.
Clarke, L. Katherine, "Recreational Reading in the Social Studies," Social Education, II, 31-34, January, 1938.
Frederick, Robert and Sheats, Paul, *Citizenship Education Through the Social Studies.* New York: Row, Peterson and Co., 1936.
  Chapter VIII. What Shall Be the Nature of the Social Studies Textbook? 164-193.
Halverson, L. H., "A Quantitative Analytical Comparison of Geography Textbooks," The Journal of Geography, XXXV, 60-67, February, 1936.
Herrington, Dorah, "The Textbook, A Great American Achievement—To Be Memorized, To Be Discarded, or To Be Consulted," Educational Method, XVII, 78-80, November, 1937.

Hogan, Marita and Yeschko, Margaret, "Latin American Countries in Children's Literature," The Elementary English Review, XVII, 230-234, 256, October, 1940; 276-285, November, 1940.

Horn, Ernest, *Methods of Instruction in the Social Studies.* New York: Charles Scribner's Sons, 1937.

Chapter V. Reading in Relation to Learning in the Social Studies, 151-205.

Chapter VI. The Textbook and Collateral Reading, 206-264.

Chapter VII. The Use of Imaginative Literature, 265-299.

Hunt, Erling, "What About Original Sources?" Education, LXI, 11-13, September, 1940.

Johnson, Henry, *Teaching of History.* New York: The Macmillan Co., 1940.

Chapter XII. Textbooks in History, 241-256.

Chapter XIII. The Use of Textbooks in History and Other Social Studies, 257-280.

Chapter XIV. The Selection and Management of Collateral Reading, 281-296.

Kepner, Tyler, The Influence of Textbooks Upon Method, *The Historical Approach to Methods of Teaching the Social Studies, Fifth Yearbook,* National Council for the Social Studies, 1935, 143-172.

Kennedy, Anna C. and Painter, Fred B., Materials for the Social Studies Program, *The Social Studies in the Elementary School, Twelfth Yearbook,* the National Council for the Social Studies, 1941, 101-156. (The last part of this reference gives many definite references.)

Levine, Michael, "The Textbook in Social Studies," Social Education, III, 318-320, May, 1939.

McKelvey, Frederick, "Utilizing Library Resources in Elementary Social Studies," Social Education, IV, 570-572, December, 1940.

Meighen, Mary, "Training Children to Use Their Geography Textbooks Efficiently," The Journal of Geography, XXXVIII, 330-332, November, 1939.

National Society for the Study of Education, the *Thirty-Second Yearbook, The Teaching of Geography.*

Chapter I. Nineteenth Century Textbooks of Geography, 3-28.

Chapter XXIX. I. Difficulties in Using Geography Texts, 475-479.

Orr, Harriet, "History Textbooks and International Attitudes," The Social Studies, XXXII, 254-255, October, 1941.

Perkins, John, "Uncle Sam's Bookshop," Social Education, IV, 177-179, March, 1940.

Perpinan, Jesus, "School Textbooks and International Relations," Social Education, II, 404-408, September, 1938.

Pilant, Richard, "Teachers, Texts, and Current Problems," Social Education, I, 487-491, October, 1937.

Sterk, Clara and Purdy, Beatrice, "A Plan for Teacher Participation in the Selection of Textbooks," The Elementary School Journal, XLI, 658-664, May, 1941.

Stormzand, M. J. and Lewis, Robert, New Methods in the Social Studies. New York: Farrar and Rinehart, 1935.

Swindler, R. E., The Contribution of Research Towards the Understanding and Solution of Collateral Reading Problems, The Contribution of Research to the Teaching of the Social Studies, Eighth Yearbook, National Council for the Social Studies, 1937, 136-168.

Taylor, Katherine, "Historical Sources and the Teaching of the Social Studies," Social Education, I, 116-118, February, 1937.

Whipple, Gertrude, "Guiding Reading in the Middle Grades," Social Education, III, 40-46, January, 1939.

Wilder, Howard, "Progress in Social Studies Textbooks," Social Education, I, 313-318, May, 1937.

Williams, Paul, "The Streamlined History Textbook," Education, LXI, 8-11, September, 1940.

Chapter Eight: SOME AUDIO-VISUAL AIDS

CHARTS

SOME TYPES of charts are maps, graphs, diagrams, table charts, and cartoons. For example, the early maps were charts which were made for navigators. They showed the position of rocks, shallow places, and other features that should be known to sailors. In this chapter, only a few kinds of charts which are used in teaching the social studies are discussed.

The table chart is sometimes used to arrange data. The time-table of a railroad is a table chart. The places where the trains stop are given in order along with the times of the arrival and departure of each train. Chronological tables of events in history are frequently given. For example, there are tables showing, in sequence, the dates of inventions, discoveries, explorations, wars, the gaining of territory, and other events.

A chart is called a tree chart when it resembles a tree and its branches. For example, the many products derived from coal are sometimes arranged in the form of a tree.

Another kind of chart resembles a stream in which the small tributaries unite to form the main stream. This is called a stream chart. The growth of the United States is often shown by a stream chart. Still another kind of chart is one which is frequently used to show the legislative, executive, and judiciary branches of our government, and the powers and organization of each branch. This is called a flow chart. This chart is something like a diagram where various parts are connected by lines.

GRAPHS

Many statistics are used in the social studies. The big problem is to present the quantitative data so that the pupils will easily understand them. Numerical facts often mean very little to a person until they are shown in some clear and interesting graphic form. In geography and some of the other social studies, numbers are often used. The pupils sometimes memorize the numbers without understanding what they represent. It is a waste of time to expect pupils to carry very many numbers in their minds, especially if the numbers are so large that they have practically no meaning to them. Numerical facts should frequently be expressed in some simple visual form which has meaning. Most pupils in the fourth grade are able to read very simple graphs. As they advance from grade to grade, their power of reading graphs increases.

During recent years much use has been made of the pictorial graph. This graph appeals to all classes of people because it shows data in the form of attractive pictures. It is easy to understand. Simple pictures are used as symbols of the real objects. One pictorial symbol represents a certain amount. Some pictorial symbols that are frequently used in the social studies are bales of cotton, shocks of wheat, bottles of milk, buckets of coal, iron rails, baskets of tomatoes, bars of gold, automobiles, locomotives, trees, ships, and people. The key gives the value of each symbol. Great ingenuity may be shown in making pictorial graphs. Pupils like to make them. Pictorial graphs give a general picture for comparative purposes, and this is what we want pupils to obtain.

The bar graph is easy to make and to read. Wide lines, bars, or narrow rectangles are drawn horizontally or vertically from a line usually marked zero. On a horizontal bar graph the scale of values is usually placed at the bottom, while on a vertical bar graph, the scale is usually at the left-hand side. The scale should be large enough so that the bars will differ in length and comparisons can be made. Usually, pupils prefer the horizontal bar graph.

Another simple graph which is easy to make and to read is the circle graph. It is sometimes called the pie graph. The entire circle represents 100 per cent. The circle is divided into parts corresponding to the correct percentages. The parts are usually colored or shaded to make them stand out. Sometimes the percentages are written in the different parts of the circle so that the reader may obtain a more nearly accurate picture. The circle graph is often used to show such information as how our government or some other organization spends its money, the uses of land in a country, and the amount of wheat or some other product produced in the chief regions of the world.

The line graph is generally found to be difficult for the pupils to understand. The line graph is widely used in books and other publications. Probably the best way of teaching pupils to read line graphs is to have them make these graphs. Some teachers have the pupils keep a record of their marks over a period of time. Later, they make a line graph showing their marks. The figures representing the time element are put along the bottom of the graph, while the figures representing the marks are placed along the left-hand side. Another good activity is to have the pupils keep a record of the temperature for a number of days. Later, they show the temperature for the given number of days on a line graph.

POSTERS

Posters are commonly used to bring some idea before the people. There are posters on a variety of subjects such as safety, travel, good health, the army, the navy, the buying of defense bonds, the raising of money, and some coming event. They are often seen on billboards and in various public buildings. They are commonly used to advertise certain products.

Posters have an important place in teaching in all grades. Pupils like to look at them and many pupils like to make them. School events are often advertised by means of posters. Pupils make posters to illustrate what they are studying. In the lower grades, the pupils make simple posters in their study of foods, clothing, shelter, primitive people, the neighborhood, the home, and many other topics. In the upper grades, they make posters in their study of various problems. There are almost an unlimited number of ideas for the making of posters.

A poster (1) should be easily seen, (2) it should catch the eye of the individual and cause him to think, and (3) it should impress upon the individual a simple story which he will not soon forget. There are various ways of making posters. Sometimes a poster has only printing on it in large letters. Other posters may be made by building up a picture out of construction paper of different colors. Still other posters may be drawings.

Enough printed material should go with a poster to make it easily understood.

CARTOONS

Some teachers are surprised to learn that cartoons have a place in the teaching of the social studies. They are accustomed to associate cartoons with newspapers and magazines and not with teaching. They have not learned the value of making use of ideas or methods which people outside the school have found to be useful in keeping themselves informed about events. Teachers may often profit by studying the methods which newspapers and magazines use in getting their readers interested in the material appearing in their publications.

Cartoons have a place in the upper grades and the high school. They are especially useful in the social studies. Pupils often like to draw cartoons as well as to read them. A cartoon should tell a striking story at a glance. It makes use of humor, satire, exaggeration, and often the ridiculous. The caption should usually be short and to the point.

Cartoons are of little value if they do not cause the pupils to reason, to weigh the various sides of the question, and to appraise the ideas obtained. In using a cartoon, the teacher should make sure that the pupils clearly get the point which it makes. They should interpret the symbols that are used and should evaluate the ideas obtained. The peculiar character of a cartoon is likely to make the pupils remember for a long time the ideas which they get.

OBJECTS AND SPECIMENS

Teachers realize that pupils should have as many concrete experiences as possible, because they enable them to understand more clearly what they are studying. Too many teachers depend upon the book to give pupils most of their information. In some cases, the words of the book convey little meaning to the pupils, unless other means are used. One very excellent way of getting concrete experiences is to visit places and obtain first-hand information. Very early man obtained most of his information by coming into contact with actual things. Even today, people like to travel and see real objects in place of reading about them. An actual trip to a place is usually many times more valuable than just to read or hear about it. This is the chief reason why excursions or journeys are often taken by teachers and pupils to as many places as possible.

Pupils study about so many objects and places that it is impossible to get first-hand information about all of them through real journeys. It is necessary for pupils to get much of their information from books and other sources. As pupils read or listen to someone talk, they should form definite mental images. The more definite the images are, the more understanding a pupil has of what he is studying. If a pupil cannot go to places to get into contact with the real things about which he is studying, the things should be brought to him whenever it is possible to do so. Such things are called objects. Various kinds of objects are brought into the classroom, such as arrowheads, tomahawks, stamps, old letters, old newspapers, tools, weapons, powder horns, old cooking utensils, checks, bonds, deeds, furniture, grain, fruit, cotton bolls, and clocks.

Sometimes it is impractical to bring objects to the classroom, so models and specimens are used. A model is a replica or representation of an object. There are models of mines, farms, houses, ships, statues, bridges, and many other objects. Specimens are parts of objects such as pieces of yarn, cloth, leather, wood, wool, paper, coal, iron, copper, and glass. Specimens are often called samples.

Objects and specimens may be collected by both the teacher and the pupils. In every community there are objects and specimens which may be had just for the asking. Most people are glad to give them to the school when they know that they will be used and appreciated.

The time to use objects and specimens is when there is a felt need or a good reason for using them, and not just any time. Only those objects and specimens should be studied which are related to the work which the pupils are studying or soon will study. A pupil frequently brings an object to school which may be used in the unit which is being studied.

Sometimes a teacher is ready to begin a new unit and someone happens to bring an object or a specimen to school in which all the pupils become interested. Problems are raised and the new unit is launched without any difficulty. When a pupil brings an object or a specimen to school which has no connection with the work which the class is studying or soon will study, it should be gratefully received and the children should be permitted to look at it if they so desire. Problems may be raised for future study. It should be put in a place where it may be used at some later time when it is needed.

Pupils enjoy coming into contact with objects and specimens. They like to see and handle them whenever it is possible to do so. It means much more to a pupil if he touches them. While he feels an object, his mind begins to get a definite image which he can carry away with him. Even adults have the desire to see and handle objects. For example, the author visited a school recently in which a class was studying about the Pacific coast. One of the pupils had brought to school some stones and shells which he had picked up along the Pacific coast of California. The rest of the pupils listened with awe while the pupil told about swimming in the Pacific Ocean and finding the stones and shells which he had brought to school. After he finished his talk, the pupils looked at the stones and shells in a new light. As they looked at them and handled them, one could see that the stones and shells were playing an important part in helping the pupils form definite mental images of the Pacific coast of California.

The teacher should follow a definite plan when objects and specimens are used, but of course he should always have a definite plan in whatever he does. It is usually not enough just to call the attention of pupils to certain objects and specimens which are on the table in the classroom. The pupils will probably look at them, but most of the children will not get very much from them. The interest of the pupils should be aroused in the objects so that they will want to look at them. They should help the pupils form more definite experiences. For example, when looking at a boll of cotton, the pupils should see more than just some white cotton fiber in which there are a few seeds. They should see, in their imagination, certain scenes connected with the cotton industry. Some may picture farms where cotton seeds are being planted, others may see farms on which cotton plants are being cultivated, while still others may see the fiber being picked or being transported to the gin. The cotton boll may even help some pupils to picture mills where cotton fiber is being woven into cloth.

Objects and specimens are needed if the pupil is going to form concrete and correct images about certain things. For example, did you know that the coconut not only has a thick shell but that it is surrounded by a thick husk when it grows on a tree? Adults are often surprised to learn that they formed many inaccurate images in school. One of the reasons why they formed so many inaccurate images is that they got too much of their information from books and not enough from real objects, specimens, and pictures. Wide-awake and experienced teachers endeavor to have numerous objects and specimens on hand so that the pupils may see and examine them, as well as read about them.

MODELS

A good model is a faithful representation of an object. The teacher should keep in mind that the model is likely to differ in size from the object which it represents. When a pupil looks at a model, he should think of the object which it represents and not of the model. He should be taught to compare the size of the model with the real object. Possibly the model is larger than the object, but usually it is much smaller. In comparing sizes, familiar terms should be used such as the size of a pencil, a ruler, a person, a schoolroom, the school building, the school yard, a farm, or the city in which he lives. For example, if the model is of a building, the size of the real building which is represented may be compared to the school building or to some other building in the community.

It is not enough to ask a pupil merely to look at a model and report on what he sees. When such an assignment is made, he is likely to miss many of the details which a model shows about a real object. The teacher should help the pupil interpret and understand a model by giving him some question to answer as he looks at it. It takes time for pupils to learn to interpret models without the aid of questions from the teacher. Of course the aim is for the pupil finally to reach the stage where he will raise the questions which are necessary for him to answer, if he is going to form in his mind an accurate and definite image of the real object. In studying a model, questions are often raised which cannot be answered at that time. Additional reading and research may be needed to give the answers. Thus, the study of models may not only lead to the forming of mental images, but it may also stimulate pupils to desire to seek additional information about given subjects.

Pupils like to look at models. They like to see how they are built and how they operate. There are some museums where pupils may go and see models operate. Sometimes guides are on hand to give any needed information and to show how the models operate. The Museum of Science and Industry in Chicago is such a museum and it is visited annually by thousands of school children. This museum contains models which appeal to people of all ages, because persons never get too old to enjoy looking at models. Some of the models may be operated by children as well as by adults.

Pupils frequently make models while studying their units. The construction of a simple model should give the pupil a better picture of the object. In order to make a model, the pupil must solve certain practical problems. The teacher should make sure that these problems do not lead the pupil too far away from the purpose of forming a definite mental picture of the object. For this reason, the model should not be too complicated and it should be completed within a reasonable time without the expenditure of too much effort. Whenever a pupil makes some· thing, it should have a direct relation to what he is studying and the making of it should contribute to the solving of his problems. Models of ships, buildings, villages, mines, airplanes, and trains are often made by children.

THE SCHOOL MUSEUM

Every school can have some kind of a museum if the teacher wants one. Children like to collect objects and with a little encouragement they will help to collect articles for a school museum. There are many schools in which the school museum was started by the pupils and teachers in the social studies classes. In some schools, the museum material is in the different classrooms. Each teacher looks after the material in his classroom and it is generally related to the work which the pupils do under the direction of the teacher. Whether a classroom has any museum material depends largely upon the interest which the class-room teacher takes in it.

In many schools, the collecting of museum material is a project in which all the teachers and pupils take part. There may be one or more rooms in which the material is kept. When a room is not available for the museum material, it is often kept in the corridors, providing they are wide enough and are well lighted. Dark or narrow corridors should not be used for exhibiting museum material. Where the library is large, a part of the room is sometimes given over to a museum.

There is no need of having museum material if it cannot be seen and used by the pupils. If possible, the material should be kept in a place where (1) it may be easily examined by pupils at various times during the day, (2) pupils may examine the material without annoying other pupils, (3) teachers feel free to get the material or return it at any time, and (4) it is protected from people who might wish to take it from the building.

It is not difficult for a teacher or a group of teachers to start a museum. Over the course of years, the museum will gradually grow as material is added to it. Pupils should always be interested in helping the school have a good museum. Some of the sources from which museum material may be obtained are (1) the people living in the community, (2) some large industrial plants, (3) Chambers of Commerce in our large cities, (4) transportation companies, (5) Fairs, (6) certain governmental agencies, (7) certain museums, and (8) schools which have materials for exchange with other schools. Many teachers are agreeably surprised at the large amount of material which may be obtained without making very much effort. As the years pass, a teacher or a group of teachers should be able to collect a vast assortment of useful materials.

There are museums in many of our large cities. Teachers should work in cooperation with them. The museums have been established to serve the people and their directors are always glad to have pupils come to study their exhibits.

THE BULLETIN BOARD

Every room in which the social studies are taught should have one or more bulletin boards. All educators and teachers believe that they can be used very effectively in teaching, yet some of them do not make much effort to put into actual practice what they believe. Some social studies rooms do not have even a single bulletin board and the teachers make no attempt in getting bulletin boards placed in their rooms. Again, in a large number of schools where there are bulletin boards in the social studies rooms, many teachers look upon them with indifference and do not make much use of them. Only occasionally is material of importance placed on them. Very often the material is kept up so long that even an energetic pupil gets into the habit of forgetting to look at the bulletin board. In some rooms, the bulletin boards are placed in dark corners or in inconspicuous places where there happens to be room for them. Sometimes they are too small to be used effectively.

Although there are some teachers who do not make much use of bulletin boards in their teaching, yet there are many teachers who do make efficient use of them. Their pupils constantly refer to the material posted on them. They are managed by the pupils who see that the material which is posted is pertinent. Bulletin boards, correctly used, create much enthusiasm and interest.

The efficient use of the bulletin board enriches learning, because material of real interest to the pupils is placed where all can easily see it. Pupils take more interest in their work and in their room. They are taught the best ways of displaying material. They come to see that any material which is worth displaying should be arranged neatly and attractively. Managing a bulletin board with all of its problems furnishes a very fine opportunity for developing cooperation and participation among the pupils. It is difficult to see how current events can be taught adequately without using the bulletin board to display clippings and other material of current interest.

1. Kinds of Bulletin Boards

Bulletin boards are commonly made of cork, soft wood, or some other solid material into which tacks or pins may be pushed easily for the purpose of displaying various kinds of material. Some bulletin boards are attached to the wall so that they cannot be moved. Others are movable and are placed wherever they are needed in the room. In order to save space, some bulletin boards have hinges and the frames open and fold like the pages of a book. In some schoolrooms, a narrow bulletin board extends along the top of the blackboard.

Many schoolrooms have a map and display rail on one or more walls. Maps, pictures, charts, papers, and other materials are hung from them. Sometimes a wire is stretched horizontally along the top of the blackboard or along the wall from which various kinds of materials are suspended. Any teacher who is willing to make the effort can find places for displaying material.

The kinds of material which may be shown on the bulletin board are almost unlimited. When one stops to make a list of the various kinds of material, he is likely to be surprised at the large number. Such a list includes clippings, cartoons, pictures, photographs, drawings, postcards, posters, maps, charts, booklets, bulletins, letters, written reports, bibliographies, specimens, creative projects, room and school announcements, assignments, and written papers.

2. *How to Use the Bulletin Board*

The best way of using the bulletin board has never been discovered and it probably never will be. We should think not of one way but of several ways of using it. As teachers gain in power to teach, they will gain in power to use the bulletin board. An energetic teacher uses it in many different ways. He carries on experiments in its use, because only by experimentation can he hope to improve his teaching. Probably there is no teacher who feels that his pupils are making the maximum use of it. It is a big problem to get every pupil interested in the bulletin board so that he will take delight in using it without undue pressure from the teacher.

The maintenance of one or more bulletin boards in a social studies room should be a cooperative project by the teacher and the pupils. The pupils should understand that the bulletin boards belong to them and it is their responsibility to see that they are used efficiently. The teacher and pupils should discuss how they are going to use them. They should decide how many bulletin boards to have in the room. They must see that they are of the correct size and are placed in conspicuous places where they are well illuminated. Sometimes the pupils and teacher find it is necessary to consult with the principal in order to have their plans carried out.

The pupils should decide what kinds of material are to be placed on each bulletin board. All the pupils should bring material for the bulletin boards, but the arranging of the material should be left to certain pupils who have been selected to do this work. The material should be displayed in an attractive manner under a well thought out plan. Pupils are likely to pay more attention to a neat bulletin board than to one poorly arranged.

Much more material is usually brought in than can be used. There must be a wise selection of the material that is to be displayed. The pupils must be able to give good reasons for their selections so that all members of the class will be completely satisfied. They may decide to divide the bulletin boards into sections for various kinds of material. Certain pupils are appointed to arrange the material in each section. A good heading should be given for each section and it should be printed at the top in large letters.

The pupils should decide the length of time for displaying any given material. Various factors determine this, but in most cases it should be only a few days, probably from two days to five days. Pupils grow tired of looking at the same material over and over. A pupil cannot be blamed for losing interest in a bulletin board if the material is not removed after the class has been given sufficient time to examine it. There should be certain times during the day when pupils may go to the board to examine the material. It is certainly poor teaching for a teacher to expect pupils to use a bulletin board when no time is given for them to study or to look at the material displayed on it.

The material on a bulletin board should be related to the work of the class and it should enter into the class discussions. If the pupils are not encouraged to make use of the material, many of them are likely to pay very little attention to it. It is also a good plan to have certain rules for evaluating the work which the pupils do in connection with the bulletin board. Due credit should be given to those who take an active part in bringing material, arranging it, and in using it.

If the class is large, it is often wise to have one or more

committees of pupils appointed to manage each bulletin board. The teacher is always on hand to advise and make suggestions. The membership of a committee should be changed from time to time so that all members of the class may have an opportunity of serving. Place the responsibility on the pupils and it is remarkable how favorably they respond.

THE BLACKBOARD

It may seem strange to some teachers that time is spent in discussing the use of blackboards, since they are so common. In many classrooms they occupy much of the wall space. When it is realized that a large number of teachers do not make efficient use of all their blackboard space, it can easily be seen why this book considers their use. Probably the chief reason why some teachers do not make the maximum use of the blackboards in their classrooms is that they have never been taught how to use them. Most educators seem to have taken for granted that since there is usually much blackboard space in every classroom, teachers are sure to use blackboards wisely without receiving any training in their efficient use. The fact is that teachers must learn to use the blackboard just like they learn to use any other tool in teaching. They should come to understand the many possibilities which blackboards offer in teaching.

Blackboards should be used by both the teacher and the pupils. When the material on the board has answered its purpose, it should be erased. Blackboards should be kept clean and free of dust. Pupils do not like to use blackboards that appear messy and poorly kept. All work should be neatly and attractively arranged, because the pupils should be taught to form good habits. It is folly to expect pupils to form good habits if the teacher does not set a good example for them.

How to Use Blackboards

Generally speaking, the blackboard should be in continual use. There are many different ways of using it. The energetic teacher is always discovering how to make better use of it in his teaching. Pupils use it in explaining their work. A pupil may wish to use the blackboard when giving a report to the class. A committee of students may use the blackboard while discussing their problems. Colored chalk is sometimes used to make certain ideas stand out more prominently.

Some of the common uses which are made of blackboards in teaching the social studies are:

(1) The teacher uses the blackboard for giving assignments, lists of references, outlines, instructions, questions, and problems to the pupils. This kind of material should be put on the blackboard before the class discussion begins.

(2) The teacher uses the blackboard to develop lines of thought with the pupils. During the class discussion he writes on the board certain ideas brought out by the pupils. He frequently shows the pronunciation or the spelling of certain words and he may stress certain data and words by writing them on the board. He sometimes makes a drawing to illustrate some point or to clear up some question. A teacher should develop the art of making drawings on the board so that the work will mean more to the pupils. At first, the beginning teacher may hesitate to make drawings, since he may think that the pupils will find fault with them. However, a little practice gives a teacher more confidence in himself. It does not take a good teacher long to form the habit of drawing illustrations on the blackboard.

(3) The teacher often writes the questions on the blackboard when he gives short examinations or tests. If the examination is long or if it is difficult for all the pupils to see the board, it is best not to write the questions on the board. They should be mimeographed or duplicated in some other way. Then a copy of the questions may be given to each pupil.

(4) The blackboard is often used by pupils in giving reports or in class discussions. They frequently give outlines of what they have done or are going to do. They may list references and give various kinds of tables. They may draw maps, pictures, graphs, and cartoons which help to explain their reports.

(5) Pupils should be encouraged to make use of the blackboard from time to time. The blackboard is in the room to use and they should be taught to make wise use of it. The work should be purposeful and the pupils should not be permitted to put just anything on the board.

(6) Sometimes the teacher and pupils develop an outline in class. One of the pupils or the teacher writes the outline on the

board. Summaries of certain problems which are worked out by the teacher and pupils may also be put on the blackboard.

THE RADIO

One of the marvels of the age is the radio. Its use has grown phenomenally during the past few years. There were only a few homes in the United States with radio sets in 1922, while at the present time many homes have radio sets. Probably three out of every four radios are in use every day, and it is estimated that the average radio is "turned on" approximately five hours daily. There are many stations broadcasting programs in our nation. No other country makes so much use of the radio as the United States.

The possibilities of using the radio in education are very great. Since radio broadcasting is only a few years old, we still have much to learn about the most efficient ways of using the radio in teaching. Many broadcasting companies and schools are experimenting on these problems and good results are being obtained. Our broadcasting companies have education departments which are under the direction of wide-awake people who really have the training of citizens at heart.

Some of our school systems throughout the country have radio departments where teachers write and produce programs suitable for the schools. For example, the radio council in the Chicago Public School System has a staff of educators trained in the use of the radio. It has several well-equipped broadcasting booths of its own and a professional library on the use of the radio in education. The council plans, writes, produces, and evaluates programs weekly for the different grade levels in the schools. It provides teachers with a wealth of supplementary materials and suggestions on how to make the best use of certain radio programs in their school work.

The radio can never take the place of a good teacher. Teachers will always be needed in a schoolroom to guide and to inspire the pupils. We should look upon the radio as an aid to good teaching. It gives new material and supplements the work which is being done. The programs furnish the pupils material which they will not likely get in any other way.

Since children and adults are almost certain to listen to radio broadcasts during a part of their leisure time, the schools should aid the pupils in forming the habit of listening to good programs when they are not in school. There are so many different kinds of programs that it is not difficult to find programs which appeal to the interests of almost any individual. Our schools should aid the pupils to develop good judgment and discrimination in listening to the various broadcasts.

Many radio programs are very helpful in teaching the social studies. Some of the more valuable programs are travel talks; news reports and comments; round table discussions, debates, and talks on current problems; historical, civic and geographical plays; talks by famous people; and accounts of events as they are actually happening.

How to Use Radio Broadcasts

During the past few years much information has been gained on how to use radio programs, but we still need much more knowledge on the ways of using them most profitably. The teacher will be able to make better use of the programs if he keeps in mind that they are to be used not for entertainment but for helping the pupils do their work. He should carefully select the programs which are going to be heard. They should generally be related to the work which the pupils are doing.

The teacher should prepare the children for listening to certain broadcasts during school time just the same as he prepares them for using any other aid. Sometimes books are read, pictures are examined, places are located on maps, new words are explained, and reports are given so that the broadcasts will be more meaningful. When a broadcast is to be a starting point from which the children will begin their study, these activities may be done after the program is given.

Very often the children become interested in doing a number of activities after listening to a broadcast. They may wish to take a trip to get first-hand information, they may bring in clippings of current events, they may read books or magazine articles, they may make maps and draw pictures, they may collect objects, they may give a play, or they may do various other activities. It is remarkable that children do a large number of activities in connection with good radio broadcasts. A broadcast is often related to several of the subjects which are being studied.

The children should usually listen to radio programs in their own classrooms and not in an auditorium where many pupils are gathered. There is a certain amount of restlessness and inattention in large groups. Again, the classroom is the normal setting and any material needed to interpret the broadcast can generally be handled more easily in the classroom than in the auditorium. Most teachers do not believe the pupils should take many notes during a broadcast, unless the program calls for note-taking. Pupils seem to learn more by being able to concentrate on what is being said. If a pupil is required to take notes, he will likely miss parts of the program.

Pupils should be encouraged to listen to good programs which are given outside of school hours. Sometimes they can receive considerable help in solving their problems by listening to such programs.

PROBLEMS FOR DISCUSSION AND RESEARCH

1. Name and illustrate the different kinds of charts.
2. Of what value are graphs? Illustrate the different kinds of graphs.
3. Discuss the use of posters in teaching the social studies.
4. Draw a cartoon to portray some point you wish to make. Discuss the value of cartoons in teaching the social studies.
5. Examine newspapers and magazines. Make a list of the types of graphs, charts, and cartoons you find. Does it seem as if newspapers and magazines are making very good use of graphs and cartoons?
6. Discuss the value of objects, specimens, and models in teaching the social studies.
7. Explain how a school may obtain a museum if it does not already have one.
8. If there is a museum close at hand, visit it and see how its material might be used in teaching the social studies.
9. Make an outline of the important facts that a teacher should know about the bulletin board and its uses.
10. Explain the various ways that the blackboard may be used by the teacher and pupils.
11. Obtain a textbook which is used by the pupils in the social studies. It may be a textbook in geography, history, civics, economics, sociology, or a combination of subjects in the social studies. Examine it carefully to see what use is made of the audio-visual aids mentioned in this chapter. Report on what you learn.

12. Make a list of radio broadcasts which are suitable for children.
13. Learn what certain large school systems are doing in respect to radio broadcasts for use in the schools.
14. Try to visit schools where the children listen to radio programs during the day. Explain how they use the programs.
15. Give some advantages and disadvantages of using radio programs in the schoolroom.

REFERENCES

Bartlett, Kenneth, *How to Use the Radio*. Washington: The National Association of Broadcasters, 1941.

Branom, Mendel and Branom, Fred, *The Teaching of Geography*. Boston: Ginn and Co., 1921.
  Part Three. The Materials of Geography, 93-132.

Callamore, Edna, "The 'Why' of Geography Exhibits," The Journal of Geography, XXVII, 152-157, April, 1928.

Dale, Edgar, "New Understanding Through Visual Aids," Education, LVIII, 65-69, October, 1937.

Davidge, Lucius, "Education on the Air," Junior College Journal, XI, 322-324, February, 1941.

Earley, Albert, "Visual Instruction," School Life, XXVI, 271-272, June, 1941.

Eiselen, Elizabeth, "The Technique of Exhibits," The Journal of Geography, XXXIX, 320-322, November, 1940.

Goldman, Louis, "Reincarnation Through a Museum," School Activities, XII, 239-240, February, 1941.

Greenwood, Roy, "How We Use the Town Meeting of the Air," New York State Education, XXVIII, 430-431, 466-488, March, 1941.

Gibbong, Hazel, "Radio and the Elementary Child," Educational Methods, XVIII, 166-170, January, 1939.

Gregory, W. M., "Radio Guidance to Geography Instruction in the Cleveland Elementary Schools," Educational Method, XVII, 65-69, November, 1937.

Hoban, Charles, Hoban, Charles, Jr., and Zisman, Samuel, *Visualizing the Curriculum*. New York: The Cordon Co., 1937. Chapters III and VI.

Horn, Ernest, *Methods of Instruction in the Social Studies*. New York: Charles Scribner's Sons, 1937.
  The Radio, 326-334.

How Schools Can Use Radio. New York: National Broadcasting Co., 1941.

How to Use the Radio in the Classroom, by a Committee of Teachers. Washington: The National Association of Broadcasters, 1941.

Knowlton, Daniel, "Graphic Methods in the Social Studies," Social Education, II, 181-186, March, 1938.

Levenson, W. B. and Randall, L. A., "Education Via F M Radio Programs," School Executive, LX, 46, June, 1941.

Lewis, Dorothy, *Broadcasting to the Youth of America*. Washington: The National Association of Broadcasters, 1941.

McKown, Harry and Roberts, Alvin, *Audio-Visual Aids to Instruction*. New York: McGraw-Hill Book Co., 1940.

Chapter IV. Objects, Specimens, and Models, 53-70.

Chapter V. Graphic Materials, 87-102.

Chapter X. Auditory Aids, 211-242.

Norsted, M. W., "Radio Listening Habits of Students," Minnesota Journal of Education, XXI, 222, January, 1941.

O'Brien, Mae, "Listen to Children," Teachers College Record, XLII, 616-634, April, 1941.

Oppenheimer, Arthur, "Education's New World of the Air," Social Education, II, 617-622, December, 1938.

Radio in Education, Reprint from Educational Method for January, 1939. Washington: Department of Supervisors and Directors of Instruction of the National Education Association.

Radio in Education, Educational Press Bulletin, November, 1940, issued by Superintendent of Public Instruction, Springfield, Ill.

Stolper, B. J., "The Bulletin Board as a Teaching Device," Teachers College Record, XL, 1-5, February, 1939.

Chapter Nine: MAPS AND HOW TO USE THEM

IMPORTANCE

MAPS ARE very important visual aids. It is impossible to teach the social studies without using maps. They contain much information which may be obtained by those who will take the time to study them. Many people merely look at maps and never realize that they often contain more information than is found on many printed pages. Only those who know how to read and interpret maps ever really get very much from them. Every map tells a story. In fact, a map may tell a number of stories and it is up to teachers to teach pupils how to read maps most efficiently.

Maps have been used from very ancient times. Man probably began to draw maps at about the same time he began to draw pictures. We have no way of knowing what the first map showed since it probably was made on a rock, the wall of a cave, a piece of wood, or the ground. It probably was a very rough sketch of some small area in the region where the person lived. As time passed, people began to travel and their knowledge of the world increased. The map grew to include more than the local region. Routes of travel and more distant places were shown.

The world of the Phoenicians, Greeks, and Romans centered around the Mediterranean Sea. Their maps included southern Europe, northern Africa, and western Asia. The Mediterranean Sea is much longer in an east and west direction than it is wide in a north and south direction. These people thought that the earth is longer in an east and west direction than in a north and south direction. The early Mediterranean navigators used longus (length) to describe the east and west distances and latus (width) to describe the north and south distances. Longitude came to be used in place of longus and it is distance measured east or west from the prime meridian. Latitude is used in place of latus and it is distance measured north or south from the equator.

After the time of Columbus, many parts of the earth came to be known and the map of the world was gradually expanded to include new lands and places. Today, explorers have visited so many different places that we are now able to draw a fairly accurate map of the entire world.

Maps are used not only in schools but in many other places. They are found on the walls of museums and in many public buildings. They are seen on billboards. Newspapers and magazines make much use of maps in giving the news. Various publications of our government contain maps. Advertising literature often have maps. In fact, some people have even gone so far as to call this period of time "the map age."

LEARNING TO INTERPRET MAPS

Since maps are so very important and common, a person might naturally think that teachers would see to it that their pupils learn to read them. However, many teachers spend very little time in teaching pupils to use maps. They seem to think that pupils will learn to use maps with very little assistance from them. This is the incorrect view to take. Probably the chief reason why teachers spend so little time in teaching map reading is because they, themselves, do not know how to get much information from maps. When they went to school their teachers never spent much time in teaching them to use maps. Hence, they never got the map habit and they do not fully realize the value of maps. A teacher cannot be expected to teach well what he does not know.

There is much more in a map than most people think. A map is not a picture of the earth or a part of the earth, but it does represent the earth or a part of it. For example, colors or different shadings may represent mountains or lowlands, but they are not pictures of mountains or lowlands. A person must learn to interpret the ways in which the real objects upon the earth are shown on a map. He must know what the symbols represent. They should enable him to form mental images of real things. Thus, the map becomes a framework for ideas and images.

KINDS OF MAPS ACCORDING TO FORM

It will aid the teacher in thinking about maps to classify them in various ways. One way is to group maps according to form and to where they are found. Those that are used chiefly in the schoolroom are found in the first five groups mentioned here.

The Globe Map. The most nearly accurate map of the world that we have is on a globe. The globe is shaped about the way the earth is shaped. Areas, shapes, and directions are represented almost accurately on a globe. Some educators think that a globe sixteen or eighteen inches in diameter is the one that most schools should buy for general use, providing they have the money. Of course those schools that lack the money should buy smaller globes. Many teachers prefer the physical-political globe because both the physical features and the political divisions are shown. A large globe costs more than a large physical-political wall map of the world.

Maps in Textbooks. A good textbook in the social studies has many maps. This is especially true of geography and history textbooks. The maps are highly selected and are related to the printed material. They need to be consulted by the pupils when studying their lessons. There are colored maps and black and white maps. They are of different sizes and show many different things. One great advantage is that every pupil using a textbook has access to a large number of good maps.

Maps in Atlases. There are various types of atlases. There are history atlases which contain many kinds of history maps, while there are geography atlases which have maps chiefly of value in teaching geography. Some maps in atlases are of value in teaching economics and sociology. The student who has the atlas habit has something which will be of great value to him all through life. Getting pupils to want to use maps should be one of the chief aims of the teacher of the social studies.

Wall Maps. Every school should have a number of well selected wall maps. The number of wall maps in most schools is determined chiefly by the interest of the teachers in maps and by the amount of money available for purchasing them. There are many kinds of wall maps which are valuable in teaching geography, history, and the other social studies. A wall map is of special value in group work or in teaching the class as a whole, although it may be used also in individual work. Places should be located and other features noted which have a bearing on the solving of a problem. A wall map should be large enough to be seen by all the pupils from their seats in a classroom of average size.

Outline Maps. Maps which show only the outlines of continents, countries, and other regions are very useful. There are slated wall outline maps on which chalk is used. When through with the map, the chalk marks are erased. There are wall outline maps on heavy paper. Charcoal, pencils, ink, colored crayons, and water colors may be used with these maps. Various kinds of data may be put on wall outline maps. Such maps are very useful for individual work, group work, or work by the entire class. Children often use wall outline maps when they make reports to the class. During a class discussion, it is a good idea to have wall outline maps on hand which may be used by any interested child or group of children. Possibly some child may wish to show the chief regions of the world raising corn or the routes of some of the early explorers.

There are slated outline globes on which chalk may be used. The marks are erased when they are no longer needed. Pupils enjoy working on slated globes.

Small outline maps on paper are very useful. They are sometimes called desk outline maps because they are small enough to be used on the desks in the schoolroom. Small outline maps are very good for individual work. Many different kinds of data may be shown, such as density of population, the number of people voting in each state, the territorial growth of the United States, and the chief regions producing certain products. A pupil is likely to remember for a longer time what he puts on an outline map, providing he thinks as he works.

There are various ways of obtaining desk outline maps. They may be purchased from map companies or certain other companies. In some schools, the teacher uses a duplicating machine to produce outline maps. Some textbooks have outline maps which the children may trace. The teacher may also give outline maps to the children to trace.

Maps in Newspapers and Magazines. Many newspapers and magazines use maps of various kinds. Many of the maps are very valuable for locating places where certain events occurred. Sometimes there are maps which show where certain products are produced. During the time when elections are held, maps may be published which show the ways that people voted at previous elections, the wards of a city, and many other facts of interest to a voter. Colored maps are published occasionally in newspapers and magazines.

Maps Showing Routes of Travel. Maps showing routes of travel are used daily by thousands of people. The road map is one of our most common maps. Oil companies, the state highway departments, and other agencies publish many road maps every year. Such maps are free and are used by millions of people in finding how to go from one place to another. Large bus companies have maps showing the routes over which their busses travel. Railroad companies have maps in their time-tables. Likewise, airplane companies have maps showing the routes over which their airplanes fly. Even steamship companies issue maps which show the routes followed by their ships.

Other Kinds of Maps. There are many local, state, and national government publications which contain maps. The United States daily weather map is read by thousands of people when it is published for general distribution. It is interesting to note when the United States is at war, the daily weather map is not published for general distribution, because the data about the weather might prove to be very useful to our enemies. Many companies realize the value of using maps in advertising.

KINDS OF MAPS ACCORDING TO DATA SHOWN

Maps may be grouped according to the data which are shown on them. Some of the more common maps are briefly discussed in the following paragraphs:

1. A political map is one in which the political divisions stand out prominently. Countries, states, and counties are called political divisions. Colors are commonly used to show the political divisions, and each political division has a color different from the one next to it.

2. A physical map is one in which the physical features stand out prominently. Mountains, plateaus, and plains are physical features and are easily located. The colors on many physical

maps represent heights of land and depths of large bodies of water. On a few physical maps the colors represent regions.

3. A political-physical map is one in which both the political divisions and the physical features are plainly indicated.

4. A relief map is one in which the relief is clearly shown. There are relief models on which the surface features are actually raised. Pupils may feel the topography and easily visualize it. Many geographies have relief maps which show the relief by black and white shading.

5. There are maps which show precipitation, pressure, winds, temperature, and the weather.

6. Vegetation maps show the location of forests, grasslands, and deserts.

7. Product maps show the location of regions producing certain products, transportation maps show routes of travel, while land use maps show how the land is used.

8. Population maps tell us something about the people. Very often a population map shows the distribution of people or the number of people to the square mile.

9. There are various kinds of maps which show historical data. Some of these maps have data about explorations, wars, territorial acquisitions, immigrants, elections, industries, and problems of government.

10. Pictorial maps are commonly used in newspapers, magazines, and books. Pictures appeal to people. Many people look at a picture map when they would never think of looking at a map that does not have pictures.

WHY MAPS ARE USED

Many teachers think that the chief use of maps is to locate places which are mentioned in geography, history, and the other social studies. It is true that maps do give pupils a knowledge of place location. Everything that has happened in history has happened somewhere upon the earth, and locating the places where events have taken place helps to relate history to certain regions on the earth. In fact, it is always a good idea to keep in mind that places about which we study are located somewhere upon the earth. They mean more to a person if they can be located on a map with some degree of definiteness. A pupil should form the habit of turning to a map to locate any new place which is mentioned. If pupils do not form the habit of locating places on maps in school, they cannot be expected to locate places on maps after they leave school.

Locating places should not be the only reason for using maps. The teacher who never gets beyond the location of places does not really understand the functions of maps. A very important function of maps is to present data. Maps give such a wealth of information that good teachers teach from them. Much of the data shown on maps may be classed as political, physical, social, economic, and historical. Political data include material about countries, states, and various civil divisions. Physical data give information on such topics as location, area, shape, surface, depths of bodies of water, elevations, soil, minerals, native vegetation, wild animal life, temperature, precipitation, pressure, winds, and ocean currents. Maps giving information about cities, density of population, races, wealth, elections, religions, language, and similar topics show social data. Economic data on maps include such information as the distribution of products of the farm, range, mine, and sea; the location of factories, railroad lines, airplane routes, and highway routes; the various uses of the land; the importance of trade; and the value of certain products. Historical data on maps give information about army campaigns, the growth and decline of countries, early routes of travel, the location of famous places, and various other events that have happened in the past.

A study of maps permits a pupil to visualize regions of various sizes. The information which a pupil obtains from maps enables him to understand more fully the possibilities of a region. They help him to do inferential thinking, because certain data suggest new ideas. Maps also permit a pupil to compare regions, thus bringing out relationships. It is almost impossible to compare regions intelligently without using maps. This is especially true if the regions are large or are far apart.

Maps fascinate many people, even though they may not be able to get much information from them. To those who have the power of unlocking some of the data which maps contain, they are more interesting than a puzzle. The more a person studies a map, the more meaning a map has. The wise use of maps promotes interest in the social studies.

QUALITIES OF MAPS

A teacher should keep in mind a number of questions when he selects maps to be used by pupils. Some of these questions are the following:

(1) Is the map clear and can it be read easily? Some maps are poorly shown and the data do not stand out clearly.

(2) Is the map accurately drawn and are the data accurate? Since most teachers do not have enough knowledge to determine these facts for themselves, they must take the advice of experts in the field. If the data have been furnished by a trained expert and if the map is published by a company that understands the making of maps, the chances are that the maps meet the requirements of accuracy.

(3) Is the map the correct size? It should be large enough for the purpose for which it is to be used. If it is a wall map, it should be easily seen by all the pupils in a classroom of average size. Many wall maps are too small for class work.

(4) Does the map have the correct amount of information? Many maps show too much. A map used in the lower grades should not have so much data as one used in the upper grades. Some maps have so much data that pupils become confused in attempting to read them. Pupils should advance from simple maps to more complex ones as they grow in power to read maps.

(5) If a map has colors, are they pleasing to the eye? Are they distinct enough to make certain regions stand out? If the colors are too bright or harsh, the map should not be used. On a colored physical map, the international color scheme is frequently used. Shades of blue are shown for depths of the oceans. Lowlands are shown by shades of green. As the land gets higher, different shades of yellow, brown, and red are used.

(6) Does the map have a good legend? The legend should contain all the information that a person needs in order to read the map correctly. The symbols and the colors that are used on the map should be explained in the legend.

MAP PROJECTIONS

All maps of the world or of a region are not drawn exactly alike. This may be told by looking at a number of different maps of the world. On some maps, the meridians are straight lines, while on other maps they are curved lines. The meridians meet at the poles on some maps of the world, while on other maps of the world they do not meet at the poles. Likewise, the parallels are straight lines on some maps while on other maps they are curved lines. The shapes and areas of the continents are determined by the way the meridians and parallels are drawn.

The projection of a map is the way the map is drawn. The way that the meridians and parallels are drawn determines the projection that is used. A globe is almost a true map of the world. The meridians and parallels are curved lines on a globe and the meridians meet at the poles. The parallels are really parallel to one another. It is well to remember that all meridians extend north and south while all parallels extend east and west.

The big problem is to draw a curved surface on a flat piece of paper. It is impossible to draw an accurate map of a nearly spherical earth on a flat piece of paper. This can be shown by taking a half of a hollow ball and trying to flatten it. As you press on the hollow half of the ball it either stretches or breaks as it becomes flattened. Something must be sacrificed in drawing a map of the world on a flat piece of paper. On some world maps, the areas of regions are not comparable. On other world maps, the shapes of land masses are not accurately drawn. On still other maps of the world, the distances are not shown accurately. In drawing a map, the cartographer must first determine what he wishes to show. Then he can decide what projection to use.

A very common map of the world which is used in many schoolrooms is the one which is drawn on the Mercator projection. This projection was first used about four hundred years ago and the map was made especially for sailors. The meridians run straight up and down and the parallels run straight across on such a map. There is much stretching on the map and the stretching becomes greater as the distances increase north and south from the equator. This stretching causes regions away from the equator to appear much larger than they actually are. In fact, in the far north and the far south, the map has been stretched so much that shapes, areas, and distances are greatly distorted. Greenland is somewhat less than one-third as large as Australia, but on a map of the world on the Mercator projection, it appears to be much larger than Australia. In fact, on such a map the poles are not shown and the area of one region cannot be compared with the areas of other regions. There is also no common scale for measuring distances on the map.

On a map of the world on the Mercator projection, north is towards the top of the map and south is towards the bottom. Pupils who use such a map are likely to get into the habit of saying up north and down south. They are likely to think that the top of all maps is north and the bottom of all maps is south. However, this is incorrect because there are some maps on which north is not at the top and south is not at the bottom. Indeed, there are maps where both west, north, and east are at the top.

On account of the defects of the Mercator projection, many teachers prefer not to use a map of the world which is drawn on this projection. There are several other projections which are commonly used. Some teachers prefer to use a hemispherical map of the world in the lower grades, while some form of an equal area projection is generally used in the other grades. A good school atlas shows maps which are drawn on various projections. The name of the projection which is used in drawing a wall map is usually printed on it.

USING MAPS

Since the earth is almost round, a globe is the most nearly accurate map of the world which we have. Areas, shapes, and distances are accurately shown on a globe. When pupils in the lower grades first need to use a map of the world they should use a globe. Frequent use of a globe usually starts in the third or fourth grade when the pupils begin studying world geography or groups of people living in various regions on the earth. Of course some teachers may introduce the globe sooner, but most teachers prefer to wait until the third or fourth grade is reached.

A globe gives a truer picture of the earth than a map on a flat piece of paper. Pupils come to see that the earth is shaped like a globe. Of course a globe is very much smaller than the earth, so we cannot expect a globe to give young people a knowledge of the size of the earth. About the only thing that can be brought out about the size of the earth in the lower grades is that it is very many times larger than the globe. The continents, oceans, and regions that are being studied may be located. Directions are taught. Going towards the North Pole is north and towards the South Pole is south. Going to the right of north is east and to the left of north is west. The equator may be traced and the pupils will see that it is a line extending around the earth halfway between the poles.

The maps in the textbooks and wall maps should be used along with the globe. In the beginning, it is a good idea to have the pupils place their textbooks on their desks so that north on the map is towards north in the room. They learn that the globe, the maps in their books, and the wall maps show similar things. The first maps that are used should be simple and should not have very much data.

As pupils advance from grade to grade, they gradually learn to read maps. The power of reading maps slowly grows on a pupil. It is not developed in any single grade, but it should be developed in all grades. Teachers should not think that pupils can learn to read maps in a few lessons. As long as pupils are in school, they should use maps whenever there is any good reason for using them. It is only through the actual use of maps over a period of years that pupils learn to use them correctly and to get very much information from them. A common fault of many teachers is that they expect pupils to use maps without ever having been taught to use them. In teaching pupils how to use maps they should be taught how to use the scale, how to use parallels and meridians, and how to use the legend.

USING THE SCALE

Most maps in a textbook and many wall maps have a scale which may be used in measuring distances. On a wall map and in some large atlases, the scale is often given in two ways: (1) the statement is made that one inch equals a certain number of miles and (2) a straight line is drawn on which the miles are marked. Due to the difficulty of drawing a simple map of the world on a flat piece of paper, some maps of the world do not have a single scale which may be used anywhere on it.

If no scale is given on a globe, it may be found easily by doing a little arithmetic. Find the circumference of the globe in inches. Since the earth has a circumference of about 25,000 miles, divide 25,000 by the number of inches that were obtained for the circumference of the globe. The answer will be the approximate number of miles that one inch represents on the globe. In a textbook, the scale of a map is usually a straight line which has been marked off in miles.

Pupils should be taught to use the scale. First, they learn where to look for the scale. After finding the scale, they learn how to use it in measuring distances. If the scale states that one inch represents a certain number of miles, the problem is simple. The distance between two places is measured in inches by using a ruler or a tape measure. Then the number of inches is multiplied by the number of miles that one inch represents.

If the scale is a straight line that has been marked off in miles, the pupils may be instructed to do the following: Take a piece of paper and place the straight edge next to the scale. Mark off the scale of miles on the paper. Now use this scale on paper in finding the distance between two places. Probably a better way to find the distance between two places is to take a piece of paper and place the straight edge so that it passes through both places. Place dots at these two places on the paper. Then apply to the scale and determine the number of miles between the two dots.

USING MERIDIANS AND PARALLELS

Meridians are the north and south lines on a map while parallels are the east and west lines. If a map is accurately drawn, the meridians meet at the poles, providing the poles are shown. The parallels are lines which are parallel to the equator. Pupils learn the north and south directions on a map by following meridians and the east and west directions by following parallels.

Most teachers believe that latitude and longitude should not be taught before the pupils reach the fifth grade. In the fourth grade, regions are located in reference to the equator or the poles. For example, a place may be near the equator, near the North Pole, or halfway between the equator and the North Pole. By the time the pupils reach the fifth grade they need to have some more nearly accurate way of measuring distance from the equator. To understand the climate of a region, a pupil should know how far it is from the equator. Since latitude tells how far a place is from the equator, fifth grade pupils may be taught the meaning of latitude.

After the pupils have been taught the meaning of latitude, they should be taught the meaning of longitude. Longitude does not tell us anything about the climate of a region, but it does help to locate a place definitely. If the latitude and the longitude of a place are given, it can be accurately located. Longitude also helps the pupils understand how time changes as a person moves east or west around the world.

USING A LEGEND OR KEY

When we speak of the legend or key, we mean the explanatory material which is given on all good maps. This explanatory material helps a person read a map. A map contains much data which are shown by various kinds of symbols. These symbols must be understood before the map can be interpreted. Hence, it is the duty of the teacher to teach his pupils the meaning of the symbols which are found on maps and to train them in their use. Pupils should form the habit of turning to the legend or key when they read maps.

Pupils should learn to tell what the different colors represent on maps. If the colors are on a political map, they represent political divisions. If they are on a physical map, they tell us something about the surface. On most physical maps, the colors represent heights of land and depths of oceans. On a precipitation map, the various colors represent different amounts of precipitation, while on a vegetation map they represent the different kinds of vegetation. Pupils come to see that colors represent different kinds of data. Sometimes, shadings are used in place of colors. When reading a map, the pupils should try to visualize what the colors or shadings represent.

The explanatory material in the legend may tell how swamps, ocean currents, winds, temperature, and other natural features are shown. It may also explain how man-made features, such as cities, railroads, canals, airplane routes, and boundaries, are designated. By showing man-made features on a physical map, the relationship between man and his physical environment may be easily understood.

USING THE GLOBE MAP

The globe map may be used to show many of the same facts which are shown on a flat map. There are a few things which can be shown better by using a globe than by using a flat map.

A globe is needed to show how rotation causes day and night. In a darkened room an electric light or a flash light may represent the sun. The globe is rotated and it is readily seen that the part of the earth facing the sun has day while the other part has night.

The earth revolves around the sun. The earth is also inclined so that the North Pole always points in the same general direction towards the North Star. A globe is needed to show these facts while explaining the seasons.

A globe is needed to give the impression to pupils that the earth is shaped like a sphere. It is impossible to teach satisfactorily the shape of the earth by using a flat map of the world. The true shapes and areas of regions are shown better on a globe than on a map of the world on flat paper.

A globe is needed to show the reasons why the time of day is not the same everywhere. The time belts may be marked off easily on a globe. The reason for the International Date Line can also be understood better by using a globe than a flat map.

A better understanding of airplane routes and sailing routes may be obtained by using a globe than a flat map. On a globe, the meaning of the great circle sailing route can clearly be seen, but on a flat map of the earth it is very difficult for pupils to visualize such a route.

MAKING A NEIGHBORHOOD MAP

Many teachers believe that the real beginning of map study should be in the third or fourth grade. Very simple maps are first made by the children. During the study of their home neighborhood they take short trips to places near the school. On returning from a trip, they sometimes make a drawing showing the schoolhouse, the place visited, and the streets over which they passed in going to and from the place. It is a good idea for the teacher and the pupils to make this drawing on a large piece of paper placed on the floor. North should be written near the north edge of the paper; east, near the east edge; south, near the south edge; and west, near the west edge. While the map is on the floor, the children may be drilled on directions. Later, the drawing may be placed on the north wall where all may see it more clearly.

The next step is to make a map of the neighborhood in which the school is located. The idea of the scale is first developed with the pupils. They are led to see that they cannot make a map as large as the neighborhood on a small piece of paper. In getting the pupils to see the need for using a scale, a drawing of the schoolroom is made, letting one inch represent a given number of feet. After the children understand how to make a drawing of their schoolroom, they are ready to proceed to make a map of the neighborhood, letting a given number of inches represent a block or a certain number of feet.

Children generally make a map of the neighborhood on the sand table or on a piece of plywood, cardboard, or wallboard placed on the floor or a table. The four main directions are kept in mind while making the map. The streets are laid out with strips of paper. The children decide what objects to show and how to show them. Various buildings are made out of construction paper or wood and are placed in their correct places. People and automobiles are placed in the streets. Telephone wires and electric wires are shown by stretching twine or thin wire on pins or toothpicks. Trees are made by placing twigs along the streets. Small pieces of green paper are glued to the branches for leaves. Sometimes shapes of green trees are cut out of green paper and are pasted to small sticks.

MAPS FROM MEMORY

Some years ago, pupils spent much effort in learning to draw maps of states and countries from memory. Much time was wasted in doing this because they did not learn much geography. Today, we do not think it is worthwhile to have pupils spend very much time in learning to draw maps from memory. If outline maps are wanted, pupils may trace them or buy them already drawn. Pupils are encouraged to make rough sketches because a rough sketch often shows what the pupil has in mind.

COPYING MAPS

Suppose a pupil or a class needs a large outline map of a country, a continent, or the world. How can such a map be obtained? One way of obtaining such a map is to buy it. Another way is to draw it free-hand, but this is difficult for most pupils.

Another way of obtaining a large outline map is to enlarge a map by using squares. Small squares are drawn over the map to be enlarged. The squares are numbered. On a big piece of paper, as many large squares are drawn as there are squares on the small map. The large squares are numbered to correspond to the numbers of the squares on the small map. Then the part of the map in each small square is drawn in the corresponding large square.

Still another way of making a large outline map is to trace or draw a small map on a glass slide or on a cellophane slide. Place the slide in the lantern and project the drawing on a large piece of white paper placed on the wall. Trace the drawing on the paper. Large outline maps may also be drawn on the blackboard by using this same method.

MAKING PICTORIAL MAPS AND PRODUCT MAPS

Pictorial maps are frequently made by pupils. A pictorial map is made by pasting or drawing pictures of objects on an outline map in the regions where they are produced.

Children also enjoy making product maps of a country or region. Products or samples of products produced in the region are put on a large outline map. Sometimes the material is wrapped in cellophane and is pasted on the map. Heavy pieces may be sewn on the map. Of course some products may be pasted directly on the map. Medicine capsules are frequently used to hold small products such as wheat and rice.

MAKING RELIEF MAPS

When pupils are old enough to study the relief of a country or a region, they are encouraged to make relief model maps. On a relief model map, the elevations and depressions are actually shown. The relief model is usually made on a thick piece of cardboard, a piece of wallboard, or a piece of one-fourth inch plywood. The relief may be shown by using several kinds of mixtures, such as (1) salt and flour, (2) papier mâché, (3) patching plaster, (4) plaster of Paris, or (5) oil clay. If patching plaster is used, it should be mixed with water until a mixture is formed which resembles a thick cream. Patching plaster makes a very good map. When plaster of Paris is used, it should be mixed with vinegar so that it will not set or become hard so quickly. Even so, it hardens too rapidly for most children to use.

A salt and flour mixture is made by using about two parts of salt and one part of flour. The salt and flour are mixed with water to form a thick mixture out of which the relief model is built. The mixture is spread on the map with a flat knife. In many schools, this is the most common mixture used for making relief maps.

Papier mâché is made by tearing some newspapers into very small pieces. The pieces of paper are soaked in hot water and beaten into a pulp. The pulp is put into a porous cloth and the water is squeezed out. The pulp is now mixed with a generous supply of thin paste which has been formed from flour and water. The paste is made by adding one cup of water to one or two tablespoonfuls of flour. The mixture is cooked until the paste becomes clear. After mixing the pulp with the paste, any surplus water is squeezed out. Then the papier mâché is ready to use.

Before starting to make a relief model, the pupil should study carefully the relief of the region which he is going to make. He should visualize the elevations and depressions and know the locations of the mountains, plateaus, plains, rivers, lakes, and other relief features. After studying the region, he is ready to begin. He draws the outline of the region on a piece of thick cardboard, wallboard, or one-fourth inch plywood. Then he takes one of the mixtures which has already been described. He builds the relief slowly by using a flat table-knife. He consults physical and relief maps as he works. He makes ridges for high mountains. He uses a sharp pointed instrument to trace the rivers before the mixture becomes hard or dry. After the map becomes dry, it may be colored with oil paints or water colors.

A pupil who makes a relief model map has a better idea of

the relief of the region than he can get just by studying maps. The chief criticism of relief model maps is that the heights of mountains and the depths of valleys are greatly exaggerated by the pupils.

PROBLEMS FOR DISCUSSION AND RESEARCH

1. What are some of the reasons why maps appeal to many people, even though they do not know much about them?

2. Tell something about the evolution of maps.

3. Explain how pupils may obtain the map habit.

4. Maps may be grouped or classified in a number of ways. Make two or more groups and describe the maps in each group.

5. Make a list of the uses of maps both in the schoolroom and outside the schoolroom.

6. Suppose you are a teacher buying maps. What are the qualities you would want the maps to have?

7. What is meant by a map projection? Describe the Mercator projection. Give the advantages and disadvantages of using a map of the world on this projection.

8. Examine wall maps and maps in atlases and see how many projections you can find. Try to learn to identify several of the map projections.

9. Why should a globe be used before a map of the world is used in the third or fourth grade?

10. Explain fully how to teach children to use the scale on a map.

11. Of what use are parallels and meridians on a map?

12. Of what importance is the legend on a map?

13. Describe how young children may make a map of the neighborhood.

14. Give some uses of a globe.

15. Of what value is it to draw maps from memory?

16. Explain how large outline maps may be obtained.

17. What is the value of copying maps?

18. Describe how children may make pictorial maps.

19. Explain how children may make a relief model map. What are the different kinds of mixtures which may be used in making a relief model map?

20. Make a list of the different kinds of maps which you find in recent newspapers and magazines.

21. Examine the advertisements which appear in newspapers, magazines, and other places. Discuss how maps are used in advertising.

REFERENCES

Aitchison, Alison and Uttley, Marguerite, "Maps: The Sign Language of Geography," Educational Method, XVII, 289-293, March, 1938.

Boggs, S. W. and Branom, F. K., *Globe Studies and Uses,* Chicago: A. J. Nystrom & Co., 1938.

Baldwin, J. W., The Use of Equipment in Teaching the Social Studies—Past and Present, *The Historical Approach to Methods of Teaching the Social Studies, Fifth Yearbook,* National Council for the Social Studies, 1935, 106-122.

Burgess, Alvin, "The Use of Maps in Developing Geographic Personalities," The Journal of Geography, XL, 57-64, February, 1941.

Burkhart, C. A., "Map Making—A Sketch," Education, LVIII, 271-278, January, 1938.

Burnham, Guy, "Map Projections as a Basis for Maps," The Journal of Geography, XXXIII, 142-147, April, 1934.

Clayton, Margie, "The Third Grade Studies Maps," The Instructor, XLIX, 25, October, 1940.

Cypher, Irene, "The Living Map," Education, LXI, 14-18, September, 1940.

DeBernardis, Amo, "Audio-Visual Aids and National Defense," Educational Screen, XIX, 55-57, February, 1941.

Delehanty, Bertha, "An Approach to Geography," School Life, XXVI, 304, July, 1941.

Dudley, Elizabeth, "An Approach to Map Study," The Journal of Geography, XXXVI, 354-356, December, 1937.

Gluck, Harold, "Maps Practically for the Asking," The Journal of Geography, XXXIX, 30-36, January, 1940.

Johnson, Henry, *Teaching of History,* New York: The Macmillan Co., 1940. Chapter XI. The Use of Maps, 220-240.

McKown, Harry and Roberts, Alvin, *Audio-Visual Aids to Instruction.* New York: McGraw-Hill Book Co., 1940.
Chapter V. Graphic Materials, 71-87.

Mikesell, Ruth, "Geographical Activities Involving the Use of Maps and Graphs," The Journal of Geography, XXXIII, 105-113, March, 1934.

Moore, Clyde and Wilcox, Lillian, *The Teaching of Geography.* New York: American Book Co., 1932. Chapter XVI, The Use of Maps, 217-227.

Moyer, Josephine and Taylor, Frances, "Introduction of the Map to Fourth Grade Children," The Journal of Geography, XXXIV, 249-252, September, 1935.

Renner, George, "The Map as an Educational Instrument," Social Education, IV, 477-483, November, 1940.

Renner, George, "The Map in Modern Education," Teachers College Record, XL, 703-724, May, 1939.

——, "Educational Revision of Wall Maps," The Journal of Geography, XL, 13-18, January, 1941.

——. "Blackboard Wall Maps," The Journal of Geography, XXXIV, 369-374, December, 1935.

Ridgley, Douglas, "A Lesson with the Globe," The Journal of Geography, XXXIII, 279-281, October, 1934.

Ristow, Walter, "Geographical Information Please," The Journal of Geography, XXXVIII, 314-318, November, 1939.

Shryock, Clara, "Gradations in Map Learning," The Journal of Geography, XXXVIII, 181-187, May, 1939.

Sorenson, Frank, "The Influence of Specific Instruction on Map Interpretation," The Journal of Geography, XXXV, 300-307, November, 1936.

The Teaching of Geography, the Thirty-Second Yearbook, National Society for the Study of Education, 1933.

  Chapter XXV, Maps and Map Standards, 395-405.

  Chapter XXIX. IV. A Study of the Ability of Elementary School Pupils to Read Maps, 486-492.

Tom, A. O., "Relief Modeling in Elementary Geography," The Journal of Geography, XXXIX, 281-284, October, 1940.

Chapter Ten: PICTURES AND THEIR USE

A PICTURE AGE

PICTURES ARE SO common today that some people speak of this period of time as the picture age. Almost everyone enjoys looking at pictures. They appeal to both the young and the old. Newspapers and magazines often illustrate their articles with pictures. Some large daily newspapers, besides having pictures distributed throughout their pages, have a page given over to pictures. These same papers often have a picture supplement once a week. There are also magazines which have so many pictures that they are known as pictorial magazines.

Many textbooks and pamphlets are illustrated with pictures. This is especially true of books in the social studies. In fact, pictures occupy from one-fourth to one-third of the space in many geography textbooks. It is a well-known fact that American textbooks in the social studies are better illustrated than the textbooks in any other country.

Advertisers believe in using pictures to tell their stories to the public. Pick up a catalog or any magazine which carries full-page advertisements and one will find pictures which the advertisers think will appeal to the readers. Millions of people attend motion picture theaters weekly and some of the pictures are highly instructive.

People are eye-minded. Much of what they learn comes to them through the eye. It is not known for certain what per cent of all sensory impressions reaches a person through the eye. What we do believe is that for most persons the eye ranks far above all other sense organs in giving sensory impressions to the body. This has been realized since very ancient times, because there is an old Chinese proverb which says, "One picture is worth a thousand words." Even today we read about the "enrichment of education through the seeing experience," and that "younger children think largely in terms of concrete visual images."

During the past, some enthusiasts made extreme statements about the importance of pictures. Some of them said that motion pictures would do much of the work that teachers are doing. A few even claimed that there would not be much need for teachers in those subjects where motion pictures were used in the classes. The idea was that students could interpret almost everything by looking at motion pictures. Naturally, when sound came into use with motion pictures, some people spoke as if the talking picture would take the place of teachers in the classrooms. Of course, these people were incorrect in their views, but for a time they caused some teachers to be alarmed about their positions.

A few teachers looked with disfavor upon motion pictures because they did not want them to take their places in the schools. They were not so keen about using them. One fortunate thing was that the great majority of teachers did not become frightened, because they could not imagine a real school for children where teachers would not be needed. They looked upon motion pictures as aids in teaching and they made use of them whenever they could. As time passed, all good teachers came to see that motion pictures are very useful and that they have an important place in teaching. All good teachers now welcome the use of pictures whenever they believe that they will aid the pupils in solving their problems or in interesting them in their work.

It must not be thought that pictures are of much use only in teaching slow pupils, or pupils who do not like to read the printed page. Pictures appeal to the bright children as well as to the slow. Neither should it be thought that pictures are chiefly for younger children. Older pupils also like to look at pictures. Good textbooks for high school pupils and for college students in geography, history, and the other social studies have pictures. Pictures appeal to all classes of pupils. However, it is generally true that pictures are used more in the social studies in the grades and high schools than in the colleges.

TYPE OF PICTURES

Pictures may be classified in many different ways. For example, all pictures may be classed as still pictures or moving pictures. Again, pictures may be classed as silent pictures or pictures accompanied by sound. Pictures may be grouped according to what they show, according to their size, and according to where found. The simple classification which is made here considers many factors, and it has been made with the hope that it will be of use to teachers, that it will cause constructive thinking, and that it will show some of the common sources of pictures. The classification is as follows:

1. Pictures in textbooks, reference books, and pamphlets
2. Pictures in newspapers and magazines
3. Pictures in advertising material with some teaching value
4. Wall pictures or large pictures for showing in the schoolroom
5. Photographs, snapshots, and post cards
6. Cartoons
7. Sketches, paintings, and posters
8. Stereographs
9. Slides
10. Motion pictures with or without sound

STANDARDS IN SELECTING PICTURES

Teachers should exercise much skill in selecting pictures for the pupils to study. There are many pictures which are of little or no teaching value. There are some pictures which would be harmful for children to study. The wise teacher is always on the lookout (1) for good pictures which the pupils may use and (2) to see that poor pictures are not placed before the pupils.

The question is, "How does a teacher go about selecting pictures for pupils to study?" He has certain standards which guide him in his selections. Let us briefly discuss some of these standards:

1. Is the picture simple enough for the pupils to understand? The picture should not contain too much, yet it should contain enough ideas so that the pupils may easily get a story or some information from it.

2. Does the picture furnish enough ideas to cause pupils to think or to perform some school activity? A good picture should raise questions and problems as well as help to answer them.

3. Is the picture attractive, large enough, and accurate? Much time is often lost and pupils come to dislike the social studies on account of having to study pictures which cannot be seen distinctly or are too small. A picture should be typical of the region or the period of history that is being studied. It should be accurate or authentic. Pupils are likely to get incorrect ideas by looking at inaccurate pictures, or at pictures that are not representative of the region or a certain period of history. For example, the painting showing Washington standing in a small boat while crossing the Delaware River might be a fine work of art, but it is likely to give the child an inacccurate picture of the actual crossing. Likewise, a picture of a snow house in the Far North may give the children the inaccurate idea that most Eskimos live in snow houses. If such pictures are used, the teacher must endeavor to see that pupils get correct ideas and images.

4. Does the picture help to explain, illustrate, or supplement the work which the pupils are doing? Is the picture related to the work which is being done? Just to show any picture is not good teaching.

5. Does the picture give any idea as to time and place? Does it show human activity in relation to the environment? Possibly the picture shows cultural adjustment or a landscape that helps a pupil to interpret a region. Maybe the picture shows something about the customs of the people.

6. Does the picture have an appropriate caption which gives enough information so that it may be interpreted by the pupils? A caption should be clear and easily understood. It should tell enough, but not too much. It should be thought-provoking and should stimulate thinking.

Some teachers prefer to use pictures without any captions, but the majority of teachers still believe that captions should accompany most pictures.

WHY USE PICTURES?

Just because a person looks at pictures is no reason that he gets very much from them. The eye may be compared to a camera and the sensitive plate or film to the brain. After the picture is taken by the camera, the film or plate must be developed before there is a picture which may be seen. Something similar is true for the eye. A person may look at a picture, but if nothing takes place in his mind to cause thinking, he gets very little from it. In order to get a clear mental picture, some thinking should take place; and the more thinking a picture causes, the more likely a person will obtain a clear mental image which will be definite and correct.

Pupils are likely to acquire the habit of observing if they are taught to use pictures. This is a very important habit which they should acquire at an early date and it should gradually be strengthened as they grow older.

It is impossible for pupils to visit all the places or to see all the objects about which they study. Hence, pictures are very valuable because they help to give a sense of reality to what pupils are studying. In many cases, if a person cannot visit a place and get first-hand information, the best thing for him to do is to look at pictures that will give him the ideas and images he should have. Knowing how to read pictures opens the door to much knowledge that a person cannot easily get by other means.

The use of pictures helps to develop the imagination. No person can get very far in life who has little imagination. Thinking and imagination go together and pictures help to form ideas that are useful in thinking. Of course the imagination should be of the type that helps a person to solve his problems. It should not be mere day-dreaming about things which are never likely to happen.

Printed matter is very valuable, but it is often impossible or very hard to make some ideas clear to a pupil by using only printed words. Hence, pictures are often used to supplement the printed material. Sometimes a pupil fails to grasp clearly the meaning of the printed material until he looks at pictures. For example, when the coal mining industry in the Appalachian Region is being discussed, a few good pictures will help to give the pupils a better idea of coal mining than if no pictures were used. In talking about the dress of the people of colonial times, pictures are often needed to give pupils an idea of what people wore in those early days.

Pictures also help to keep pupils from forming incorrect

images and ideas. For example, how can a pupil be expected to form an accurate image of a mountain if he has never seen mountains or pictures of mountains? Some people occasionally say that they learned many things in school that their travels later showed to be incorrect. Of course, no teacher can expect to have all his pupils form correct ideas and images about everything they study, because no one is a perfect teacher and each child has an independent mind of his own. Yet, if the right pictures are used skilfully and at the most opportune time, they would help in causing the pupils to form correct ideas and vivid, concrete images.

Pictures aid in helping to raise questions and problems. Pupils cannot think without having questions arise in their minds, so the more thinking that takes place in the minds of the pupils, the more questions there are to answer. Since this is true, teachers sometimes use pictures to introduce a unit of work. The pupils become interested in what they see in the pictures and the interest causes them to want to study the units.

Pictures are very valuable in helping to recall certain ideas or facts. In interpreting pictures, pupils are sure to recall facts which they have learned in previous lessons. In using facts over and over, pupils are more likely to remember them. If facts are important, they should be used frequently by the pupils. Pictures are very useful in reviews and in making summaries.

HOW TO USE PICTURES IN TEXTBOOKS

Pictures make up an important part of every good textbook in geography and history. During the past few years great improvements have been made in the selection of pictures. Since they are a valuable part of any book, pupils should learn to read pictures just as they learn to read printed material. They should form the habit of turning to pictures for information, and after turning to them they should know how to proceed in interpreting them. Many teachers pay very little attention to pictures because they, themselves, have never formed the habit of studying pictures. Such teachers cannot be expected to teach their pupils to read pictures correctly. In fact, many children never receive any worthwhile instruction about using pictures. How can pupils be expected to use pictures correctly if they receive very little instruction in their use? Of course, the answer is that they cannot be expected to use them correctly. They should be taught how to read pictures intelligently.

Every good teacher uses pictures and he encourages his pupils to use them. He considers pictures as one of the important sources of information which pupils use when studying their problems. It takes time to teach pupils to use pictures, but such time is very well spent.

Pupils should study the pictures in their textbooks. The teacher should help them learn how to study pictures. Gradually they come to rely less and less upon the teacher as they learn how to study. If there are captions with the pictures they should be read and studied. The captions may contain questions which are given to help the pupils get information from the pictures. The teacher often asks questions to guide the pupils in studying pictures.

Pupils should learn that many of the pictures in a book give information that they cannot get from the printed page. They should understand that one of the main purposes of pictures is to help them get information for solving their problems. They should see the relation of the pictures to their classwork. Occasionally, the teacher may ask the pupils if a certain picture in the textbook is a good one and if it makes the work seem more nearly real.

SOME WAYS OF USING LOOSE PICTURES

One common way of using loose pictures is to pass them around the room during the class discussion. The pupils are supposed to study them briefly and to note important things. This is usually a poor way of using them since the passing of pictures is likely to detract the attention of the pupils from the discussion. Most pupils do not get much from studying pictures and trying to listen to the class discussion at the same time.

Another common way of using a picture is to hold it in front of the class while it is being described or explained. This may be a good way if it is large enough for all pupils to see it distinctly, or if the purpose is to arouse interest in the picture so that they will wish to study it. However, it is usually of questionable value to hold before the class a picture which is too small for most of the pupils to see distinctly. Pupils should see the picture clearly if they are expected to study it.

One good way of using pictures is to place them on the work table where pupils may go to study them during their study time. Each pupil may spend as much time as he wishes at the table. The pictures may or may not have captions. They may have questions written by the teacher which will aid the pupils in studying them. The pupils may be asked to write a few questions about each picture, the answers of which may be obtained by studying it. Occasionally they may be asked to write a short story on what they see in a certain picture.

Some teachers get pupils interested in a new unit through looking at pictures. A few good pictures are placed on the bulletin board, on the wall, or in some other place where they may be easily seen. When the pupils first see the pictures they become curious about them and they stop to look at them. During the discussion period, questions are raised about the pictures. This is what the teacher wishes the pupils to do. If the discussion is conducted successfully, the pupils become interested in finding the answers to their questions. One question calls for another one, and it is not long before the children are hard at work on the unit.

Pupils should be encouraged to collect pictures. Some children may bring pictures to class which are a real contribution to the work which is being studied. Picture booklets are often made by the children. Likewise, the teacher collects pictures. He should mount his best pictures on cardboard or on heavy paper so that they will not get damaged. The most valuable pictures should be put away for future use. They should be kept in a place which is easily accessible. If a teacher puts his pictures in a place that is hard to reach, the chances are he will seldom go to the trouble of getting them. If the true history of teaching is ever written, there might be a chapter on "Hidden Materials That Lie Unused."

Some teachers make sets of twenty or thirty good pictures on certain units. The pictures are numbered and are accompanied by objective tests or questions. When not in use they are put in strong manila envelopes and filed away in some place where they may be obtained when needed. Any active teacher may build up a library of pictures which may be used by the pupils at various times during the year.

USING PICTURES FOR TESTING

There are numerous ways of using pictures in testing. One way is to give the pupils a set of pictures and tell them to write a story about each one of the pictures, bringing out the chief things that each picture shows or suggests. Another way is to have the pupils write a list of questions about each picture. They should write the answers to the questions to make certain that they are not asking just anything that comes to their minds. Still a third way is to give the pupils a set of pictures with questions accompanying each picture. They are to write the correct answers to the questions.

Another interesting test is to have the pupils place the correct caption with each picture. The captions are written on separate slips of paper. They are placed in a pile with a number of pictures. The pupil takes a caption, reads it, and then attaches it to the right picture.

Still another test is to have a number of pictures which are to be grouped according to some order by the pupils. If the pictures are geographic, they may be arranged according to certain geographic regions which the pupils have studied. For example, pictures on cold deserts might be put with the polar regions; those on growing bananas might be put with the tropical, moist regions; and other pictures might be grouped accordingly. If the pictures are historic, they might be grouped according to certain periods in history. For example, pictures of colonial Virginia might be put with colonial life in Virginia; those typical of the pilgrims and Puritans might be put with life in the New England colonies; and other pictures might be grouped in a similar manner. A resourceful teacher can think of a number of ways that pictures may be grouped.

Some pupils like to draw pictures. They should be encouraged to illustrate their work by drawings whenever it is of advantage to do so. In discussing a problem, they may draw pictures to explain certain ideas. A picture often shows whether a pupil has the right idea in mind. In testing, pupils may be required to draw a set of pictures, such as showing the chief steps in the growing of wheat or the chief events in the history of the settlement of Virginia.

CARTOONS

The cartoon has some value in teaching the social studies. It is a picture that has been drawn to tell a story or to sell an idea. It may ridicule or praise. Many newspapers have cartoons. Pupils should be encouraged to draw cartoons, especially those pupils who have ideas and can draw. Sometimes several pupils work together in drawing a cartoon. In some schools, the ideas for cartoons are developed in the social studies classes but the actual drawing is done in the art classes under the supervision of the art teachers. Many pupils color their cartoons.

HOW TO USE STEREOGRAPHS

A stereograph is a pair of nearly identical pictures on a single cardboard. The stereograph is placed in a stereoscope with two lenses. When the stereoscope is placed at the correct distance from the eyes, with the light falling upon the stereograph, the pair of pictures appear as one. The picture as seen through the stereoscope has depth and it seems more nearly real than an ordinary picture. Most pupils like to use stereographs if they are not required to use them too often. Again, the stereoscope is a sort of novelty to the children and it somewhat fascinates them.

How should stereographs be used? One way is to pass them around the class during the discussion period. This is of questionable value and there are the same objections to this procedure as there are to passing any other pictures around the class during the discussion period.

Another method that is occasionally used is to have one pupil look at a stereograph and describe what he sees to the other pupils. If the pupil describes the picture so vividly that his classmates wish to see it, this is good proof that the stereograph is being used in the right way. However, if a pupil is not able to interest the class by his description of the picture, this method should not be used.

Probably the best method of using stereographs is to place

a few of them and one or more stereoscopes on the work table or in some place where the pupils may study the pictures during their study periods. Only those stereographs should be used that are related to the problems being studied. There may be questions which will aid the pupils in studying the pictures. The teacher will decide if questions are needed.

Sometimes the pupils may have an appreciation lesson. They look at stereographs and other pictures for pure enjoyment without any thought of getting information for the solving of problems.

HOW TO USE LANTERN SLIDES

Well selected filmstrips and slides are very useful in teaching. The pictures are shown by means of a lantern on a curtain and are large enough to be seen by the entire class at one time. Such pictures are adapted for group work or class work. The resourceful teacher uses lantern slides in a number of ways. Some of the common ways of using slides follow:

1. A set of slides on a given topic or problem may be shown at the beginning of the unit to get the pupils interested in the work which they are ready to start. The slides should be well selected and should give the pupils an idea of the unit which they are going to study. They should show enough about the unit to arouse the interests of the pupils. The teacher should prepare an interesting discussion to go along with the slides. Now and then the pupils might take part in the discussion. Many questions are raised. Some of the questions can be answered easily by the pupils, but others cannot be answered without further study.

2. A set of slides may be shown as a review at the end of the unit or series of lessons. The pictures help the pupils sum up what they have learned. Most teachers prefer to have the pupils discuss the slides as they are shown. In some cases, one or more slides are given to each pupil in the class for discussion. In other cases, the discussion of the slides may be given by a group of pupils. Of course, the teacher may enter into the discussion whenever he wishes. The main idea is to let the children take part in the discussion whenever they are able to do so. Usually the pupils who are going to discuss the slides are given

an opportunity of studying them before they are shown to the class.

3. Many teachers like to use lantern slides at various places during the study of the unit. Only a few slides are shown at a time. Let us suppose that the pupils are studying about the New England states and that the teacher has forty slides that are about New England. There may be three slides on building stones. These three slides will be shown when the pupils discuss quarrying. Likewise, the slides on fishing will be shown when the fishing industry is discussed.

Lantern slides may be used in testing. As a slide is shown, the pupils may be required to answer questions, to write what they see, or to do any other work which the teacher may require.

HOW TO USE MOTION PICTURES

Motion pictures appeal to almost everyone. A large per cent of the people who attend motion picture shows are children. Some motion pictures are not suitable for children, but there are many excellent films which children do enjoy. An increasing number of films are being produced which are suitable for children. Again, newsreels are often shown which are instructive to both the young and the old.

Some years ago it was difficult to get good films in the social studies for use in the schoolroom. Today, if the school has a motion picture machine, it is easy to get good films. Some of the departments of our government at Washington and certain state universities have films to lend to teachers. Some large companies lend films. There are also places where films may be purchased or rented.

Many people have motion picture cameras. They take pictures of various scenes when they travel. The parents of some of the children take pictures and are glad to lend them to the school so that the pupils may see them. Some teachers take motion pictures so that they may use them in their work.

Whenever motion is needed in a picture, the motion picture is superior to a still picture. A motion picture shows some processes very much better than still pictures. It makes them seem more nearly real. One picture follows another without a break. The pictures give much information about certain objects in a very short time. In some cases, motion pictures aid in recall and in the retention of knowledge much better than still pictures. The motion picture helps to clear up incorrect ideas, gives much information, raises new problems, and brings joy to the pupils.

Sound motion pictures are very useful, providing the discussion that accompanies the picture is simple enough for pupils to understand. The description should be given by a person who understands children and who knows what needs explaining in the picture. Many schools cannot afford to buy a machine for showing sound pictures, but those who have such machines should make use of them.

There are various ways of using motion pictures just as there are various ways of using other pictures. A motion picture may be shown at the beginning of the class to introduce the unit, at the end of the class as a review or summary, and at other times for gaining new information.

A motion picture may be shown more than once to the same class. The first showing may be given so that the pupils will get a general idea of the field that the picture covers. The second showing may be made at or near the end of the unit. By this time the pupils are able to interpret the picture much better than during the first showing. Parts of the picture might also be shown when certain information is desired. Probably some questions arise about what the pupils saw in the picture. Showing the picture another time would clear up any questions that might have arisen. Whether all of a picture or a part of a picture should be shown more than once will be determined by the interest of the class. There is no need of repeating a picture if nothing is to be gained. It must be remembered that there is danger of killing the interest of any group of children by aimless repetition of anything, whether it is seeing a motion picture a second time, repeating a trip to a museum, or re-reading a chapter in a book.

MAKING LANTERN SLIDES

There are various places where excellent lantern slides may be purchased, rented, or borrowed. Sometimes pupils wish to make simple lantern slides to go with the work which they are doing. A class may be studying some such topic as fire prevention or safety. The pupils may wish to make some pictures or drawings on slides to bring home more forcefully some of the lessons learned. Again, a map may be needed to accompany the work which some students are doing. One of the pupils may make a map on a slide. In some upper-grade classes, pupils often draw cartoons on lantern slides. A little color adds much to a cartoon. Making simple lantern slides and showing them to the entire class are very valuable experiences, both to the makers and to those who are observing the slides.

The making of simple lantern slides by pupils is an easy task, providing they have the necessary materials and they enjoy making them. Care must be taken not to make the drawing on the slide too large. The ordinary slide is $3\frac{1}{4}$ inches by 4 inches, but the drawing on the slide should not be this large. The drawing must not be any larger than the opening in the frame which receives the slide. The drawing on the slide should be one-half inch from the edge of the slide. This makes a drawing $2\frac{1}{4}$ inches by 3 inches. The wider part of the slide is from left to right and the narrower part is from top to bottom, because the slide goes into the lantern in this way. Hence, the distance from top to bottom of any drawing that is put upon a slide should not be more than $2\frac{1}{4}$ inches while the distance from left to right of the drawing should not be more than 3 inches.

Before a drawing is made on a slide, it is best to make it first on a piece of paper. It should be made the size that it is going to be on the slide. After the drawing has been approved by the teacher, it is ready to be put on the slide. Place the slide over the drawing and trace it. Sometimes a pupil finds a picture, drawing, or map which is just the size that he wants. If the teacher permits him to reproduce it, all that is necessary is for the pupil to place the slide over the picture, drawing, or map and trace it. A pupil learns to make slides by experience.

KIND OF SLIDES

1. Plain Glass Slides. Place a plain glass slide over the picture, map, or drawing. Use a fine pen and trace with India ink. Be careful that the ink does not spread. A "China marking" pencil or any other special pencil that will mark on glass may be used in place of ink. The slide may be colored by using a fine camel's hair brush and transparent water colors. Do not put the colors on too thickly.

2. *Bon Ami Slides.* Take a plain glass slide and cover one side with Bon Ami. Let the Bon Ami dry on the slide. Trace the drawing on the Bon Ami side of the slide with a nail or some other sharp pointed object. Do not use ink or colors on this slide.

3. *Gelatin Slides.* To make about twenty-five slides, dissolve one teaspoonful of ordinary colorless cooking gelatin in a cup of hot water. When the gelatin gets about as thick as honey, spread a thin coat of it over one side of a clean glass slide. The gelatin may be spread evenly by using a small piece of cotton or the fingers. Let the gelatin dry on the slide before using. Place the slide over the drawing with the gelatin side up. Use a fine pen and India ink to make the drawing. Transparent water colors may be applied with a fine camel's hair brush. Children like to use these slides because the gelatin helps to keep the ink from spreading.

After the pupils get through with the slides which have been mentioned, they may be cleaned so that they may be used in another unit. Gelatin, Bon Ami, ink, water colors, and pencil marks may be removed from the glass slides by washing them in hot, soapy water.

4. *Silhouette Slides.* "Cut-outs" of black paper or any opaque paper may be made by the pupils. The "cut-outs" are not larger than 2¼ inches by 3 inches and are pasted on plain glass slides. When the pupils are through with the silhouette slides the paper may be removed, and the glass slides washed so that they may be used again. Sometimes pictures are drawn, cut out, and pasted on slides. The children may be tested by giving the names of the pictures.

5. *Cellophane Slides.* Clear cellophane makes very excellent slides. Cut the cellophane the same size as a glass slide, 3¼ inches by 4 inches. Use India ink, a fine pen, and work rather rapidly but carefully. Transparent water colors may be used, if the slides are to be colored.

Place the cellophane slide over the picture or drawing and trace it with India ink. Now apply transparent water colors with a fine camel's hair brush. A piece of colored cellophane may be placed over the clear cellophane slide to obtain a colored effect. Pieces of cellophane of the right colors may be placed over certain parts of the slide to show such things as a blue sky and green grass. The edges of the cellophane may be held together by a little paste.

When the cellophane slide is to be shown, it should be placed in a glass booklet. A glass booklet may be made by fastening the edges of two plain glass slides together with adhesive tape so that they will open and close as a book. It is easy to place a cellophane slide in a glass booklet before placing it in the lantern.

6. *Typewritten Slides.* Take a clear cellophane slide $3\frac{1}{4}$ inches by 4 inches. Fold a piece of black or red carbon paper over the cellophane slide, the carbon being next to each side of the slide. Place the carbon paper and slide in a typewriter. Remove the ribbon from the typewriter. Then type on the slide, leaving a margin of $\frac{1}{2}$ inch around the edge. Remove the carbon paper from the slide. Put the slide in a glass booklet before placing in the lantern.

7. *Plastacele Slides.* Plastacele is a chemical product. The kind that is frosted on one side makes very good slides. Plastacele comes in sheets and it should be cut into pieces, $3\frac{1}{4}$ inches by 4 inches. A pencil may be used to make the drawings. Colors may be shown by using transparent indelible pencils. The same method may be used for making slides on etched or frosted glass.

This discussion of lantern slides has been brief, but it is hoped that enough has been said to get the reader interested in making slides. Only by experience will the teacher gain the information which he should possess if he is going to have his pupils make slides. By experimenting he will learn what colors to use, how to apply them, and many other useful things about making slides.

PROBLEMS FOR DISCUSSION AND RESEARCH

1. Discuss the importance of using pictures in teaching the social studies.

2. Examine newspapers and magazines. Discuss this topic, "The use which newspapers and magazines make of pictures."

3. What are the standards which a teacher should use in selecting pictures to be used by the pupils?

4. Examine the pictures in several textbooks which pupils use in the social studies. Try to determine why the pictures are in the books. Are they generally good pictures? Discuss this question, "How valuable are the pictures in the textbooks of the social studies?"

5. Describe how pupils should be taught to use the pictures in their textbooks.

6. What are the advantages and the disadvantages of encouraging the pupils to collect pictures?

7. How should individual pictures be used?

8. Explain the different ways of using pictures in testing.

9. Of what value are stereographs? Explain how they may be used.

10. Give the various ways of using lantern slides.

11. How should the motion picture be used in the social studies?

12. Discuss the question, "Is the motion picture or the lantern slide the more valuable in teaching the social studies?"

13. Why should children be encouraged to make lantern slides? Make a few lantern slides according to the instructions given in this chapter.

14. Make a list of the sources from which teachers may obtain pictures.

15. If possible, learn how to operate the lantern and the motion picture machine.

REFERENCES

Angell, Della, "Making Slides in Elementary School," Social Education, III, 122-124, February, 1939.

Bell, Reginald, Cain, Leo, Lamoreaux, L. and others, Motion Pictures in a Modern Curriculum. Washington: American Council on Education, May, 1941.

Bining, Arthur and Bining, David, Teaching the Social Studies in the Secondary Schools. New York: McGraw-Hill Book Co., 1941
Chapter XV. Visual Aids to Teaching, 275-295.

Brumbaugh, Donald, "An Experiment in the Use of Motion Pictures in Teaching Current Events," Colorado School Journal, LVI, 10-11, November, 1940.

Bureau of Mines Experiment Station, 4800 Forbes Street, Pittsburgh, Pa. Write to learn what pictures may be borrowed.

Clark, Albert, "Activities in Pictures," The Instructor, L, 21, October, 1941.

Dale, Edgar and Ramseyer, Lloyd, Teaching with Motion Pictures; A Handbook of Administrative Practice. Washington: American Council on Education.

Eisen, Edna, "Aerial Views—Aids to Geographic Study," Educational Method, XVII, 285-286, March, 1938.

——, "Use of Silhouettes," The Journal of Geography, XXXVII, 27-34, January, 1933.

Glick, Annette, The Use of Visual Aids in Teaching the Social Studies—Past and Present, The Historical Approach to Methods of Teaching the Social Studies, Fifth Yearbook, National Council for the Social Studies, 1935, 123-142.

Gluck, Harold, "The Use of Toy Projection Aids in the Teaching of Geography," The Journal of Geography, XXXVIII, 58-64, February, 1939.

Greenan, John, "Using the Movies in the Teaching of History and the Social Studies," Education, LXI, 22-25, September, 1940.

Hamilton, G. E., How to Make Handmade Lantern Slides. Meadville: Keystone View Co., 1940.

Hartley, William H., Selected Films for American History and Problems. New York: Teachers College, Columbia University, 1940.

Hile, Martha, "The Use of Photographic Material in the Teaching of Geography," The Journal of Geography, XXXVII, 55-63, February, 1938.

Hoban, Charles, Hoban, Charles, Jr., and Zisman, Samuel, Visualizing the Curriculum. New York: The Cordon Co., 1937.
Chapter IV. The Motion Picture, 93-146.
Chapter V. Arresting Life With the Camera—The Still Picture, 147-210.

Horn, Ernest, Methods of Instruction in the Social Studies. New York: Charles Scribner's Sons, 1937.
Chapter IX. Visual Aids, 359-392.

Johnson, Henry, Teaching of History. New York: The Macmillan Co., 1940.
Chapter IX. The Use of Models and Pictures, 182-202.

Kennedy, Anna Clark and Painter, Fred B., Materials for the Social Studies Program, The Social Studies in the Elementary School, Twelfth Yearbook, National Council for the Social Studies, 1941, 101-153. Very good for sources of films and lantern slides.

Knowlton, Daniel, "The Factor of Selection in the Use of Visual Aids," Educational Screen, XIX, 53-54, February, 1941.

Lee, Kathleen, "Democracy at Work Through Visual Education," Educational Screen, XX, 231-232, June, 1941.

Lemos, John, "How to Make Good Posters," The Grade Teacher, LIX, 52, 82, October, 1941.

Livermon, Ruth, "Living with Chinese Children," The Educational Screen, 278-281, September, 1941.

March, Leland, "Pictures in Social Studies Teaching," Social Education, V, 26-31, January, 1941.

March, Leland, "Pupil-Made Lantern Slides in the Social Studies," Social Education, III, 609-612, December, 1939.

McKown, Harry and Roberts, Alvin, *Audio-Visual Aids to Instruction.* New York: McGraw-Hill Book Co., 1940.
Chapters VI, VII, VIII.

Melbo, Irving and Waterman, Ivan, "Pictures in Geography Textbooks," Elementary School Journal, XXXVI, 362-376, January, 1936.

Merton, Mineta, "Effective Use of Still Pictures in Elementary Social Studies," Social Education, IV, 489-493, November, 1940.

Nietz, John, Visual Aids in Teaching the Social Studies, *The Contribution of Research to the Teaching of the Social Studies, Eighth Yearbook,* National Council for the Social Studies, 1937, 169-187.

Nolen, Luella, "Check Lists for Use by Teachers and Pupils in the Evaluation of Geographic Tools," The Journal of Geography, XXXVIII, 205-208, May, 1939.

Price, W. T. R., "How to Make Lantern Slides," Education, LVIII, 501-507, April, 1938.

Probst, Ella, "The Lantern and Slide as a Teaching Device," Educational Method, XV, 264-269, February, 1936.

Riley, Noma, "A Picture Library and Its Use," The Journal of Geography, XXXVII, 202-205, May, 1938.

Roberts, Alvin, "Ten Commandments and a Film," The Educational Screen, XX, 326-328, 352, October, 1941.

Smith, Charles T., "There's No Excuse for Not Using Visual Aids," School Executive, LXI, 24-26, September, 1941.

Sources of Visual Aids for Instructional Use in Schools, U. S. Office of Education, No. 80. Washington: Superintendent of Documents.

Stadtlander, Elizabeth, "An Experiment in Individual Versus Group Study of Pictures in Geography," The Journal of Geography, XXXV, 360-364, December, 1936.

The Teaching of Geography, Thirty-Second Yearbook, National Society for the Study of Education. Bloomington: Public School Publishing Co., 1933.
Chapter XXIV. Materials for Visual Instruction in Geography, 385-394.
Chapter XXX. I. Systematizing the Use of Pictures in Teaching Sixth Grade Geography, 507-519.

Vayette, Kenneth, "A Study of Children's Responses to Geography Pictures," The Journal of Geography, XL, 262-273, October, 1941.

Wesley, Edgar, *Teaching the Social Studies.* New York: D. C. Heath and Co., 1937.
Chapter XVII. Visual Aids: Pictures, Maps, and Graphs, 340-378.

West, Seymour, *Visual Aids for Pupil Adventure in the Realm of Geography,* Montclair: New Jersey State Teachers College, 1940.

Chapter Eleven: METHODS IN TEACHING

THE SOCIAL SCIENCES

WHAT IS METHOD?

METHOD IS the plan which a teacher uses in teaching. When we talk about the methods employed by teachers we have in mind the means they use to get pupils interested and to keep them interested in activities which result in learning. It should be remembered that in discussing methods we must consider the teacher, the pupils, the subject matter to be taught, and what goes on when learning is taking place or is supposed to be taking place.

Some methods are successful, while others are unsuccessful. If the pupils make satisfactory progress, the teacher knows that his method is successful, but if they make unsatisfactory progress, he realizes that his method is unsuccessful and it should be overhauled or changed. An energetic teacher is always striving to improve his methods of teaching. Occasionally he tries some new method which seems to have much promise. He may find it to be an improvement over the methods which he has been using. On the other hand, he may find it to be less satisfactory. A teacher should keep on using those methods which he finds to be good. He should reject those methods which do not produce the desired results. It is by experimenting with new methods and by improving old methods that a teacher becomes more efficient in his teaching.

THE TEACHER AND METHOD

A teacher plays a leading part in determining the success of any method. All teachers do not have the same ability of teaching. A poor teacher can never hope to get the results that a good teacher obtains with his pupils, even though both teachers use the same methods. Skilful teaching will likely result in much learning, while poor teaching generally will produce little learning. It must be remembered that teaching does not necessarily mean satisfactory learning on the part of the pupils. Poor teaching may cause the pupils to get incorrect information and to form low ideals, wrong attitudes, and poor habits of study.

The great problem of the teacher is to direct the activities of the pupils so that the right kind and the right amount of learning will take place. Teaching is an art which can be truly developed only by those who have the highest kind of vision. A teacher must be sincere and he must have faith in himself. He must believe in the methods which he is using and he must have confidence that he can stimulate and encourage pupils to learn. He who does not have the power of causing other pupils to learn will never make a good teacher.

A teacher should study carefully the methods which he uses so that they become almost a part of him. No teacher can take the methods of some other teacher and use them successfully, until he has studied them and has made certain changes which he deems necessary. No two people see exactly alike, and it is too much to expect two teachers to use exactly the same method without modifications, no matter how slight the changes may be. The methods may be similar, but each teacher has certain peculiarities which will surely cause him to make certain changes which no other teacher would make.

A good method must be related to the experiences of the learner. Pupils must be able to understand the plan which is being used so that they will perform the desired activities. Hence, a teacher must understand many of the problems of the learners. Good teaching is well thought out. It is the deliberate attempt of a teacher to direct the activities of pupils along highly desirable lines. If pupils are to do their best work and to be guided in their thinking, they must be able to understand clearly the method which is being used.

KNOWING THE CONTENT

Which is more important, method or content? This is a question which is always coming up at meetings of teachers. Some teachers who have specialized in the field of education do not realize the importance of content, while some others who have specialized in content do not realize the importance of method. In discussing the question, two other questions must be considered. (1) Can a teacher teach what he does not know? (2) Do all excellent scholars make good teachers?

If teaching induces pupils to learn, it can be seen that a teacher may cause a pupil to learn some things which he, himself, does not know. For example, a teacher cannot know the answer to every question which arises in the classroom. He may direct his pupils to books or other sources of information for the desired information. They get the required information and report back to the class. Again, as a pupil learns, his horizon is gradually expanding. His interests are directed along various lines. Hence, a pupil often gains information which his teacher does not possess. Many pupils frequently get interested in certain problems in their class work which cause them to go beyond what is required of them in their school work. Very often we hear some teacher make the remark that a certain pupil knows more about some phase of a subject than he does.

From what has just been said, it is seen that a teacher may cause a pupil to learn facts that he, himself, does not know. However, we must not go too far along this line of thinking. A teacher who knows very little subject matter could not go very far in teaching children intelligently. He would not be able to know whether his pupils were gaining accurate or inaccurate information. Indeed, his pupils would likely gain a mass of inaccurate facts which would cause them to do faulty thinking. If a teacher is going to teach successfully, he must know that his pupils are gaining accurate information, and the one sure way that he has of ascertaining this fact is for himself to have as much information as possible. Even a well-informed teacher cannot hope to know everything, but he can make an honest attempt to be as intelligent as possible.

Probably one reason why so many people think so unintelligently about everyday problems is that they do not realize that intelligent thinking calls for accurate information. Many teachers know too little about what they are attempting to teach. Knowledge is gained by much studying and thinking. The wide-awake teacher is always on the lookout for more information.

If a teacher does not know what he is teaching, he cannot make sure that his pupils are learning the right things. For example, many poorly informed geography teachers believe that the sun is directly overhead at noon (standard time) in continental United States, so they allow their children to get the idea that the sun is directly above them at noon. A little observation will show that the sun is never directly overhead at noon (standard time) in continental United States, but it is always to the south of the observer. The question may be asked, "Why do not such teachers have the children observe the sun at noon and see where it is?" Probably the answer is that many teachers do not realize the importance of teaching the children to obtain accurate information by observing.

Again, the author once visited a seventh grade class in which the pupils were studying about business depressions. The teacher remarked that the pupils had learned the causes of depressions and how to prevent them. After listening to the class discussion for a few minutes, it was easily seen that the pupils were forming inaccurate ideas and wrong conclusions. The teacher had very little knowledge of business depressions and their causes, so she was not able to guide intelligently the thinking of her pupils. To teach the social studies wisely and well, a teacher must know the subject matter. He must not only have a love and an understanding of children but he must have a rich background of content. This idea is well stated on page 283 of the Social Studies Curriculum, Fourteenth Yearbook of the Department of Superintendence, where we read the following statement, "There is no substitute for a wide and deep knowledge of the subject which the teacher is to present."

KNOWING WHAT METHODS TO USE

Knowing a subject does not necessarily mean that a person can teach it successfully. All scholars do not make good teachers. Examples could be given of poor teaching by persons who knew their subject matter, but had very little knowledge of method. A very fine athlete does not always make a successful coach. Likewise, a person well versed in the social studies, but lacking in method, will probably do poor teaching. A teacher must know how to present material so that the pupils will do their best work. He must not only know the best methods of teaching, but he must be able to use them effectively.

The author once visited a classroom in which a teacher was doing poor work. This teacher had been recommended highly by her instructors in college as a very good student. After watching the person teach, it was soon evident that the teacher did not understand children and how to teach them. She seemed to be well informed on the subject matter, but she was not able to interest the children in what they were supposed to be doing. In other words, this teacher was weak in methods. Among other things, the teacher was advised (1) to read certain books and articles on teaching the social studies, (2) to talk to other teachers about how they presented the subject matter, and (3) to take a course in the teaching of social studies during the summer or in the evening classes after school.

RELATION OF CONTENT TO METHOD

It only seems logical to conclude that content and method go hand in hand in teaching. One is as important as the other. If one is lacking, a teacher is bound to do poor work. Practically all good educators and teachers realize this. Our teachers colleges understand this because they encourage their students to take content courses as well as method courses. It is a good thing to know the latest ideas concerning teaching, but it should be remembered that they have little practical use except as they are related to definite materials to be taught. Method should never be separated from content.

THE DEVELOPMENT OF METHOD

The beginning of method may be traced back to very early times. Method has always been used wherever any teaching has been done. Throughout the ages, teachers have continually altered their methods to meet changing conditions. Today, changes in methods are still going on and they will continue to go on as long as teachers make progress in the art of teaching. Teachers are continually improving old methods, trying new methods, and discarding those methods which no longer prove to be satisfactory.

It is the history of teaching that some people have greater visions of progress than other people. Such teachers are never fully satisfied with the methods which are being used, so they advocate new methods. They play an important part in keeping the schools in closer contact with changing conditions.

Until near the close of the nineteenth century, the social studies in the United States were taught chiefly as memory studies. The textbook method of teaching was mainly used. Pupils did very little thinking while studying. They prepared themselves to answer questions which were based on their books. Very often the answers to the questions were worded in the phraseology of the book. Pupils with good memories were able to memorize their work very easily and they usually made the best marks. Very little attention was given to thinking. Indeed, pupils were not encouraged to ask questions, and most teachers considered children to be unruly if they persisted in asking questions or in talking about events which were not mentioned in their books.

Until recent years, most of the geography which was taught was descriptive, locational, and factual. A pupil was supposed to remember fact after fact, he had to be able to locate a large number of places, and he usually had to draw the outlines of the states and countries. In studying a country, an outline was commonly used. The outline generally had such topics as location, area, surface, soil, rivers, climate, minerals, plant life, animal life, occupations, and government. Much stress was put upon the physical features, and the relation between the physical features and life was poorly developed. Very little effort was made to separate essential facts from non-essential facts.

History was usually studied in a chronological order. Much attention was given to wars. Dates were considered to be important. Facts were stressed and very little attention was given to the idea of relating the past to the present.

During the past fifty years, many committees have been appointed to study the various phases of the social studies. The reports of the committees have been very helpful and stimulating to teachers. They have aided teachers in obtaining new viewpoints and in adapting their methods of teaching to changing conditions. They have helped them to see that learning is an active process and that pupil activity is the important thing to keep in mind. More responsibility is being placed upon the pupil, and this is where it rightly belongs. At the same time, pupils are made to realize that they live in groups, and the socializing of the individual is stressed.

Today, pupils are led to think when they are studying the social studies. They are encouraged to raise problems and to get information from various sources in solving them. Isolated facts are no longer considered to be of much real value. Pupils are taught how to live together and to cooperate with one another. History is studied primarily with the idea of better understanding the present by learning about some of the events of the past. The study of geography aids pupils to see that many of man's activities are influenced by the natural environment. Likewise, civics gives the pupils a knowledge of the different governmental agencies and of social problems connected with the welfare of the community.

THE IMPORTANCE OF LEARNING

Since learning plays such an important part in every schoolroom, the teacher should understand something of its nature. Some of the factors which determine the rate of learning are the individual pupil, the difficulty of the material to be learned, the way the material is presented to the pupils, and the physical surroundings. All pupils do not learn with the same degree of ease. Likewise, the more difficult the material is to the pupil, the more time it takes to learn it. Some teachers never seem to comprehend that the way the material is presented has an important bearing upon the rate of learning. Methods play a far more important part in learning than many teachers realize.

Learning by pupils is aided in the following ways:

1. Learning is aided when the pupil feels a need for knowing the material. Hence, the teacher should try to get the pupil to want to learn it. If the pupil realizes the need for learning, he will study more diligently and will make an honest effort to get the material.

2. Material is more easily learned when it is understood by the pupil. He is more likely to make the right associations with material which has meaning to him. He must be able to relate what he is learning to his own experiences. The more success he has of relating new experiences to old experiences, the greater

the possibility that learning will result. The material should be adapted to the age level of the child.

3. Learning is aided when the material is interesting to the pupil. If he is interested in the material, he will enter into learning it in a whole-hearted manner. Interest is catching. If the teacher shows an interest in the material, the pupils are likely to become interested.

4. Learning is often aided when the study period and the recitation period are combined or when the study period directly follows the recitation period. Problems raised during the recitation may be studied shortly afterwards while they are still fresh in the mind of the pupil.

5. Learning is often aided by a few words of praise on the part of the teacher. All children like to know that their efforts are appreciated. The teacher does not need to use many words in showing a pupil that his work is satisfactory. Just a nod of his head, a smile, or a word or two are often all that are needed.

6. Learning is aided when the pupil knows that he is having success in solving his problems. Making progress gives encouragement to a pupil, while making mistakes discourages him. When a pupil makes an error and knows that it is an error, he should correct it immediately. Otherwise, it is likely to cause incorrect learning. It is a wise policy to have pupils correct their mistakes as soon as possible after they are made.

7. Learning is aided when the pupil is in good physical condition and when the conditions of his surroundings are of the right kind. We know that the way a person feels has an important bearing upon the work he does. If a pupil is sick, or has had a recent accident, or is under some emotional strain, he cannot be expected to enter wholeheartedly into his work. Sometimes the condition of the room has a leading part in learning. The air may be too hot or too cold. The room may be unattractive. There may be too much noise. The teacher should strive to make the surroundings as favorable for study as possible.

INDIVIDUAL DIFFERENCES

All pupils in a given class do not have the same ability. They differ from one another in many ways. In any class where the same amount of work is required of all pupils, there are some pupils who get their work completed long before the slowest one in the class. Pupils form bad habits of study and do not have their talents properly developed if they have time to waste. All children should work according to their ability. Hence, the individual differences of pupils should be considered by teachers.

Teachers use many different methods of taking care of individual differences. No plan has been discovered which is entirely satisfactory, yet much progress has been made. (1) A very common plan that is practiced in many schools is to give individual aid to pupils when they need it. (2) Some schools have opportunity rooms where the pupils may go to work on their problems. An opportunity room is under the supervision of a teacher, who is on hand to give aid whenever it is needed. (3) Pupils are sometimes grouped in classes according to their abilities. (4) Some teachers try the plan of making assignments on three levels. The minimum assignment is done by the slowest pupils. The maximum assignment is for the superior pupils. The average assignment is for the pupils who are neither slow nor superior, but are considered to be average. (5) Many schools use some form of the activity program to care for individual differences. Pupils engage in activities according to their abilities. (6) Some teachers think that the laboratory method, the workshop plan, or some other individual method is especially adapted for individual differences.

ORGANIZATION OF THE CLASS

a. The Class as a Whole

A problem which confronts every teacher is how to organize the class. There are a number of ways of organizing the class. It may be organized as a whole, in groups, by individuals, or in some combination of these three ways.

A very common organization is the class as a whole. All the pupils have the same assignment and they study the same problems. Each pupil is responsible for getting all the work done. During the recitation period, the pupils discuss their problems. Those pupils who do not understand the work get assistance from those who do understand it. The pupils have an opportunity of raising questions and problems for discussion and study. The recitation period may be looked upon as an open forum where all children take an active part.

Many teachers like to conduct the class as a whole because they can make sure that every pupil studies certain definite problems. When called upon to discuss one of the problems, the lazy pupils cannot give the excuse that they were not supposed to have studied the problem. However, the teacher must make sure that the class discussions do not become monotonous and that the pupils in reciting do not merely repeat what everyone already knows. There is no need of conducting a class if no new ideas are introduced.

b. The Class in Groups

Some teachers believe that pupils can do better work by dividing the class into groups. The unit which the pupils are studying is divided into a number of parts, and each group works on a certain part. At certain times, all the pupils meet to discuss problems which are common to each group. When a group is ready to give the results of its work, the pupils meet to hear its report.

There are many ways of dividing the class into groups. (1) Sometimes the teacher divides the class into groups. He may have certain reasons for grouping the children. For example, he may group the pupils so that they will not form cliques. Again, he may wish to make certain that the backward pupils are in the right groups so that they will find themselves. (2) It is often a wise policy to let the children form their own groups under the guidance of the teacher. (3) Certain leaders or chairmen are appointed by the pupils. Each chairman selects his own group. (4) Still another way of dividing the class into groups is to write the topics on the blackboard which the pupils may study. Then the pupils form groups to study the topics. Care must be taken by the teacher to see that pupils do not form the same group each time that a new unit is taken. Pupils should learn to work with one another. By having the opportunity of working with many different persons, a pupil is likely to develop the spirit of true cooperation.

In group work, each pupil should do his share of the work.

It is often easy for a lazy person to loaf and to let the others do the work. No one or two pupils in the group should be allowed to do most of the work.

Group reports should be given in language which can be easily understood by the pupils. The group giving the report should be careful to see that its work is well organized. The speakers should talk so that they can be heard and they should try to make their talks interesting. They should give reports in their own words and not in the words of some book. It is usually best not to read a report. Sometimes in giving its report, a group follows an outline which it has put on the blackboard.

Pupils should pay attention when the reports are given. They must learn the art of listening and of gaining information when others speak. They may ask questions of those giving reports, or they may question any of the statements. Sometimes the class is given a test to see if the pupils really obtained anything of much value from a report.

One objection which many teachers have to group reports is that most of the pupils are unable to give their reports so that the other pupils receive much help or inspiration from them. Very often only the pupil making a report receives much good from it. Another objection is that many of the reports are purposeless, since the pupils often do not know what the important facts are which should go in their reports. Where group work is used, the teacher should guard against these dangers and any others which may arise.

c. The Class as Individuals

Many teachers only occasionally conduct the class on an individual basis. They assign different topics to each pupil, who usually is required to make a report on what he studies. The pupil is given an opportunity of learning to work by himself.

Some teachers have the class entirely organized on the individual plan. Certain methods of teaching make use of this way of teaching. Sometimes contracts or written instructions are given to the children. They work at their own rate of speed. Where the individual plan is used, the teacher should see that the pupils come together at certain times for class discussion. One objection which many teachers have to the individual plan is that it does not furnish enough opportunity for pupils to learn to cooperate and to work together. Teachers using this plan must make sure that this objection is not a valid one.

d. A Combination of Several Plans

Many teachers like to make use of all three ways of conducting the class. They think that a certain part of the work should be done by all pupils. A problem often arises which interests only one pupil who is assigned to work on it. Sometimes certain parts of a unit may be studied by groups. Thus in studying a given unit, there are times when all the pupils are doing the same work. At other times, individual assignments and group assignments are made. Activity work generally calls for much group work and individual work.

If there is certain information which all the pupils should have, probably the material should be studied by conducting the class as a whole. If the teacher thinks the pupils need training in cooperation and working together, probably group work should be used. If the pupils need training in learning to work independently, the teacher may decide to use individual work. The needs of the pupils and the type of material are two of the chief factors in determining how the class will be conducted.

MANY KINDS OF METHODS

The word "method" is loosely used by many teachers and educators. There are many plans used in teaching. One method is generally related to a number of other methods, since some of the elements of any good method are usually found in several other methods.

Schools exist for pupils, and everything should be done with this thought in mind. All good methods should provide for the growth of the child and they should enable him to get those habits, ideals, skills, generalizations, and understandings which he needs in getting along as a good citizen.

A good method helps the learner select those things which he should study. It includes a list of the objectives which the teacher intends to develop. It is important that the objectives are well thought out and are worthwhile. In the past, there seems to have been a desire on the part of some teachers to think of a long list of objectives. There were sometimes so many objectives that most of them had very little meaning. A short list of pertinent objectives is much more desirable than a long list of high-sounding, but meaningless ones. Many teachers try to teach too much, and what they do teach often has little connection with present-day problems.

After a teacher determines the method he is going to use, he should make it meet present-day conditions. The best methods are interesting and stimulating to the pupil, they provide for his initiative and self-activity, they develop his judging and thinking powers, and they arouse in him a desire to be a good citizen.

Some of the reasons why many teachers prefer to use a number of methods during the year are the following:

(1) To use one method all the time would probably cause the work to become monotonous to both the pupils and teacher. It is fun to try new ways.

(2) One unit of work may be best taught by using a given method while another unit of work may be best taught by using some other method.

(3) Sometimes the needs of the pupils can be best met by using a certain method. For example, if the teacher decides that the pupils need extra training in using maps he should employ a method which gives special attention in the use of maps.

(4) A teacher never advances very far if he is always content to use the same method month after month. Progress can only be made by trying something which seems to be an improvement over the old.

Some of the special methods which teachers claim they use are the contract method, the problem method, the project method, the textbook method, the workbook method, the directed-study method, the topical outline method, the type study method, the lecture method, the question and answer method, the Morrison five-step method, the individual method, the source method, the laboratory method, the Dalton method, the Winnetka method, the socialized lesson, supervised study, the workshop plan, the story method, the dramatization method, and the comparison lesson.

Although a rather long list of methods has been given, the teacher must not expect to find each method distinct from all the others. Experienced teachers well know that all methods have certain elements in common. One teacher may call the plan he is using by one name, while another teacher who is using almost the same plan may call it by another name. Each teacher makes his own plan, and he draws on various sources while making it. When the plan is completed, it is often a composite of several plans which have been mentioned in this chapter. Whether the method that is being used should be called by one name or by another name is not the important question. The main question is whether the method is the best one that the teacher is able to use.

NOTEBOOKS

Should pupils be encouraged to keep notebooks? Those teachers who were forced to keep notebooks when they went to school and who never saw any value in keeping them are likely to say no. Those teachers who enjoyed keeping notebooks when they were in school and who found them to be useful are likely to say yes. The correct answer is that notebooks should be kept by those children who feel a real need for them. If correctly kept, a notebook will prove valuable and helpful to a pupil. On the other hand, if he is forced to keep a notebook without seeing the value of it, the notebook will prove to be a disappointment to both pupil and teacher. It will probably be only busy work.

Some teachers have children keep notebooks in the lower grades, while others do not. If notebooks are kept in these grades, they should be simple and should not include too much. Maps, drawings, pictures, outlines, tests, and short descriptions may be kept in the notebook.

Many teachers encourage their pupils to keep notebooks in the upper grades. They discuss with the pupils (1) the value of a good notebook, (2) the material which should go into a notebook, and (3) the arrangement of the materials. A good notebook kept by an upper grade pupil may be divided into a number of parts. One part may be given over to notes taken hurriedly. The pupil takes these notes for his own benefit and they are not to be graded by the teacher.

A second part of a notebook may be given over to work which will be checked and marked by the teacher. Book reports, notes taken in class, notes taken on excursions, class discussions, lists of important names and dates, and outlines of selected readings are included in this section. The work should be neatly arranged and carefully done. The teacher should not require more work than he has time to examine and mark.

A third section of the book may contain a record of the progress which is being made by the pupil. He records the grades which he gets in his work. The teacher should give suggestions to the pupil concerning what to include in this part of his notebook so that his progress may be noted.

PROBLEMS FOR DISCUSSION AND RESEARCH

1. Clearly explain what is meant when we talk about methods in teaching.
2. Discuss the statement that method is just as important as content.
3. Discuss the question, "Can a teacher teach what he does not know?"
4. What are some of the reasons why all good scholars do not make good teachers?
5. Discuss the evolution of methods in teaching the social studies.
6. What are some of the different ways in which learning is aided?
7. Give five or six ways of caring for individual differences.
8. Give three or four plans of organizing a class. What are the advantages and disadvantages of each plan? Which plan do you prefer? Why?
9. Consult teachers and library references. Make a list of the methods which teachers use in teaching the social studies.
10. Why should not all teachers use the same method?
11. Why may a teacher wish to use several methods during the term?
12. Discuss the value of keeping notebooks.

REFERENCES

Andrews, G. G., "Stimulating Interest in Historical Study," Social Education, III, 307-312, May, 1939.
Andrus, Ruth, The Social Development of Children; How Children Live and Grow and Learn, The Social Studies in the Elementary School, Twelfth Year, National Council for the Social Studies, 1941, 3-17.
Association of Social Studies Teachers of New York City, A Teaching Guide for the Social Studies. New York: College Entrance Book Co., 1941.
  I. Essential Phases of the Lesson, 1-20.

II. Types of Lessons, 21-29.

IV. Notes from a Supervisor's Files, 35-53.

V. Lesson Plans, 54-162.

Bennett, H. K., "Teaching How to Study," The Grade Teacher, LIX, 66-67, October, 1941.

Bining, Arthur, Mohr, Walter, and McFeely, Richard, *Organizing the Social Studies in Secondary Schools*. New York: McGraw-Hill Book Co., 1941.

Chapter II. The Importance of Guidance, 19-45.

Bining, Arthur and Bining, David, *Teaching the Social Studies in the Secondary Schools*. New York: McGraw-Hill Book Co., 1941.

Chapter XII. Teacher Planning, 223-239.

Branom, M. E. and Branom, F. K., *The Teaching of Geography*. Boston: Ginn and Co., 1921.

Part II. The Course of Study, 75-92.

Part III. The Materials of Geography, 93-132.

Part IV. The Class, 132-164.

Part V. The Project, or Active Method, 165-264.

Burr, Phillips, Investigations in the Field of Method, *The Contribution of Research to the Teaching of the Social Studies, Eighth Yearbook*, National Council for the Social Studies, 1937, 44-74.

Conclusions and Recommendations by the Commission on the Social Studies of the American Historical Society. New York: Charles Scribner's Sons, 1934.

Chapters I, II, III, IV, V.

Cutright, Prudence, The School as a Social Agency for the Nurture of Children: The Place of the School in the Living and Education of Children, *The Social Studies in the Elementary School, Twelfth Yearbook*, National Council for the Social Studies, 1941, 18-28.

Eisen, Edna, "Making the Teaching of Geography Effective," The Journal of Geography, XXXVI, 132-139, April, 1937.

Fancler, D. G. and Crawford, C. C., *Teaching the Social Studies,* Los Angeles: C. C. Crawford, 1932.

Fox, James, "Newer Instructional Practice," School and Society, LIV, 49-52, July 26, 1941.

Frederick, Robert and Sheats, Paul, *Citizenship Education Through the Social Studies*. New York: Row, Peterson and Co., 1936.

Chapters IV, V, VI.

Garfinkel, Maurice, "Modern Tendencies in the Teaching of Geography," The Journal of Geography, XXXIII, 187-194, May, 1934.

Gilland, Erna, "A Supervisory Procedure in Geographic Education," Educational Method, XVII, 297-300, March, 1938.

——, "Some Trends in the New Geographic Education," Educational Method, XVII, 262-269, March, 1938.

Gregg, F. M., "An Important Principle in Teaching Primary Grade Geography," The Elementary School Journal, XLI, 665-670, May, 1941.

Grilli, Helen, "Teaching Slow Learning Children," Social Education, III, 169-173, March, 1939.

Guyton, David, "Let's Tie Up Teaching with Everyday Living," The Journal of the National Education Association, XXX, 234-236, November, 1941.

Hahn, H., "Why Failures in the Study of Geography?" The Journal of Geography, XXXV, 225-234, September, 1936.

Harper, Charles, "This Matter of Method," Social Education, II, 392-394, September, 1938.

Harrington, Eldred, "On the Teaching of Geography," Educational Method, XV, 255-258, February, 1936.

Hockett, John, "Are the Social Studies Skill Subjects?" Social Education, II, 321-323, May, 1938.

Hodgkins, George, "Skills in the Social Studies," Social Education, IV, 194-200, March, 1940.

———, "A Skill-Training Program for the Social Studies," Social Education, IV, 562-568, December, 1940.

Horn, Ernest, Methods of Instruction in the Social Studies. New York: Charles Scribner's Sons, 1937.
    Chapters I, II, III, IV.

Horrocks, John, "Classroom Committees," Social Education, III, 244-246, April, 1939.

Hunt, Erling, "Problems in the Teaching of Modern History," Social Education, I, 552-557, November, 1937.

Kelty, Mary, Learning and Teaching History in the Middle Grades. Boston: Ginn and Co., 1936.
    Principles of Organization, etc., 19-98.

Kennedy, Anna Clark and Painter, Fred B., Materials for the Social Studies Program, The Social Studies in the Elementary School, Twelfth Yearbook, National Council for the Social Studies, 1941, 101-156.

Knowlton, Daniel, History and the Other Social Studies. New York: Charles Scribner's Sons, 1926.

Klapper, Paul, The Teaching of History. New York: D. Appleton and Co., 1926.

Kusch, Monica, "Geography: A Laboratory Subject," The Journal of Geography, XXXIX, 203-206, May, 1940.

Lacey, Joy, Teaching the Social Studies in the Elementary School. Minneapolis: Burgess Publishing Co., 1941.

Lawson, Douglas E., "Geography Then and Now," Elementary School Journal, XLI, 597-604, April, 1941.

Levi, Herman, "Ineffective Geography Teaching—Why?" The Journal of Geography, XXXVII, 185-187, May, 1938.

Long, Forrest and Halter, Helen, "Individualization in the Social Studies," Social Education, III, 402-408, September, 1939.

Lowengrund, Edith, "Making Junior High School History Real," The Social Studies, XXVIII, 17-20, January, 1937.

Lucas, W. C., "Making Geography Teaching Click," The Journal of Geography, XXXVIII, 349-354, December, 1939.

Martin, Neil, "Equipping a High School Geography Room," The Journal of Geography, XXXVIII, 226-232, September, 1939.

McGuire, Edna, "Social Studies Skills in Elementary Schools," Social Education, I, 569-574, November, 1937.

McHale, Catherine, "Vocabulary Building in Junior High School," Social Education, III, 612-620, December, 1939.

Moore, Clyde and Wilcox, Lillian, The Teaching of Geography. New York: American Book Co., 1932. Part II. Methods and Procedures, 101-182.

Park, Joe, "A Practical Social Studies Notebook," The Journal of the National Education Association, XXVII, 88, March, 1938.

Powers, Pauline, "Ah, Geography," The Journal of Geography, XXXVII, 274-277, October, 1938.

Reeder, Edwin, "Social Studies in the Elementary School," National Elementary Principal, XX, 137-140, April, 1941.

———, Geography for Public School Administrators. New York: Bureau of Publications, Teachers College, 1931.

Research Bulletin of the National Education Association, XV, November, 1937, Improving Social Studies Instruction. Chapter IV. Methods and Aids in Teaching, 211-217.

Schutte, T. H., Teaching the Social Studies on the Secondary School Level. New York: Prentice-Hall, 1938. Chapter VI.

Schwarz, John, Social Study in the Elementary School. New York: Prentice-Hall, 1938. Chapters VII and VIII.

Selsky, Marcella and Smuck, L. Merle, "Enrichment in Geography," Baltimore Bulletin of Education, XVIII, 57-63, September-October, 1940.

Shannon, J. R., "Elements of Excellence in Teaching," Educational Administration and Supervision, XXVII, 168-176, March, 1941.

Simpson, I. Jewell, "Social Studies in Maryland's Elementary Schools," Curriculum Journal, XII, 26-28, January, 1941.

Stephenson, O. W., "Articulation in the Social Studies," Social Education, I, 351-355, May, 1937.

Stormzand, M. J. and Lewis, Robert, New Methods in the Social Studies. New York: Farrar and Rinehart, 1935.

Taylor, Walter, "Follow-Thru," The Journal of Geography, XXXVIII, 213-216, September, 1939.

Teachers' Guide to Child Development, California State Curriculum Committee. Sacramento: State Department of Education, 1936.

The Social Studies Curriculum, Fourteenth Yearbook, Department of Superintendence of the National Education Association, 1936.
Chapter XII. The Teacher and Classroom Techniques, 281-311.

The Teaching of Geography, Thirty-Second Yearbook, National Society for the Study of Education, 1933.
Chapter XX. Method in Geography, 315-332.

Thralls, Zoe and Reeder, Edwin, Geography in the Elementary School. Chicago: Rand McNally and Co. 1932.
Chapter X. What Are the Various Means of Organizing Geographic Materials for Instructional Purposes? 355-379.

Wilson, Howard and Murra, Wilbur, Contributions of Research to Special Methods: The Social Studies, Thirty-Seventh Yearbook, Part II, the National Society for the Study of Education, 1938.

Wirth, Fremont, "Some Recent Trends in the Teaching of History," Education, LVIII, 23-25, September, 1937.

Wittkop, Norman, "Methods of Motivating Geography Teaching," The Journal of Geography, XXXVII, 205-207, May, 1938.

Zafra, Carlos, "Homogeneous Grouping in the Social Studies," Social Education, IV, 493-497, November, 1940.

———, "The Ninth Grade Studies Local Government," Social Education, III, 551-554, November, 1939.

Zeleny, Leslie, "Group Learning," Social Education, IV, 317-321, May, 1940.

Chapter Twelve: THE UNIT IN

THE SOCIAL STUDIES

WHAT IS A UNIT?

DURING RECENT years, very much has been written and said about units and the unit method of teaching. Many teachers say that they are teaching units and many textbooks claim that their subject matter is written around units. Likewise, courses of study have been made with the unit idea in mind. Since so many teachers and educators are thinking in terms of unit, one might naturally suppose that there would be common agreement concerning the definition of a unit. However, it seems impossible to give a simple definition of a unit which will please all educators.

It is true that teachers and educators agree in a general way on many of the points about a unit, but it is also true that they disagree among themselves on a number of points. Some teachers call almost any topic or block of work a unit. A few textbook writers apparently think that the chapter headings are units. Some teachers see no difference between the terms "unit," "project," "problem," and "activity." A few teachers believe that a unit must be stated in a certain way. Others believe that the statement is of little importance.

There are several reasons why the ordinary teacher is likely to become confused if he reads much of the literature which has been written about the unit. One reason is that so many different terms are used by various writers. For example, we read about (1) the unit, (2) the unit of learning, (3) the unit of teaching, (4) the unit assignment, (5) the unit of work, (6) the unit of understanding, (7) learning units, (8) source units, (9) student units, (10) units of social significance, (11) the traditional subject matter unit, (12) the functional subject matter unit, (13) the possible child-experience unit, (14) the immediate child-experience unit, (15) the center of interest unit, (16) the unit of adaptation, (17) the unit for teachers, and (18) the unit method. Teachers who specialize in education easily understand all the preceding terms. The everyday teacher, who has had only the average amount of education in his training, is likely to become confused in his thinking when he tries to understand all these terms.

Another reason for confusion over the meaning of the term "unit" is because many writers have been unable to define it in simple words, or to define it in such a way that it will have much meaning to the ordinary classroom teacher. It should be remembered that the classroom teacher is a busy individual who must study subject matter as well as methods of teaching. If an article is not clear to a teacher on first reading, he may not have time to read it a second time. Hence, educators who write articles for classroom teachers should strive to make them clear. This does not mean that they should be written in very simple language, but it does mean that they should be written in language which an average classroom teacher can understand.

Dr. Henry Morrison in "The Practice of Teaching in the Secondary School" defines a unit of learning as "a comprehensive and significant aspect of the environment, of an organized science, of an art, or of conduct, which being learned results in an adaptation in personality." James Michener and Harold Long in "The Unit in the Social Studies" state that "a social-studies unit, whether for teacher or student, is an organization of information and activities focused upon the development of some significant understanding, attitude, or appreciation which will modify behavior."

Since it is very difficult to give a simple definition of a unit in a few words, the definition which is given here will probably be unsatisfactory to some. The following definition does have simplicity, and in a general way it is what many teachers believe a unit to be. A unit in the social studies is a body of closely related worthwhile materials, which can be studied as a whole and which cause pupils to perform different activities, that help to give them those experiences which are needed in everyday living.

A chapter heading or a topic is not usually a unit. One chapter is usually very much related to other chapters in a book, and it generally should not be studied by itself, but in relation to the other chapters. The same is true for topics. One topic generally can only be understood as it is studied in relation to other topics. A unit usually includes more than a chapter or a topic. Of course, there are cases of a chapter or a topic being a unit. It depends upon what is included in the chapter or topic and how the pupils develop it in their study.

WORKING OUT A UNIT

The teacher who uses the unit organization is kept busy while the pupils are studying a unit. There is no one commonly accepted method of teaching a unit, although writers and speakers often mention the unit method. There are a number of methods which may be used. Each teacher selects his own method, and the method he uses successfully is correctly called a unit method. Thus there is no single method of teaching which can be called the unit method.

One of the important problems that confronts a teacher is to determine the units which the pupils will study during the year. In some places, the course of study does this for the teacher. In other places, the teacher is given considerable leeway in determining the units which he teaches.

The teacher should determine the approximate time to be spent on a unit. Some units may occupy only a few days, while others may occupy a number of weeks. Many teachers like to have the pupils work three or four weeks on a unit. They believe this is a long enough period of time for the pupils to do a good piece of work. They prefer to have them study a number of units during the year. There should not be too many units studied by the pupils, neither should there be too few. The number of units which the pupils study during the year are determined by such factors as the maturity of the pupils, the nature of the units, the course of study, the attitude of the teacher, and the time given over to the social studies.

In studying a unit, the pupils do many different kinds of activities in gaining the experience which they need in solving their problems. The recitation period is no longer merely a place where pupils meet to answer questions asked by the teacher. Some of the recitation periods or parts of them may be used as study periods, where pupils are at work solving problems under the supervision of the teacher. The teacher moves here and there, observing what each pupil is doing, offering words of encouragement, and giving aid and suggestions wherever they are needed. Pupils learn to work together. Each one contributes his share in the solving of problems. Tests are given whenever they are needed. In some schools, the teachers give written or oral instructions for the pupils to follow. These instructions are clear and definite and they aid the pupils in doing their work. The instructions may contain questions, problems, suggested activities, and references.

STEPS IN THE PREPARATION OF A UNIT OF WORK FOR TEACHING

The following outline is only suggestive. It shows what a teacher may do in preparing to teach a unit.

I. Understanding what is meant by a unit
   A. Talk to teachers and others
   B. Consult the course of study
   C. Read articles which have been published in magazines and books on units
   D. Read articles on units which have been written, but not published
   E. Visit classes where units are used

II. Selecting the unit
   A. Consult the course of study
      1. To learn what units are taught in a given grade
      2. To learn the approximate time to be spent on any one unit
      3. To obtain references for pupils to read
      4. To get suggestions about teaching the unit
      5. To get any additional helpful information
   B. If a course of study is not followed, approval for taking a unit should be obtained from the principal or the person who is in charge of the school
      1. Unit should be worthwhile
      2. Unit should appeal to the pupils

3. Unit should be selected according to some general plan of what the pupils have studied in previous terms and will likely study in later terms

III. Studying and analyzing the unit
A. Determine what to teach and then master it
    1. Consult the course of study to learn what the unit includes
    2. Consider the pupils who are to be taught
        a. Needs of the pupils, their ages, what they have already studied, what they will probably study in later years, the ability of the pupils for work, individual differences, the amount of time which can be given to the unit, etc.
    3. Study carefully the subject matter, talk with people about the unit, attend lectures, take field trips, listen to appropriate radio programs, read newspapers and magazines, study books, collect material which may be of help in learning about the unit. A teacher should know what he is teaching, so mastery of the unit by the teacher is very important
B. Get acquainted with books and other references written for the pupils
C. Determine the methods to use
    1. Various ways of conducting the class
        a. Class as a whole
        b. Groups or committees
        c. Individual assignments
        d. Combinations of the above three ways
    2. Various methods or plans which may be used in teaching the unit
        a. Project method, problem method
        b. Textbook method, workbook method
        c. Morrison unit method
        d. Question and answer method, the topical outline, the type study
        e. Individual instruction, the laboratory

method, workshop method, contract method, Winnetka plan, directed study procedure, supervised study

    f. Dramatization, the journey method, the story method, the lecture method

    g. The comparison lesson

    h. Socialized lessons, panel discussions, drills and games

  3. Visit classes to see various methods in use

D. Consider how to use various tools and aids
  1. Textbooks
  2. Supplementary books or books for collateral reading
  3. Maps, globes, atlases
  4. Pictures
  5. Graphs, charts, tables of statistics
  6. Museum materials, models, exhibits
  7. Radio
  8. Bulletin boards
  9. Newspapers, magazines, pamphlets

E. Think of the various activities which individual pupils or groups of pupils may do
  1. Reading books and other printed materials
  2. Making posters
  3. Making drawings
  4. Making collections of pictures, museum materials, cartoons, and various other materials
  5. Making booklets
  6. Making various kinds of maps
  7. Mounting pictures and other materials on cardboard
  8. Filling in outline maps
  9. Making lantern slides
  10. Making models
  11. Making a movie
  12. Making diagrams, writing tests
  13. Making objects out of clay
  14. Conducting an election, holding a convention, making a survey of conditions in the community

15. Giving an assembly program, managing a bulletin board
16. Conducting a debate
17. Writing a class newspaper
18. Writing summaries of articles read
19. Forming a club
20. Interviewing people and attending meetings
21. Taking trips to various places
22. Writing stories, plays, and poems
23. Listening to radio broadcasts
24. Constructing scenes on the table and in boxes
25. Giving talks and reports
26. Playing educational games
27. Dramatizing scenes
28. Reading suitable material

F. Think of the problem of testing
1. Why tests should be given
2. What qualities are to be measured
3. When to give tests
4. Kinds of tests
   a. Essay type
   b. Objective type
      (1) True-false; yes-no
      (2) Matching
      (3) Multiple choice
      (4) Arrangement
      (5) Completion
      (6) Others

G. Consider references and materials which the pupils may consult and study
1. Books and pamphlets
2. Maps, pictures, and other visual materials
3. Newspapers and magazines
4. Good radio programs and motion pictures
5. Neighborhood resources

IV. Organizing the unit for teaching
A. Putting everything together as a whole
B. Outline may be as long as the teacher wishes to make it

   C. Recommended order of procedure
  1. Objectives
  2. Suggested ways of approach
  3. Outline of suggested problems
  4. Suggested activities and methods of attack
  5. Suggested tests
  6. References

THE HERBARTIAN PLAN

During the early 1890's the Herbartian theory of education came to be accepted by many educational leaders. The Herbartian method has five steps. They are:

1. Preparation: By recalling certain facts and in various other ways, the pupils are prepared for the new lesson.

2. Presentation: The new material may be presented to the pupils in a variety of ways.

3. Comparison: The new material is compared and related to old material.

4. Generalization: From a study of the material, the class comes to a certain conclusion or generalization.

5. Application: The generalization is applied to new situations.

The Herbartian method was much used in our country for twenty or thirty years. Today, this method is no longer commonly used, although its influence may still be seen. New methods have taken its place. It gave too much attention to the work of the teacher and not enough to the pupil.

THE MORRISON UNIT PLAN

Dr. Morrison of the University of Chicago developed a plan for teaching a unit which covers several days or a few weeks of work by the pupils. It has five steps.

1. Exploration: The teacher tries to learn what the pupils know about the new unit. He may do this by a written test, an oral test, or a class discussion. The exploration test may show that it is unnecessary for some pupils to study certain topics that other pupils need to study. It helps the teacher to know what materials to present. The exploration period usually takes one or two periods.

2. *Presentation:* The teacher gives a brief oral description of the unit. He tries to get the class interested in it. After presenting a preview of the entire unit, the pupils are given a test to see if they have gained the correct understandings. Those pupils who fail in the test have the material presented to them until the teacher feels satisfied that they have got it. The presentation period may take thirty minutes, but the time depends upon the ease with which the pupils grasp the preview given by the teacher.

3. *Assimilation:* The pupils study the unit. They do much reading and various kinds of activities. Sometimes they have study sheets to guide them in their work. The teacher should be careful to see that the study sheets are not regarded by the pupils as having lists of things that they must do. The study sheets are merely guides for aiding the pupils to get the needed understandings. During this period, the teacher gives help where it is needed. Tests are given to see if the pupils have mastered the material being presented. Discussions may frequently help. The presentation period may last from a few days to a number of weeks.

4. *Organization:* When the class is thought to have put enough time on studying the unit, the pupils are required to organize their material. If any pupil fails to organize the material satisfactorily, it should be retaught until he gets it. One or two periods are usually enough for organizing the material.

5. *Recitation:* The pupils are now ready to give the results of their work before the class in the form of talks or written papers. Usually there is not time for more than a few of the pupils to give oral recitations, so most of them may prepare written reports. The recitation step takes about two days.

Morrison believes that a teacher of the social studies should teach for mastery of the unit, so he has this mastery plan: (1) pre-test, (2) teach, (3) test for the desired outcomes, (4) if a pupil fails, find out why he failed and change the teaching procedure, (5) re-teach, (6) re-test, and keep on re-teaching and re-testing until a pupil gains the necessary understanding and information.

Sometimes it is difficult to determine just how well the pupils have mastered the acquiring of good ideals, attitudes, habits of work, enriched experiences, and the ability to study independently and to work cooperatively in groups. Even the testing for information is not so easy as some people may think. Just how far into a subject should the pupils go? What are the important facts that pupils should collect and think about? It stands to reason that the pupils in the eighth grade should go more fully into a subject than the pupils in the fifth grade. Again, what seems to be important today may not be important tomorrow. All teachers do not agree on what things are important. Hence, it is impossible to master problems in the social studies in the same way that problems in mathematics are mastered. Mastery is important in the social studies, but teachers must remember that it includes much more than the acquiring of certain bits of information.

The Morrison unit plan is used by some teachers, but there have been numerous adaptations of his plans to other methods. As has already been stated, teachers use different methods in teaching a unit. Numerous experiments have been carried out to determine the best method of teaching a unit, but as yet there is no proof that one method is better than some of the others. There are a number of good methods. However, there are some methods that are so poor that they should never be used.

ADVANTAGES OF THE UNIT ORGANIZATION

It is well to remember that no plan is self-teaching. Teachers are needed to put any plan into effect. Again, no plan can be expected to produce very good results in the hands of a poor teacher. Hence, even the best plan needs a good teacher to see that the pupils follow it wisely. People have been on this earth for hundreds of years and changes come about slowly. We must not expect great changes in our methods of teaching to take place over night. They come about gradually and are due to a number of forces, many of which affect us unconsciously.

A few of the advantages claimed for the unit organization are:

1. It is easy to provide for individual differences. In some schools, the classroom becomes an active laboratory where pupils work out their own problems.

2. The lessons are socialized and each pupil works at his own rate of speed.

3. The pupils have a motive for doing their work, and it is easy to keep them interested in what they are doing.

4. Since the work is so well planned, the pupils know what to do and there need be no question about the assignments for the next day. There should be no wasting of time.

5. Pupils gain experiences, the ability to do things, and good habits of work.

6. Related information in place of unrelated information is obtained and as much of the work as possible is connected with life outside the schoolroom.

7. Different methods of procedures in teaching the unit keep the work from getting monotonous.

8. It provides a splendid opportunity for pupils to learn to look up materials and to learn to depend upon themselves.

9. Pupils learn to make efficient use of various kinds of materials such as books, pamphlets, magazines, pictures, maps, graphs, and charts.

10. Good training is furnished in making outlines and reviews.

11. It provides splendid opportunity for individual work and group work.

12. Ample opportunity is furnished for doing various kinds of creative work.

13. It helps to keep the teacher from getting into a rut, because he must be well informed on many things if he is going to direct intelligently the work of the pupils.

14. It can be carried out successfully in any classroom; providing the teacher believes in the plan.

DISADVANTAGES OF THE UNIT ORGANIZATION

The unit organization has certain limitations. A skilful teacher understands the limitations and he makes his plans with them in mind. The poor teacher pays little attention to the limitations and the results of his teaching may be anything but satisfactory. Some of the limitations or disadvantages are the following:

1. There are some things which the pupils should learn which do not fit well into unit organization.

2. Where study guides are used, pupils may come to depend too much upon them and poor habits of study may be formed.

3. Pupils should learn to work together in groups and to co-

operate. Hence, all the work should not be on an individual basis.

4. If a teacher is not careful, there will not be enough opportunity for discussion among the pupils. Pupils must be given time to discuss their problems.

5. Pupils often become tired of following the same plan day after day, or of writing summaries of the work which they have studied. Thus the work may become monotonous.

6. If the teacher is not careful, the pupils will not receive help when they need it. Very often a pupil will waste much time before he asks the teacher for help. Unless the supervision is well done by the teacher, the pupils may form poor habits of work.

7. If careful watch is not made, the pupils are likely to work chiefly for the gaining of facts. Very often the tests are chiefly for facts. Good attitudes, ideals, habits of work, enriched experiences, and the ability for work should be obtained as well as information.

PROBLEMS FOR DISCUSSION AND RESEARCH

1. After much reading and thinking, explain what is meant by a unit in the social studies.

2. What are some of the problems that a teacher must consider who uses the unit method of teaching?

3. Describe the steps in the preparation of a unit for teaching.

4. How does the Herbartian plan of teaching resemble the Morrison unit plan?

5. Describe the Morrison unit plan.

6. Is there any one plan which may be called the unit method of teaching?

7. Give the chief advantages of the unit organization.

8. Give some of the disadvantages of the unit organization.

REFERENCES

Abild, Ruth, "Alaska, A Social Studies Unit of Activity," The Grade Teacher, LIX, 54-55, 89, October, 1941.
Bailey, Grace, "Pupil-Teacher Planning in the Intermediate Grades," Social Education, IV, 258-261, April, 1940.
Bard, Harry, Emenheiser, B. F., and Parker, Mary, "Enrichment in

History," Baltimore Bulletin of Education, XVIII, 84-93, 96-97, September-October, 1940.

Bining, Arthur and Bining, David, *Teaching the Social Studies in the Secondary Schools*, New York: McGraw-Hill Book Co., 1941. Chapter IX. Unit Procedure, 166-183.

Bining, Arthur, Mohr, Walter, and McFeely, Richard, *Organizing the Social Studies in Secondary Schools*. New York: McGraw-Hill Book Co., 1941. Chapter III. Organizing the Materials of Instruction, 46-62.

Blood, Pearl, "The Preparation of Geography Units by Student Teachers," The Journal of Geography, XXXV, 18-24, January, 1936.

Brown, Bessie, "A Unit on the Library," The Instructor, LI, 18-19, November, 1941.

Brown, Florence, "Southeastern Asia," The Journal of Geography, XXXVIII, 141-150, April, 1939.

Carter, Harriet, "Our National Forests—A Social Problem," The Journal of Geography, XXXIX, 151-155, April, 1940.

———, "Saving Our Soils—A Unit of Study for Junior and Senior High Schools," The Journal of Geography, XXXVII, 308-318, November, 1938.

Conlon, Florence, "The Integration of Art and Social Studies in the Elementary School," Educational Methods, XV, 209-214, January, 1936.

Crewson, Walter, "Teaching Unit: A Type Area in the Los Angeles Citrus Fruit District," The Journal of Geography, XXXV, 24-30, January, 1936.

———, "Teaching Unit on Japan," The Journal of Geography, XXXII, 27-34, January, 1933.

Davey, J. and Hill, H., The Unit and the Unit Method in the Social Studies, *Eighth Yearbook, National Council for the Social Studies*, 1937, 1-20.

Davis, Mary and Scholz, La Velle, "Mexico—Land of the Sombrero," The Instructor, XLIX, 17, 65, 73, April, 1940.

Diehl, Ivan, "A Problem Plan for Organizing a Teaching Unit in Geography," The Journal of Geography, XXXIX, 323-325, November, 1940.

Eldridge, Lillian, "Procedures in Teaching History," Social Education, III, 394-401, September, 1939.

Emerson, Cora, "A Fifth Grade Studies Chocolate," American Childhood Education, XXII, 5-7, February, 1937.

Farthing, Dorothy, "A Teaching Unit on Alaska," Social Education, IV, 39-44, January, 1940.

Few, Louise, "A Third Grade Studies Wool," American Childhood, XXII, 8-10, 51, January, 1937.

Firth, Roxie, "Christmas Sharing," The Instructor, LI, 22-23, December, 1941.

Fleming, Eleanor, "The Pioneer Unit," The Grade Teacher, LIX, 38, 79, November, 1941.

Fuller, Alice, "Fire Prevention, Safety Lessons for Little Children," The Grade Teacher, LIX, 26, 77, October, 1941.

Gage, Fenton, "A Unit on Propaganda Analysis," Social Education, IV, 483-489, November, 1940.

Gooden, Olive, "The Heavenly Creations," The Instructor, LI, 24, 68, December, 1941.

Grant, L. S., "The Story of New France," The Grade Teacher, LIX, 48-49, 83, October, 1941.

Guy, Dorothy, "The Ancient Greeks," The Instructor, L, 23, 77, October, 1941.

Harap, Henry, "What Is the Consumer Moment?" Frontiers of Democracy, VII, 48-50, November 15, 1940.

Hileman, Mary, "A Visit to Reindeer Land," The Journal of Geography, XXXVII, 278-283, October, 1938.

——, "Adios for Mexico, A Social Studies Unit for the Third Grade," The Journal of Geography, XXXVIII, 359-363, December, 1939.

Hodgkins, George, A Guide to Newer Methods in Teaching the Social Studies. Washington: National Council for the Social Studies, 1936. 38, 42-46.

Hunolt, Domitilla, "Unitary Organization," Social Education, III, 115, 121, February, 1939.

Jennings, Vivian, "Unit Organization and Laboratory Procedures," Social Education, IV, 180-182, March, 1940.

Kelty, Mary, Learning and Teaching History in the Middle Grades. Boston: Ginn and Co., 1936. 115-654.

Kenigson, Dorothy and Choffey, Evelyn, "Colonial Life in New England," LI, 24, 29, 70, November, 1941.

Knight, W. E., "Reasoning Through Social Studies," Kentucky School Journal, XIX, 22-24, December, 1940.

Mapes, Carl, "Creative Map Making in the Teaching of Historico-Geographical Units," The Journal of Geography, XXXIX, 156-160, April, 1940.

Martin, Mary, "We Study the School," The Instructor, L, 12-13, 79, November, 1940.

——, "A Unit on the Post Office," The Instructor, LI, 16, 66, December, 1941.

Michener, James and Long, Harold, The Unit in the Social Studies. Cambridge: Graduate School of Education, Harvard Uni., 1940.

Milyard, Beulah, "A Unit on the Public Schools," The Instructor, LI, 27, 63, November, 1941.

Painter, Florence, "The Conservation Unit," The Grade Teacher, LVIII, 42-43, 88-89.

Perlman, Herbert, "Basic Tools in the Social Studies," High Points, XXIII, 50-52, February, 1941.

Purnell, Louise, "A Unit on Switzerland," The Journal of Geography, XXXVIII, 200-204, May, 1931.

Relyea, Marion, "Desert—And Oasis Life," The Grade Teacher, LIX, 44-45, 70, November, 1941.

Renner, George, "Conservation as a Unit of Study in Geography," Education, LVIII, 283-290, January, 1934.

Schapiro, Eleanor, "Publishing a Local History," Social Education, III, 25-29, January, 1939.

Sister M. Bernetta, "Unit Teaching Material: The Polar Regions," The Journal of Geography, XXXIX, 10-16, January, 1940.

Smallenburg, Carol, Teaching Social Studies in the Upper Grades: A Unit on Community Recreation, Twelfth Yearbook of the National Council for the Social Studies, 1941, 200-214.

Soper, Eugene, "A Unit on Columbus," The Grade Teacher, 46, 88, October, 1941.

Storm, Grace, The Social Studies in the Primary Grades. Chicago: Lyons and Carnahan, 1931.

Symonds, Janet, "A Unit on the Ojibwa Indians," The Instructor, XLIX, 21, 68, 77, October, 1940.

Taylor, Ethel, "The Farm in the Fall," The Instructor, L, 19, 68-69, October, 1941.

Teachers' Lesson Units published by Teachers College, Columbia University, New York City.

Waddell, Charles, Seeds, Corinne, and White, Natalie, Major Units in the Social Studies for the Intermediate Grades. New York: John Day, 1932.

Waltermire, Helen, "Brazil," The Grade Teacher, LVIII, 40-41, 82, 83, April, 1941.

Ward, Jesse, "The Earmarks of a Unit," Education, LVI, 630-631, June, 1936.

Wesley, Edgar, Teaching the Social Studies. New York: D. C. Heath and Co., 1937.
  Chapter XXIX. The Unit Procedure, 518-528.

Wilder, Ira, "How to Teach by the Unit Method," The Social Studies, XXXII, 67-69, February, 1941.

Willcuts, Virginia, "A Unit in Sixth Grade Geography," The Journal of Geography, XXXVIII, 115-117, March, 1939.

Chapter Thirteen: PROBLEMS, PROJECTS,

AND ACTIVITIES

1. PROBLEMS

THE IMPORTANCE OF PROBLEMS

EVERY GOOD teacher tries to get his pupils to think, and fortunate is he who succeeds in doing so. It is much easier for most people to take something for granted in place of endeavoring to work out the solution for themselves. The same is true for pupils. They will generally follow the least lines of resistance in studying, unless they are shown that it will pay them to take some other line. It does take some effort to think and it is the business of the teacher to lead his pupils to see that it pays them to think. The thinking person is the one who will most likely succeed and who may become a leader among men, while the unthinking one is prepared to be only a follower. Of course, all thinking persons understand that they must know when to follow as well as when to lead. In a democracy, a thinking person is both a leader and a follower. Hence, it is the business of the school to train pupils to be both followers and leaders.

One way of getting pupils to think is to have them solve problems. The problem method is not new. Probably the first school teacher in the far distant past made use of problems. During the years that have passed since the dawn of teaching, great changes have come about in methods, yet teachers use problems and they will probably still be using them in the years to come. It is only natural to teach the pupils how to study problems, since everyone who is old enough to think is continually confronted with problems. He who solves his problems successfully is on the road to success, while he who does not is on the road to failure. To prepare pupils for present-day living as well as for future living, they must be given training in solving worth-while problems.

Anyone who is able to read this book intelligently does not need to be given a definition of a problem, because he knows what it is from actual experience. A problem is sometimes said to be a question that requires considerable thinking in answering it. The more difficult the problem, the more thinking that will likely be needed in studying it. A problem offers a challenge to a pupil to see if he can really solve it. It arouses his curiosity and he makes an attempt to find the correct solution. The greater the curiosity of the pupil, the more diligently he will work in getting a satisfactory answer. A problem must be real to a pupil; otherwise it is not a problem to him. Neither does he have a problem if his curiosity is not aroused.

Too many teachers fool themselves by thinking that their pupils have problems when actually they do not have them. Very often the pupils do not enter into the work wholeheartedly and they do very little thinking. In many cases, they memorize what their books say and they let the authors of the books do most of their thinking. Even though the work which they are doing is stated in the form of a question or problem, this does not neces-sarily mean that the problem is real and vital to them. A fine flow of words by a pupil does not always indicate that he has done very much thinking. Some pupils recite very nicely as long as they are permitted to use the words which they have memorized from their textbooks, but they are lost when told to use their own words. The problem method is not memory work, but it is thinking where past experiences are recalled and are related to new experiences.

HOW TO STATE PROBLEMS

There are various ways of stating a problem. The way a prob-lem is stated is important to the pupils, but its importance is sometimes overestimated. The chief thing is for the teacher to see that a given problem means something to the pupils and that they are actually interested in studying it. It generally takes much more than the statement of a problem to get the pupils interested in it. A teacher who teaches by problems must be alert at all times to make use of any experiences which the pupils may have.

Since a problem presents a challenge to the pupils, it is commonly stated in the form of a question. Such questions often begin with why, how, or what. Examples of problems are (1) "Why is New York a great port?" (2) "Why do we celebrate Thanksgiving?" (3) "How are the British Isles influenced by the ocean?" (4) "How did America come to be settled?" (5) "What are some of the factors which influence manufacturing?" (6) "What are some of the reasons for the Revolutionary War?"

Sometimes the pupils decide to have a debate over some problem that has arisen. Then the problem is stated in the form of a debate such as "Resolved that more substitutes should be used in place of lumber." Occasionally a problem is stated in a few words such as "A study of transportation in the United States," or "A study of the settling of the Far West." In studying the main problem, subproblems arise. In using an outline in studying, the main topics should become problems and the minor topics should be subproblems.

SOME CHARACTERISTICS OF A GOOD PROBLEM

First of all, a problem should be interesting to the pupils. No pupil can be expected to get much out of any study if he is not interested in it. Interest causes a pupil to study diligently and to work without being prodded by the teacher. The teacher should think of various ways of arousing the interest and of keeping the pupils interested until their problem is solved.

A problem should be easily understood by the pupils. If a problem is too difficult, they will probably become discouraged and will lose much time in trying to study it. On the other hand, the problem should not be too easy because anything that is too easy is likely to cause pupils to form poor habits of work. The ages of the pupils and their ability to solve problems determine to a large extent the kind of problems that may be studied profitably.

The teacher should make sure that the pupils may obtain plenty of material for the solving of most of their problems. If pupils are unable to find material after a reasonable search, they are likely to become disheartened and lose all interest in studying; unless they are permitted to drop the problem and take another one. A teacher occasionally allows the pupils to take a problem on which they cannot easily find material, just to show them that there are problems that cannot readily be solved.

What is the difference between a question and a problem? Let us suppose that the pupils are using a good textbook in history. In the course of the discussion, they want to know when the cotton gin was invented. They have raised a simple question because all anyone needs to do is to turn to his book and find the answer with very little difficulty. After some discussion the pupils become interested in learning what effect the cotton gin had on the development of the South. They now have raised a problem because much thinking and considerable study must be done in finding the answer.

Whether the term "problem" or "question" should be used depends upon the amount of thinking and studying that the pupils do. Where very little thinking and studying takes place, most teachers would use the term "question" in place of "problem." When there is a problem, the challenging must be great enough to cause the pupils to do a reasonable amount of work in its solution. As pupils advance in age and in the power to solve problems, they should be expected to be able to do more studying and research work. A problem on the level of an eighth or a ninth grade child requires much more thinking than on the level of a fourth or a fifth grade child.

All the problems studied by pupils should be worthwhile. They should get the pupils interested in other activities. Every problem should also be stated definitely and clearly so that the pupils will have no difficulty in understanding its meaning.

RELATION OF MEMORY WORK TO PROBLEM SOLVING

It is difficult for people to keep from going to the extremes. It is hard to stay in the middle of the road and to steer a straight and true path. Some years ago, our schools paid too much attention to memory work, and not enough attention to reasoning and thinking. The children memorized the words in their books and thinking was at a premium. Along came educators who condemned pure memory work and advocated that the pupils should be taught to think and to learn to depend upon themselves. Some educators even led a few teachers to think that a good memory was no longer needed by the pupils and that pupils should not be required to remember facts. Such educators went too far in their condemnation of memory work.

He who remembers nothing is unable to reason and to think intelligently. In order to reason and to think, a person must be able to recall certain past experiences. A good memory for past events is certainly a good asset for any person to have. The trouble with many people today is that they do not have enough facts to permit them to think correctly and they do not have a strong desire to get the facts. They are willing to base their thinking on an insufficient number of facts or on inaccurate facts. In a modern school, both memory work and thinking are stressed, because one is very closely related to the other.

Pupils in a school, like people in the world at large, may be grouped into two classes, the thinkers and the non-thinkers. Some pupils are content to be non-thinkers. They do not seem to have the ability or the urge to do much thinking. It is the duty of the teacher to try to get all his pupils to think. Even under the best of conditions, a teacher cannot hope to get all his pupils to be good thinkers, but he can hope to help them increase their power to think. The correct kind of training can do much to stimulate the weak as well as the strong.

In order to think, a pupil must recall past experiences and relate them to new experiences. A poor memory retards thinking, but a pupil who has facts at his disposal and is able to use them at the right time is the one who is likely to get the best solutions to his problems. In thinking, a pupil accumulates new material and he fixes more firmly in mind the old material. This kind of memory work is approved by our best teachers. The pupil has a reason for trying to remember certain ideas because he has thought them out. They have been found to be useful and they will likely be useful time after time. Hence, memorizing is still important, but it is brought about in a different way today than it was done some years ago. However, the most important thing is for pupils to have the ability, the desire, and the opportunity to use their knowledge in the solution of new problems.

THE STEPS IN PROBLEM SOLVING

The four chief steps in problem solving are (1) raising the problem, (2) stating the problem, (3) gathering and studying the materials, and (4) coming to definite conclusions and verifying them.

The first thing the teacher has to consider is how to arouse the interest of the pupils in a problem so that they will want to study it. Sometimes the teacher gives a problem to the class to study and the pupils immediately become interested in it. Under such circumstances it would be a waste of time for the teacher to spend any effort in trying to arouse an interest, since it already exists. However, if the interest does not exist, the teacher should present sufficient material to get the pupils interested. He may do this in various ways such as giving a short preview of the problem, having a class discussion, or showing pictures or other objects. For example, a teacher got his pupils interested in Mexico by showing them articles which he had collected in Mexico. He put the articles on a table in the schoolroom. The children examined them and asked many questions. They soon had problems about Mexico which they wished to study.

Pupils often raise problems without any help from the teacher. They frequently come to class with problems that interest them. Sometimes the solving of one problem calls forth other problems. Class discussions often raise numerous problems. It is not always wise to let the pupils take a problem, just because one or more pupils happen to think of it. The teacher should have some general plan in mind which he follows.

After the pupils have raised a problem and become interested in it, the second thing is to state it clearly and definitely so that it is understood by all. Some teachers write the problem on the blackboard where all the pupils may see it. This helps them keep the problem in mind when studying it. It is easy for pupils to get off the problem in their discussions. When this happens, the attention of the pupils may be called to the problem and they may be asked to state it again.

The third step in solving a problem is the gathering and the studying of materials. Books are read and information is obtained from many sources. The teacher should be on hand to help the pupils. Books may be suggested for the pupils to read and certain pupils may be encouraged to take trips, listen to certain radio programs, consult people, and do other kinds of work.

In working on a problem, the pupils may work individually, in groups, or as a whole class. The chief idea is to have each pupil work according to his ability and to study enough material so that he will come to a conclusion on the problem.

The fourth step in the solution of a problem is arriving at definite conclusions and verifying them. The pupils may reach their conclusions in a class discussion after collecting and interpreting data on the subject. They may check their conclusions by consulting the teacher, the textbook, or some other authority. If their conclusions are approved by the teacher or agree with the textbook, the pupils may feel very sure that they have solved the problem successfully. If the conclusions are found to be incorrect, more information should be sought on the subject. As pupils learn to solve problems and to work independently, they come to depend less upon the teacher. A class in the lower grades generally needs much more help in selecting and interpreting materials than does a class in the upper grades. However, all pupils need the help of the teacher from time to time.

WHAT ARE THE LIMITATIONS OF THE PROBLEM METHOD?

The problem method has certain limitations which should be recognized by all teachers. Most of the limitations may be overcome by wise teachers. Some of the chief limitations are the following:

1. The problem method is not the only method that should be used. Some of the work which pupils do may be taught better by using another method. It cannot be repeated too often that there is no one best method.

2. The problem method involves much thinking or mental work. Pupils are likely to get tired of using this method all the time. This means that as the pupils grow weary of using the problem method, they do less thinking and more memorizing.

3. Teachers frequently expect too much out of the problem method when pupils first begin to use it. Results are usually slow in the beginning and inexperienced teachers often grow impa-

tient. It should be understood that pupils must grow accustomed to using the problem method before they can be expected to obtain the best results.

4. It is difficult for some teachers to keep the pupils on the problem while it is being discussed. Pupils are likely to discuss many things which are unrelated to the problem if they are not required to stay on it. The teacher must be able to determine when a pupil has wandered off the problem and he should be quick to see that he gets back on it.

5. Some teachers, on account of their inability to think quickly and to hold in mind the various points that the pupils make in their discussions, are unable to use successfully the problem method. A slow thinking teacher usually can get better results by using some other method.

6. If the teacher is not careful, pupils using the problem method may form poor habits of reading books. If a pupil is studying a problem, he will only read carefully the material in a book that pertains to the problem. This often means that only a few pages or perhaps a few paragraphs will be read. The rest of the book will probably be cast aside as having no interest to the pupil, since the material is not on the problem which he is studying. Through the course of time a pupil may form the habit of reading only a few pages in any one book. This is a very bad habit for a person to have because he never has the inclination to finish a book after he starts to read it. Many books are worth reading from cover to cover.

WHAT ARE THE ADVANTAGES OF THE PROBLEM METHOD?

Teachers give many advantages for the problem method. Some of the advantages are:

1. It is a natural way of teaching since every person who is old enough to think intelligently is called upon to solve problems in his everyday life outside of school. The solving of problems is merely doing in the schoolroom what people are doing outside the schoolroom.

2. Problem solving involves various kinds of student activity, since a pupil tries to look at the problem in different ways. Even the weakest student will likely find something he can do well.

The various abilities of a pupil are developed. If a reasonable amount of problem solving is done, a pupil will probably find the work to be interesting and enjoyable.

3. The solving of problems develops judgment, trains initiative, and encourages the formation of good habits of study.

4. A real problem gives a challenge to a pupil which stimulates him to study diligently until he gets a satisfactory answer to it. The pupil gets a certain amount of satisfaction out of the solving of a problem.

5. Problem solving teaches a pupil a very good way of studying. It shows him how to collect, interpret, and weigh material.

6. The problem method may be used in any schoolroom.

7. A problem gives a pupil something definite to study. It may be adapted to various age levels. A teacher may have his class study problems which require only a short time for solving, or they may take problems which require several days for their solution.

2. PROJECTS AND ACTIVITIES

WHAT IS A PROJECT?

Some years ago, nearly all educators and educational magazines were discussing the project method of teaching. Using the project method was generally supposed to be a sign that a teacher was progressive. Hence, almost every teacher claimed that he was using the project method. Nearly every kind of activity which the pupils did was called a project by some teacher. Educators and teachers did not always agree among themselves on just what activities should be called projects. What were called projects by one teacher were not always called projects by other teachers. Various definitions and ideas were given concerning projects. As a result, inexperienced teachers and many others got confused in their thinking and they wondered what projects really were. Even today, there is no common definition of a project which is accepted by all good teachers.

New terms come into use as the years pass. Very often a new term has about the same meaning as an old term. Ernest Horn in "Methods of Instruction in the Social Studies" makes this clear. He states that about thirty years ago the setting of a hen by a primary class was called a problem. Some years later it was called a project. Still later other terms were used to describe the setting of a hen. Today, it is called an activity by many teachers. The children still have the same general purposes and interests and their knowledge is being expanded in about the same way, even though their teachers may use a new term to describe what they are doing.

The word "project" was used by engineers and some others before educators began to use it. The building of a bridge was a project. The term was used in 1900 to describe certain work that was being done in manual training. Some years later, it was used to describe a task done at home in some agricultural classes. Raising chickens or growing vegetables was a home task. The idea was that such projects involved planning on the part of the pupil and some physical activity.

As the years passed, teaching by projects in various subjects became common. During the 1920's and the 1930's, the project method of teaching was the center of interest and it is still of much importance. Sometimes the term "project-problem" or "problem-project" is used, because projects always involve problems and problems often cause the pupils to become interested in projects. Many teachers even make no difference between a problem and a project; because they are so much alike and in many cases it is difficult for them to tell one from the other. In the long run it actually makes no difference to a teacher whether the activity is called a problem or a project, providing the pupils are working efficiently and getting good results.

A project is a unit of activity with a well-defined, worthwhile purpose and, in its study, problems and activities arise and are considered by the pupils. A project is of interest to the pupils. It involves much planning, and results in some activity. Learning takes place while a project is being developed, because a project cannot be completed without studying a number of problems. Projects help to make the work more interesting to the pupils.

AN EXAMPLE OF A PROJECT OR AN ACTIVITY

Some teachers believe we should interpret the term "project" somewhat narrowly. To them, a project stresses the practical or concrete side of the thing to be done, while a problem suggests the mental solution which takes place in the minds of the pupils. For example, planning a model of a Swiss village would be a problem, but the actual making of it would be a project. Hence, these teachers prefer to use the term "problem-project" because problems always accompany projects.

It is an old but true saying that children learn by doing. The schoolroom should be a busy place where children are engaged in many different activities in doing their work. During recent years, much has been said and written about the activity program. The term "activity" is often used in place of the term "project."

A good example of a project on purifying water is given by Ruth Wagner in Social Education for January, 1941. Her school was located on the shore of Lake Michigan and the people in the region got their drinking water from the lake. A storm caused the water of Lake Michigan near the intake or water crib to have more germs than usual. For a few days it was necessary to boil the water before drinking it. The children got interested in studying about their drinking water on this account. From a discussion of boiling the water to kill the germs, the children got interested in how the water from Lake Michigan is made safe to drink. Many questions arose.

The teacher made a thorough study of the water supply. Then she explained to the children the treatment of the water to purify it. The children got water from Lake Michigan. They let the water settle and poured the good water into a jar. They then mixed the good water with lime and alum and let it settle. They poured off the good water into another jar. They made a filter by putting sand and gravel in a pan which had holes in the bottom. They poured the good water into their filter. The water came out clear. This activity led the children to want to see how the city actually purified the water.

The pupils took a trip to the filtration plant where they were shown how the water is purified. They asked many questions and learned much. Later, they visited the harbor front to get a view of the harbor. Then they went on top of a tall building to get a good view of the harbor and its location in relation to the filtration plant.

KINDS OF ACTIVITIES

There are many different kinds of worthwhile activities which pupils have done. Some of these are the following:

1. Making various kinds of maps
2. Making models of villages, houses, castles, bridges, boats, stagecoaches, covered wagons, farms, airplanes, and oil fields
3. Making a frieze
4. Making a mountain scene
5. Making a bird house and houses for animals
6. Constructing furniture, weaving rugs, and making pottery
7. Dressing dolls
8. Making a zoo
9. Making a collection of minerals, stamps, shells, rocks, clothing materials, forest products, and food products
10. Making a museum
11. Collecting pictures and various materials
12. Making booklets
13. Constructing posters and drawing cartoons, charts, graphs, and pictures
14. Managing a bulletin board
15. Dramatizing certain events
16. Giving an assembly program
17. Managing a class newspaper
18. Writing plays, poems, stories, and songs
19. Planning and conducting a fair
20. Making a survey of the community and taking field trips
21. Managing a school election
22. Running a "safety first" or a "clean-up week" campaign
23. Making various scenes on the sand table
24. Making puppets
25. Carving objects out of soap
26. Interviewing people
27. Making butter, bread, and candy
28. Making moving pictures and lantern slides
29. Giving a party or tea to parents and friends
30. Raising silkworms, plants, and animals

WORK OF THE TEACHER

The four chief steps in the development of an activity are (1) selecting the activity, (2) planning the activity, (3) working to complete the activity, and (4) judging the results.

The teacher plays an important part in activity work. He should aid the pupils in selecting the right activities. When he suggests activities for the pupils to study, he should make sure that they become interested in those they actually take. The pupils often think of worthwhile activities with very little or no aid from the teacher. If pupils are really interested in their work and if each one is working according to his ability, the teacher does not need to worry about what activities the pupils may take. They will suggest many more activities than they have time to do.

After the pupils begin work on their activities, they need aid in deciding what to do. They must do as much of the planning as possible. A discussion may be held where various pupils give their ideas. The teacher becomes one of the group and he gives his ideas and suggestions when they are needed. The experienced teacher can lead his pupils to think of many things which they might otherwise omit. By skilfully questioning the pupils and by giving needful explanations, the teacher is a great help to any class of pupils. For example, in many schools the pupils put on assembly programs. In place of the teacher suggesting the program and planning it for the pupils, he calls them together and lets them decide what they want to do. Under his direction, the pupils plan the nature of the program and what it will include.

Individual pupils often work out their own activities. Before starting to work on an activity, the student generally discusses his plans with the teacher. The teacher is often able to suggest ways in which the pupil may improve his plans. When the pupil reaches a place in his activity where he needs help, the teacher should be on hand to give it.

After the pupils have planned what they are going to do, they start to work on their activities. The teacher supervises the work and gives help and suggestions where they are needed. He sees that each proceeds along the right lines and does not waste time.

The last step in activity work is judging the completed work.

Each pupil examines his work carefully to determine whether he has left out anything or whether he can add any improvements. After this, he is ready to present his work to his classmates and to the teacher. The teacher should be careful to judge the work in such a way that the pupil will be benefited by his remarks and at the same time be encouraged. The right kind of encouragement goes a long way in getting a person to do good work.

ADVANTAGES AND DISADVANTAGES OF THE ACTIVITY METHOD

The activity, or project method has about the same advantages as were given for the problem method. Activities are definite and pupils can see the progress they are making and can tell when they have completed their work. Pupils learn to depend upon themselves and to think. It develops the creative ability of children, and gives them training in working out problems and in making something that other people may see. Initiative and responsibility are developed.

Since projects should be completed, pupils learn to persevere, to respect the opinions of others, to be open-minded, and to be satisfied with only the best which they can do. They learn to cooperate with one another.

In doing activity work, pupils should not be permitted to waste time. If the teacher has too little control over the pupils, the work will tend to become aimless and haphazard. The activities should be worthwhile and the pupils should be interested in working on them. Just to do any activity for the sake of keeping busy should never be allowed. All activity work should be related to the objectives of the unit being studied. Neither should activity work be done by the pupils chiefly for display work. Pupils should learn while working on a project. They should not be working on something that is neither too easy nor too difficult for them. They should have a well-thought-out plan. All activities which are undertaken by pupils should be completed or completed as nearly as possible. Otherwise, poor habits of work will probably result. It should always be kept in mind that the activities should be carried out by the pupils and not by the teacher.

The activity program requires a resourceful and highly skilled teacher in every room. Many teachers do not meet these requirements. Hence, they fail to carry out successfully the activity program. The teacher must always make sure that the activity is a means to an end and not the end itself.

PROBLEMS FOR DISCUSSION AND RESEARCH

1. What is your idea of a problem in the social studies? Give several good problems.
2. Show how problems cause a pupil to think.
3. Discuss the different ways of stating a problem. Illustrate each way by stating a problem.
4. List the essentials of a good problem.
5. Give the steps in problem solving and discuss each step.
6. Give the advantages and disadvantages of the problem method.
7. When may a question be called a problem?
8. What is a project? Show how the term "project" gradually came to be used.
9. What is meant by the activity method? Make a list of some activities which you think are practical.
10. What is the function of the teacher in a room where the activity method is used?
11. What are some of the advantages and disadvantages of the activity method?
12. Visit a number of schools or talk to children who go to school. Do the children make use of the activity method? Make a list of the activities which the children say they are doing or have recently done.

REFERENCES

Base, Ruth, "Making History Meaningful," The Chicago Schools Journal, XIX, 123-127, January-February, 1938.

Bining, Arthur and Bining, David, Teaching the Social Studies in the Secondary Schools. New York: McGraw-Hill Book Co., 1941.

Chapter V. The Project and Problem Methods, 88-109.

Chapter XVI. Special Activities, 296-312.

Bozarth, Ruth, "Map Making in the Snow," The Journal of Geography, XXXIX, 325-326, November, 1940.

Branom, M. E., Branom, F. K., The Teaching of Geography. Boston: Ginn and Co., 1921.

Part V. The Project, or Active, Method, 165-265.

Branom, Mendel, *A Teacher's Geography*. New York: The Macmillan Co., 1926.

Burrow, Sarah and Seeds, Corinne, Teaching Social Studies in the Primary Grades: Community Living Through an Ongoing Interest in Airplanes, *Twelfth Yearbook of the National Council for the Social Studies,* 1941, 157-171.

Cox, Howard, "A Group of Maladjusted Boys Within a Regular Junior High School Program," Social Education, IV, 408-413, October, 1940.

Crawford, Claude and McDonald, Lois, *Modern Methods in Teaching Geography*. Boston: Houghton Mifflin Co., 1929.
Chapters X and XI.

Crewson, Walter, "Suggestions for Teaching a Phase of the Banana Industry of Central America," The Journal of Geography, XXXVII, 164-167, April, 1938.

Fairbanks, Grace and Heyl, Helen, Teaching Social Studies in the Primary Grades: Activities Developing Economic Understandings, *Twelfth Yearbook of the National Council for the Social Studies,* 1941, 172-189.

Fishback, Erma, "Building Citizenship," The Grade Teacher, LVIII, 64, January, 1941.

Fowler, Burton, Buckles, Cecile, and Perdew, R., The Activities Program in Its Relation to the Social Studies, *Sixth Yearbook, National Council for the Social Studies,* 1936, 158-170.

Galford, Mary, "Activities in Geography Classwork," The Journal of Geography, XL, 64-66, February, 1941.

Gluck, Harold, "Toyland and Geography," The Journal of Geography, XL, 24-29, January, 1941.

Harlan, Elaine, "An Old World Museum Activity Unit," The Journal of Geography, XXXVIII, 19-25, January, 1939.

Hodgkins, George, *A Guide to the Newer Methods in Teaching the Social Studies*. Washington: National Council for the Social Studies, 1936.
Projects and Activities, 46-51.
The Problem Method, 53-57.

Jackson, Anna, "A School Community Project in Historic Georgetown," Social Education, IV, 417-419, October, 1940.

James, Linnie, "Junior High School Geography," The Journal of Geography, XXXVII, 269-274, October, 1938.

Judd, Romie, "The Activity Unit," The Grade Teacher, LVIII, 62, January, 1941.

Kay, Sylvia, "We Learn to Live Together," The Chicago Schools Journal, XXIII, 17-19, September-October, 1941.

Kesselman, William, "An Effective Problem Method," The Journal of Geography, XXXVI, 369-373, December, 1937.

Koehring, Dorothy, "Social Studies in the Nursery School and Kindergarten," Childhood Education, XVII, 181-182, December, 1940.

Lane, Robert, "The Activity Program and Its Teaching Methods," Education, LVII, 322-324, February, 1937.

Lathrope, Frances, "Class Discussion of a Problem," The Journal of Geography, XXXIX, 165-168, April, 1940.

Loftus, John, "The Activity Program as a Means of Vitalizing the Teaching of Geography," The Journal of Geography, XXXIV, 349-356, December, 1935.

Mallory, Clara, "A Trip Around the World, A Project," The Journal of Geography, XXVI, 74-76, February, 1927.

Marsh, Mary, "An Indian Project," The Grade Teacher, LIX, 32-33, 77, October, 1941.

Mason, Carol and Rutz, Winifred, "A Hopi Indian Project," The Journal of Geography, XXXVIII, 75-81, February, 1939.

Mason, Marcella, "Group Activity in the Elementary School," Social Education, 635-637, December, 1939.

McDade, James, "Why the Activity School?" The Chicago Schools Journal, XVI, 10-12, September, 1934-February, 1935.

Miller, George, editor, Activities in Geography. Bloomington: McKnight and McKnight, 1937.

Morse, R. E., "A Problem Lesson in United States History for the Seventh Grade," The Social Studies, XXVIII, 62-65, February, 1937.

Newkirk, Louis, Integrated Handwork for Elementary Schools. New York: Silver Burdett Co., 1940.

——, "Hand-Work Related to an Activity Program," The Chicago Schools Journal, XVI, 12-18, September, 1934-February, 1935.

Novak, Pauline, "A Colonial Kitchen," The Instructor, LI, 34-35, November, 1941.

Oberle, Frieda and Bader, Edith, Teaching Social Studies in the Intermediate Grades: A Unit on Boats, Twelfth Yearbook of the National Council for the Social Studies, 1941, 190-199.

Parrott, Hazel, "The Greeks—the Enlighteners," Social Education, I, 109-113, February, 1937.

Rhyne, Conway, "A Flexible American Problems Course," Social Education, V, 273-277, April, 1941.

Ross, Frances and Mohme, Wilhelmine, "A Third Grade Operates a Real Store," The Journal of the National Education Association, XXIX, 49-50, February, 1940.

Rothwell, Ethel, "How the Curriculum Grows: The Study of Cocoa, An Example," The Journal of Geography, XXXVII, 15-19, January, 1938.

Rothwell, Ethel, "How a Study of Cocoa Led to a Study of Other Foods," The Journal of Geography, XXXVII, 91-97, March, 1938.

Schwarz, Emma, "Living as Pioneers," The Journal of the National Education Association, XXVIII, 36-37, February, 1939.

Schwarz, John, *Social Study in the Elementary School*. New York: Prentice-Hall, 1938. Chapter IX.

Smith, Donnal, "Nature of Social Problem Study," Social Education, II, 471-477, October, 1938.

Starrak, James, "The Problem Technique," Education, LVII, 335-341, February, 1937.

Thrasher, Arienne, "Our Japanese Project," American Childhood, XXII, 5-7, 52, April, 1937.

Todd, Jessie, "Pilgrims," The Instructor, LI, 38-39, 78, November, 1941.

Vogt, Mary, "Stamps: The Hobby of Kids and Kings," The Journal of Geography, XL, 234-236, September, 1941.

Wagner, Ruth, "Purifying Water: A Second Grade Project," Social Education, 45-47, January, 1941.

Weltzin, Edith, "The Grocery Store, an Integrated Activity for the First Grade," The Chicago Schools Journal, XXI, 78-80, November, 1939.

Wesley, Edgar, *Teaching the Social Studies*. New York: D. C. Heath and Co., 1937.

Chapter XXX. Problems and Projects, 529-540.

Willcuts, Virginia, "Uses of Rivers to Man," The Journal of Geography, XXXV, 367-368, December, 1936.

Chapter Fourteen: QUESTIONS AND ANSWERS,

THE OUTLINE, THE COMPARISON

METHOD, AND THE TYPE STUDY

1. QUESTIONS AND ANSWERS

IMPORTANCE

THE QUESTION and answer method is used to a greater or less extent in every school. During the past one hundred years, some form of the question and answer recitation has been the most important method of teaching in our schools. A few years ago, it was estimated by some authorities that more than two-thirds of the school time was given over to questions and answers. Although so much time may not now be given over to questions and answers, yet it is safe to say that the question and answer method is still the most prevalent method of teaching in the vast majority of schools.

Probably no method has been more condemned than the question and answer method, yet it is still in use and it will undoubtedly be in use for years to come. Questions are a part of any good method. It is impossible to use any approved method of teaching without some questions. Hence, we will always have questions and answers in our schools. They may be condemned, misused, abused, or overworked, yet they will always have a leading part in any good school program.

Children learn by asking questions. Any normal child is always asking questions concerning things which interest him, and his interests wander from one thing to another. It is only natural for the teacher to ask questions of the pupils since he is using a method which is already familiar to the children. The right use of questions and answers brings the teacher and pupils into closer contact with one another, because they seem to have a common interest in the same problems. Through questions, the skilful teacher can lead his pupils to solve successfully many of their problems which at first may seem difficult.

Some teachers never become skilled in asking questions. Questioning involves quick thinking on the part of the teacher. A slow-thinking teacher will probably never be able to use the question and answer method very successfully. Questions should lead the pupils to think and they should aid them in doing their work. A poor teacher generally asks questions which involve chiefly memory work and little thinking. A superior teacher asks questions which involve much thinking and little memory work, except as it is needed in thinking out a problem.

WHY DO TEACHERS USE QUESTIONS?

One of the uses of questions is for testing. Many pupils believe that the chief reason why teachers give tests is to determine what marks to give them. There is a good basis for this belief, since some teachers pay too much attention to marks and not enough attention to the other important aspects of teaching. Tests do help the teacher evaluate the work of the pupils, but this is only one of the reasons for giving them.

Sometimes the teacher gives a short test to learn if the pupils have the assignment and if they clearly understand what they are studying. From time to time, the teacher gives questions to the pupils to see what headway they are making. Questions help the teacher determine if his methods of presentation are satisfactory. They help to clear up any misunderstanding that the pupils have. They are a great help in showing the pupils how much they know about certain topics.

Questions are very useful in carrying on drill or in reviewing the work. They aid the pupils in recalling what they know or what they have learned. Teachers employ questions in developing a unit or a problem. They enable a teacher to develop a topic in its natural order and to stress any part of a problem. They stimulate pupils to think and they help to hold their attention on the problem being studied. They are useful in motivation. Lazy and indolent pupils often need questions to keep them at work by supplying certain definite incentives. Both written and oral work are often based upon questions.

WHAT ARE GOOD QUESTIONS?

All questions should be adapted to the ability of the pupils for whom they are intended. They should be neither too easy nor too difficult. They should be clear and their meaning easily understood. Generally, only one idea should be brought out in a question. Long questions should usually be avoided. The meaning of the words used in questions should be known to the pupils.

The teacher should study what objectives he has in mind before giving questions to the pupils. After thinking of a question, it is sometimes a good plan for the teacher to answer it himself before giving it to the pupils. Then he will be sure that the question implies what he thinks it does. A good question does not suggest its answer. Neither should questions be asked which require pupils to memorize the words of the book.

Questions should be definite enough so that their answers will be meaningful. For example, the following questions are very indefinite: "What do you know about the Eskimos?" "Why is Chicago a great city?"

Some questions appeal chiefly to the memory and are called memory questions. An example of a memory question is "What is the capital of Pennsylvania?" Other questions require considerable thought in answering them and are called thought questions. An example of a thought question is "How did the location of Spain and Portugal favor these countries in the search for a new route to the East?" To some pupils a question may be a memory question, while to other pupils it may be a thought question. It depends upon how much thinking is needed in answering it.

WHAT PART DOES THE TEACHER
PLAY IN QUESTIONING?

The teacher should keep in mind many things when he uses the question and answer method. He should state the question in a clear voice loud enough to be heard by all. He should not form the habit of repeating questions for the sake of those pupils who fail to hear on account of inattention.

Questions should be stated in language which pupils understand. There are some questions which may be answered by one word. Other questions require more lengthy explanations. Pupils should form the habit of giving complete answers. They should be given ample time to answer a question. Some teachers fire questions at the pupils in so rapid an order that they do not have time to think. Such questions may be called "machine gun" questions. Some teachers seem to think that good teaching demands the asking of many questions. This is not true. Good teaching requires no definite number of questions.

Pupils should learn to raise questions as well as to answer them. They will form bad habits of study if the teacher requires them to answer too many questions. Some pupils rely so much upon questions asked by the teacher that they are at a loss in expressing themselves when placed upon their own initiative. Hence, questioning requires more skill and thought than most teachers realize, because an important aim of education is to train boys and girls to rely upon themselves.

There is no regular order which teachers generally use in calling upon pupils to answer questions. If a certain order is used, a pupil is likely not to pay much attention until his time comes to answer a question. Sometimes it is a good plan to call upon the same pupil a number of times during the class period. However, no pupil should be slighted and all of the class should have the opportunity of answering questions. It is a good plan to give the question before a pupil is called upon to answer it. This will tend to make the pupils more attentive.

A teacher should be careful not to give any clue to the answer of a question by nodding his head or in some other way. If a pupil answers incorrectly, some member of the class should usually be called upon to give the correct answer. Indefinite questions, catch questions, and poorly worded questions should be avoided.

Much time is often wasted in those rooms where the teachers rely chiefly upon the question and answer method of holding the daily recitations. Pupils sit patiently, but often lifelessly, and listen to their classmates answer various questions which are based upon the work which everyone is supposed to have studied. Usually most of the pupils can answer the questions. It is a needless waste of time for pupils to be required to sit and listen to their classmates answer questions to which they already know the answers. There are too many recitations in which the majority of pupils receive no help or inspiration. The teacher should try to find some way of making the recitations profitable to every pupil. In many cases, the teacher should give extra help to the slow pupils at some other time than during the recitation period. The time of the whole class should not be taken up with the drilling of only a few students who are unable to get their work.

2. THE OUTLINE

WHO SHOULD MAKE THE OUTLINE?

Outlines are frequently used by pupils in studying their lessons. An outline is a systematic arrangement of topics or problems. Generally, it is unwise for the teacher to give an outline to the pupils and tell them to follow it in studying a given unit. The pupils are likely to have little interest in such an outline. They follow it just because they are told to do so.

When an outline is used by the pupils, they should usually have a leading part in making it. They then feel as if it is their outline and they take a more active interest in following it. They have a reason for using it because they made it with the expectation that it would be useful in doing their work.

The teacher should help the pupils in making an outline, or at least he should be on hand to give them help whenever it is needed. A good plan that is followed by some teachers is to have the pupils make a list of the things they would like to know about the unit they are starting to study. The teacher first gets the pupils interested in studying the unit. Then they are asked what they would like to know about it. While carrying on the discussion about what they want to know, they recall their past experiences. They look at pictures and glance at the printed matter in their books. The teacher or a pupil writes the questions on the blackboard as they are given by the pupils. Later, the questions are arranged by the pupils in the order which they wish to study them. When the pupils actually begin to study their questions, many additional ones will be raised, because one question often calls up another one.

QUESTIONS ASKED BY CHILDREN

The pupils in a fourth grade became interested in studying about the Eskimos. They looked at a few pictures and briefly examined their textbooks with the aid of their teacher. Then under the direction of the teacher they made the following list of questions which they wished to study:

1. Where is Eskimoland?
2. What direction is Eskimoland from Chicago?
3. How would we go to get to Eskimoland?
4. What does Eskimoland look like?
5. What do the Eskimos look like?
6. In what kinds of houses do the Eskimos live?
7. How is a snow house built?
8. How is a tent built?
9. How do they keep the houses warm in winter?
10. What do the Eskimos wear to keep warm?
11. From what is the clothing made?
12. What do the Eskimos eat?
13. What animals are found in Eskimoland?
14. How do the Eskimos hunt the animals?
15. How do the Eskimos fish?
16. Why do the Eskimos have dogs?
17. What do the dogs eat?
18. Of what use is the reindeer?
19. How do the Eskimos travel?
20. What kinds of boats do the Eskimos have?
21. What kinds of furniture do the Eskimos have?
22. What work does an Eskimo do?
23. What games do the Eskimo children play?
24. Is it always cold in Eskimoland?
25. What other people live in the Far North?

The preceding list of questions might not be called an outline by most people, but nevertheless it is closely related to an outline. The topics in an outline should become questions or problems to the pupils when they begin to study them.

SOME USES OF OUTLINES

In the upper grades the pupils are often able to make an outline which may be used in studying. For example, let us suppose that the pupils are studying the regions of South America. After they have studied carefully one or more regions, they should be able to make an outline which could be used in studying the remaining regions. Such an outline might contain topics on (1) population, (2) location, (3) area, (4) surface, (5) soil, (6) climate, (7) resources, (8) occupations, (9) transportation, (10) animal life, (11) plant life, (12) trade, (13) relations to the United States, (14) advancement of the people, and (15) government. Of course the pupils will arrange the topics to suit themselves.

An outline is often made by the pupils when they want to summarize the work which they have been doing. The outline helps the pupils arrange the work systematically in their minds. It also aids in helping them see that all sides of the problem have been studied and no important facts have been omitted.

Outlines are very useful in reviews. There is probably no better way of reviewing the work that has been studied than by making an outline of it.

It is very helpful to use an outline when making a report to the class. The outline may be put on paper and given to each member of the class or it may be written on the blackboard. When the report is given, the topics in the outline are discussed. The pupils are able to follow the speaker more easily. The outline also aids the speaker in giving his report in a systematic order and it tends to keep him from forgetting some of the essential facts. An outline acts as a spur to the speaker because his fellow classmates expect him to discuss the points of the outline. It is up to him to make good.

DANGERS IN USING OUTLINES

There are certain dangers which should be avoided in using outlines. Some of the more important ones are the following:

1. Outlines should not be forced upon the pupils. Whenever outlines are used, pupils should see the need for them and want to use them.

2. In most cases, pupils should not be made to use outlines which they did not help to make. Pupils are likely to take little interest in outlines which are made by other people and given to them to use. The best outlines are those which are made by the pupils with the help of the teacher.

3. Pupils should not be forced or encouraged to outline everything which they study. The use of outlines should not be permitted to become monotonous. The teacher should have on hand various plans which may be used from time to time.

4. Pupils should understand that it is not always necessary to follow the order of the topics in an outline in their study of a problem or in class discussions. In making an outline, some order must be followed in putting down the topics. However, no two persons or groups of pupils are likely to follow exactly the same order. In a class discussion, the teacher and pupils will decide the order in which the topics are to be discussed. It may be that the last topic or the middle topic in an outline will be the first one to be discussed in class.

5. The pupils should not form the idea that an outline contains everything on the subject, and that nothing remains outside the outline to be studied. Neither must they get the idea that after they have studied the last topic in their outline, they have learned everything about the subject. Many things will be omitted which they will not have time to study.

6. Pupils should not use an outline in a mechanical way. The topics should become questions or problems to the pupils.

7. Topics should be studied in relation to one another. Pupils should not isolate one topic and study it by itself. All topics in an outline are related to one another.

8. Most outlines are brief and the pupils should be taught to read much meaning from them. Too many general statements should not be accepted. There is often a tendency for a pupil to discuss a topic very briefly and in general terms, unless he is checked by the teacher.

3. TEACHING THROUGH COMPARISON

VALUE OF COMPARISONS

We read meaning into anything by relating it to some past experience which we have had. We learn by relating the new to the old, by recalling past experiences, and by making comparisons in our own minds. The teacher should always be on the alert to see that the pupils are making the needed comparisons in studying their problems. The pupils should continually be raising such problems as: "How does this region resemble other regions?" "How does this region differ from other regions?" "How does this period in history resemble other periods in history?" "How does this period in history differ from other periods in history?" "How does the government of a given country differ from the government of some other country?"

Life is a complex affair. We are frequently making decisions and we are often called upon to defend these decisions. Why do we proceed along certain lines and not along other lines? Why do we have certain ideas about something and not other ideas? If our actions are determined by our thinking, it will be found that they are based upon the proper evaluation of certain factors which involves the comparison of many ideas and facts. One of the requirements of everyday living is that a person be able to collect facts, weigh them carefully and accurately, make certain comparisons, and come to the right conclusions. Hence, in the schoolroom, pupils should constantly be taught to make comparisons, no matter what method is being used.

Some lessons are especially good for making comparisons. This is especially true in the study of two regions, or two periods of history that have many resemblances. Sometimes the main comparisons may be made as a review. This is frequently a good way to have a review, providing the comparison method was not used in studying the unit.

Let us suppose that the pupils have just completed a study of two groups of islands such as the Hawaiian Islands and the Philippine Islands. In reviewing these two groups of islands, the pupils may compare them in respect to such factors as location, area, surface, climate, population, kind of people, history, government, farming, mining, power resources, manufacturing, fishing, lumbering, imports, imports from the United States, exports, and exports to the United States. When each factor is studied, a brief statement containing the chief points of resemblances and differences between the two groups of islands is given. After all factors have been studied carefully, the pupils review what they have learned. Then they make a brief summary for each group of islands.

DEBATES

The debate is a kind of comparison lesson. Most pupils in the upper grades and high school like to debate. They like to have the chance of proving what they think is right and to match their wits with one another. A debater is interested in proving his point and he endeavors to persuade his audience to accept his views. He tries to overcome the statements made by his opponents with statements of his own. Pupils learn to evaluate material by debating and listening to debates.

The subject for a debate should be selected very carefully. Just any topic should not be taken. Only those topics should be chosen which are simple enough for the pupils to understand, and on which thoughtful people actually differ. A question which may be easily answered by examining a textbook or some reference book should not be debated. Neither should a subject be debated upon which there is general agreement.

The main reasons for having a debate in the social studies are to teach the pupils (1) to search for material in the solving of problems, (2) to form good habits of study, (3) to weigh the opinions of others, and (4) to come to their own conclusions after careful reflection and thinking. A pupil should not be permitted to say just anything that comes to his mind. He should not make untrue statements in order to win a debate. When a student makes untrue statements, the teacher should ask him to cite his references for such statements. If he cannot play the game fairly, he should not be allowed to participate in the debate. Occasionally, cases occur where the debaters on a certain side change their minds and agree with those on the other side after studying the problem. When this happens, there is no longer any need for a debate.

It is not always necessary for the class to come to a definite decision on every question that is debated. Sometimes the class votes on the question after listening to the debate. At other times, each member of the class draws his own conclusion without voting on the issue. The members of the class should learn how to evaluate data as they listen to the debaters.

4. THE TYPE STUDY

The type study is especially valuable in teaching geography. It is a detailed study of a region, an industry, or some topic which is representative of a number of regions, industries, or topics. For example, lumbering is carried on in a number of places in the United States. In place of teaching lumbering a number of times, this industry is only taught once in detail in studying some region. When lumbering is encountered again in another region, it is only briefly discussed. The children recall the chief points they have learned about lumbering and add any new material. A study of coal mining in western Pennsylvania is representative of coal mining in most other parts of the country.

The type study saves time. It enables the pupils to go more into detail into the study of certain problems. This abundance of detail makes the work more interesting. It helps the pupils to learn essential facts and it avoids much needless repetition.

SOME PROBLEMS FOR DISCUSSION AND RESEARCH

1. Is it possible to teach without questions being asked by someone?
2. Discuss the statement that questioning is the normal way of teaching.
3. Give examples of good questions and tell why they are good.
4. Give examples of poor questions and tell why they are poor.
5. How does unwise questioning waste the time of the pupils during a class discussion?
6. List the essentials of a good question.
7. Discuss the use of an outline by pupils studying the social studies.
8. Who should make the outline which pupils use in studying a unit?
9. List the advantages and the disadvantages of the outline method.
10. Why should comparisons be made continually by pupils?
11. Suppose the pupils are studying the South American countries of Paraguay and Uruguay and are using the comparison method. Make a list of the points which may be compared.
12. Why are debates valuable in the social studies?

13. What are some of the problems a teacher should consider when his class gives a debate?

14. Make a list of questions which may be debated with profit by pupils in the social studies.

15. Discuss the use of the type study in teaching the social studies.

REFERENCES

A Teaching Guide for the Social Studies by the Association of Social Studies Teachers of New York City, 1941, 11-16, 40.

Coulter, Kenneth, "The Question Method in Teaching History," The Social Studies, XXXI, 75-76, February, 1940.

Horn, Ernest, *Methods of Instruction in the Social Studies*. New York: Charles Scribner's Sons, 1937.
   Chapter VIII. Oral Instruction, 300-358.

Mears, Louise, "Teaching Geography Through Comparison: The Philippine Islands and the Hawaiian Islands," The Journal of Geography, XXXVII, 173-179, May, 1938.

Wesley, Edgar, *Teaching the Social Studies*. New York: D. C. Heath and Co., 1937.
   Chapter XXV. Questions and Answers, 482-490.

Chapter Fifteen: THE IMAGINARY JOURNEY,

DRAMATIZATION, AND THE STORY

1. THE IMAGINARY JOURNEY

VITALIZING GEOGRAPHY

DURING RECENT years, teachers have come to realize that much time and thought should be spent in making the work of their pupils more vital and interesting. One way of doing this is to take real journeys to some of the places about which they are studying. Real journeys are very valuable, but it is impossible to visit many places outside the community. The expense, being away over night, the problem of caring for the children, and many other factors make long journeys impractical for most schools. Hence, children must get much of their knowledge in some other way than by actual travel.

Children like to travel and to see things for themselves. Trains, automobiles, airplanes, and ships make it possible for people to travel from place to place with little inconvenience. Almost every child has traveled some distance from home. We are living in a traveling age. It is only natural for children to enjoy traveling and visiting places and to be curious about the world in which they live.

In place of taking real trips, a class may take imaginary trips. Under the guide of a skilful and enthusiastic teacher, children often like to study some of their geography by taking imaginary journeys. The world is made more real to them and they build up clear and vivid concepts of places and people. They come to see that they live in the world and not merely in a spot which is called a village, a town, or a city. The imaginary journey is best adapted for the lower grades, although it may be used in any grade. It is only one way of teaching and its use should not be overdone.

PLACES TO WHICH JOURNEYS MAY BE TAKEN

Pupils may take imaginary journeys to almost any region about which they study. In the lower grades journey geography is especially effective in teaching about those distant lands which are very different from ours. Children often take imaginary journeys to the Northland, the Hawaiian Islands, the Congo Region, the Amazon Region, the Sahara, the Alps, and other places. As they travel over these regions in their imagination, they see how other people live in different kinds of environment. In studying these regions, pupils cannot help but learn how such natural factors as location, climate, surface, soil, plant life, and animal life, influence the development of the people. One such region generally offers great contrasts to all the other regions, yet the children see that the people in each region have the same general problem of making a living. Each region that the children visit is usually typical or representative of a number of regions located elsewhere on the earth. They gradually accumulate information which may be used in understanding the geography of any region about which they may study.

Imaginary journeys may be taken by land, water, or air. Some children like to imagine that they are in an automobile traveling over one of our great highways. Other children prefer to ride by airplane, boat, or streamlined train. In some places, they may even imagine they are traveling on foot or on the backs of animals. Some imaginary journeys may be taken and completed during a class period. Others may occupy several days. Whether the imaginary journey is long or short, the pupils must be sure to get the fundamentals of the unit being studied and not pay too much attention to the minor incidents of travel.

WHAT TO LEARN ABOUT A REGION

It is a wise idea to discuss with the pupils what they expect to learn on their imaginary journey. Some such list of questions may be made for the fifth or sixth grade:

1. What kind of country are we studying? Is it mountainous,

hilly, rolling, or nearly level? Are there many streams? Is traveling easy in the region?

2. What kind of climate does the region have? Does the region have much or little precipitation? Is there enough precipitation for crops? Describe the temperature in summer and in winter. Is the growing season long enough for crops?

3. Does the region have many people? In what kind of houses do the people live? Are there many cities? Is it easy to reach the cities? What are some of the occupations of the people?

4. Is the region good for farming? What crops are grown? What is done with the crops? What farm animals are raised and of how much importance are they?

5. Try to learn some interesting facts about farming.

6. Is the region forested? If so, how important is lumbering? What are some forest products? Is there anything worth noting concerning the vegetation?

7. What minerals are mined? What is done with the minerals? Describe mining.

8. Describe fishing if it is of much importance.

9. What wild animals live in the region? Describe hunting if it is of importance.

10. Does manufacturing seem to be of much importance? If so, try to learn a few interesting facts about manufacturing.

11. What other interesting facts can we learn about the country?

STEPS IN THE JOURNEY METHOD

The imaginary journey should be made as much as possible to resemble a real journey. The pupils should first discuss with the teacher any trips which they have taken. They bring out that people prepare for a journey before starting on it, and that they must care for certain details while on the trip. The pupils apply the points which they develop to the imaginary trip which they are going to take. Some of the steps in the imaginary journey method are the following:

1. The place to be visited should be located definitely on the map by the pupils. The direction of the place from the school and the approximate distance should be given. The teacher and pupils must realize that although the journey to the place is imaginary, the place is not imaginary. They should think of it

as a real place where people actually live and work and to which people travel during the year. If the journey is to be a trip along a highway or over a river, the highway or river should be definitely located and some of the cities along or near the route should be pointed out.

2. The pupils should determine how they are to get to the place. They consult maps in their books, road maps, railroad folders, steamship folders, airplane folders, and travelers. They decide what methods of transportation to use and give reasons for their choice. For example, if the pupils are going to the Amazon Region of South America, they might decide to go by bus, train, or airplane to New York City or to some other seaport. Then they would take a steamship or airplane to Belem (Pará), near the mouth of the Amazon River. They also try to estimate the cost of such a trip.

3. The pupils determine what clothing to take along. They look at their maps and books to learn if the region is hot, moderately warm, or cold and whether much or little precipitation falls. Since cleanliness is always taught, the pupils decide to take along with them such toilet articles as soap, tooth brushes, and combs. Another problem is how much money to carry with them. Since a person may lose his money, the pupils will likely decide not to take very much cash with them. They learn about travelers' checks and other ways of getting money when they need it on a trip. Another important article is a camera. People like to take pictures when on a journey.

4. After making careful preparations, the pupils are ready to start on their journey. In traveling from their home city to the place which they are going to visit, they describe what they see on the route. They tell about the surface of the land, the kinds of transportation which the people are using, the types of houses they pass, and the work of the people. They trace on a map their route and frequently give the direction they are traveling.

5. When the pupils arrive in the region which they have selected to study, the main part of their work begins. They read books and other references, study pictures, and gather information in various other ways. They do numerous kinds of activities such as writing letters to friends back home, keeping diaries, drawing pictures, making booklets, constructing scenes, and preparing maps.

SOME DANGERS

Skilful teachers report good results in using the imaginary journey, while unskilful teachers generally have poor results. The latter group of teachers are unable to avoid some of the dangers or difficulties involved in this method.

Some teachers let the pupils spend too much time in preparing for the journey and in studying minor facts. Unless carefully guided, the pupils are likely to waste much time and to form poor habits of study. They are likely to select unimportant topics for study and to neglect the larger and more important details. Hence, they are likely to obtain a superficial knowledge of the region. If poorly taught, the pupils will not learn how to solve problems. They will form conclusions on insufficient data. Like all other methods, the journey method should not be used continuously by a teacher. It should be abandoned when the interest lags. If the pupils fail to get interested in studying a unit through the imaginary journey, this method should not be used.

2. DRAMATIZATION

THE DESIRE TO DRAMATIZE

The dramatic instinct plays an important part in our lives. From earliest times to the present, people have employed dramatization for mere enjoyment or to bring about certain objectives. Almost every child enjoys acting. In order to test the truth of this statement, all a person needs to do is to watch children at play. Small children like to play going to school, running a store, and keeping house. Even large children are not together long before some of them make use of the dramatic instinct in putting across different ideas. Of course, the chilren do not think of what they are doing as dramatization. They are merely having a good time and only acting naturally. All of us have a touch of the dramatic instinct, but it is much more strongly developed in some than in others. The teacher should make use of this instinct by using it in the teaching of the social studies.

IMPORTANCE

Dramatization vitalizes the work and makes it much more interesting to the pupils. Sometimes dramatization is the spark that is needed to put life and interest in what the pupils are doing. A slow, backward pupil may become very much awake and excited when he is given the opportunity to portray the life of some noted man or to take part in dramatizing some scene. He begins to feel as if he is an important person after all and it is up to him to prove to his fellow-pupils that he can do his share of the work. The confidence which a pupil gains by dramatization may be the means of overcoming his backwardness in his schoolwork and in meeting other children.

There are usually some pupils in a class who have tendencies to put themselves forward too much. They always want to be leaders or to be near the front in every movement. Dramatization helps to keep such pupils in their right places, because each pupil must work with all the others in making the lesson a success. Each pupil taking part has an opportunity of displaying his talent to his fellow-pupils. Pupils learn to cooperate with one another and they come to see that team work is very important. Group work is developed and the social relations of the entire class are improved.

Dramatization aids a pupil in developing his creative ability. He has to face a practical situation and it is left to him to meet it satisfactorily. Oftentimes he must decide what to do without help from anyone. He realizes that the responsibility of putting across his part of the act rests upon himself. He will do his best to do his part well. Creative ability is also developed by allowing the children to determine what scenery to use and what costumes to wear. Very often, they just imagine that they have certain scenery or are wearing certain costumes. With a little encouragement, children are able to think of various ways of meeting almost any situation.

Pupils often write their own plays. In such cases, they have the opportunity of deciding just what they will do. They are given practice in expressing their thoughts in writing so that they can be easily understood by others. They learn to express themselves accurately and clearly.

When the pupils practice dramatization, they receive training in oral expression. They learn to speak clearly and distinctly and in a voice loud enough to be heard. It is a sad but a true fact, that many children go through our schools without being taught how to speak fluently and distinctly.

MATERIALS FOR DRAMATIZATION

The social studies offer a fine opportunity for dramatization, since there is much material which may be dramatized by the pupils. History, civics, and geography are especially rich in such materials. Current events frequently furnish material for dramatization. In studying geography, pupils often dramatize scenes from foreign countries. They may also dramatize scenes from industry and commerce. Music, dances, and songs are often used in dramatization. Phases of colonial life, the making of the Constitution of the United States, the settling of the West, and the gold rush to California are a few scenes from history that have been dramatized. Sometimes the dramatization of history scenes is centered around famous men, such as Washington and Lincoln. Managing an election and holding a meeting of the city council are frequently dramatized in civics.

Not all material in the social studies is appropriate for dramatization. Neither will the pupils have the time nor the desire to dramatize all suitable materials. The teacher should try to prevent the pupils from dramatizing anything that is beyond their understanding. If the pupils do not become a part of the scene and feel that they are experiencing what is being dramatized, it is a very good sign that the material is unsuitable for dramatization or that the teacher is failing to present it satisfactorily.

PREPARING THE MATERIAL

There are various ways of preparing material for dramatization. Some of the more common ways follow:

1. Sometimes the children dramatize what they have been studying without going to very much trouble. They agree among themselves on what characters to have, who will represent the characters, and the number of scenes. They do not write a play, but each actor says what comes to his mind when it is his turn to take part. The play is put on with no elaborate preparations or stage properties. A chair may become a steamboat or a number of chairs in a row may be a train. A paper hat may be all that is needed to transform a pupil into an actor. The children use their imagination and make use of the things they have in

the room. Many of the scenes which small children act often take only a few minutes. Probably the children have been discussing how the Eskimo hunts. Two or three children may imagine themselves to be Eskimo hunters and put on a little act of their own. Sometimes the teacher tells or reads a story to the class, after which certain members act out the story.

One topic which should be stressed in all grades is safety. Thousands of our people are killed or injured every year by accidents which would never have happened if everyone had been careful. One of the most effective ways of getting the children to understand the importance of safety is to have them dramatize certain scenes in which safety is stressed.

Recently, a class in the second grade was visited in which the children were studying safety. Two north and south streets and two east and west streets were marked on the floor. One of the pupils represented a policeman. He had a star on his coat and stood at the intersection of two of the streets. Two other children represented patrol boys and they guarded two of the other three intersections of the street. One intersection was left unguarded. Two children had brought their small automobiles to school which were operated by foot power. A few of the children had roller skates.

The children walked or skated on the walks. The two children in their automobiles rode on the streets. The policeman and the patrol boys directed traffic. The policeman had a stop and go sign on which were a large circle colored red, a large circle colored orange, and a large circle colored green. The circles represented lights, and they could be covered so that all of them would not show at the same time. The children had much fun in learning how to use the streets safely. They were taught to watch the lights and to cross the streets safely. They were taught to cross only when the green light was showing. They learned to obey the patrol boys and not to cross the streets except at the intersections. They also learned to stop and look all ways before crossing a street.

Children in the lower grades enjoy acting. They play certain parts in a scene with no thought of costumes or scenery, except what they have on hand. Older children are more self-conscious and are likely to want costumes and more realistic scenery than just what they happen to have in the classroom.

2. The pupils decide to write a play based upon the work which they have been studying. They determine the number of scenes and characters. If the class is small, all the pupils may have a part in writing the play. During class time, they come together and discuss what should go into the play. One member suggests certain statements, other members propose other statements. The class decides what statements to use. The teacher or some member of the class writes the lines as they are developed.

If the class is large, it may decide to appoint a committee to write the play. After it is written, it is placed before the entire class for approval. Certain changes may be made by the class. After the play is accepted, the class determines what pupils will take part in it.

When the pupils write their own play, they have an opportunity of developing their creative ability and of expressing themselves. They are likely to take a more active interest in it because it was written by them. Again, topics which are not clear to certain pupils before writing the play are likely to become clear as the pupils discuss what they write. In most cases, it is advisable for pupils to write their own plays, even though they are somewhat crudely written. Teachers should always remember that the pupils are the ones who should have the experience of doing activities in school.

3. The teacher may write a play and give it to the pupils to act. The theory is that he should be able to write a very good play since he knows the chief facts which the pupils should learn. For reasons which have already been given, it is usually better for the play to be written by the pupils under the direction of the teacher.

4. A class may find a good play which has been written by pupils in another school. Short plays are frequently published in certain educational magazines. Just what use should a teacher permit his pupils to make of such plays? If the main purpose of the teacher is to put on a good performance and to give the children training in dramatics, it does not matter from what source the play is obtained, providing it is a good one. However, the teacher of the social studies has much more in mind than mere training in dramatics. He is teaching his pupils to solve problems, to get information, and to form certain ideals, habits, skills, and attitudes. Such training can best be brought about by

having the pupils do various kinds of activity work. If they need a play, they may write it in place of depending upon some outside source. Pupils learn by doing. This does not mean that pupils should not get ideas from plays written by others, but it does mean that they should not let others do for them what they can and should do for themselves.

There are times when it may be desirable for a class to use a play which was not written by its members. Suppose a class is invited to take part in a program which does not include any of the work which the pupils have been studying. There may not be time for the pupils to study the topic and to write a play, so they have to select one already written. If the play is a good one, the audience will receive some benefit from it.

Again, the teacher and pupils may not wish to take the time to write a play on the work they have been doing, since they have more valuable work to do. They may find a suitable play which will help them review their work and will give them a better understanding of what they have been doing.

THE AUDIENCE

When dramatization is employed, it should be usually a part of the regular school work, and the spectators are members of the class. Looking at dramatization in this light, it can be easily seen that it is only another method of teaching the social studies. Sometimes it is a good plan for the class to invite the pupils of a neighboring room or of the entire school to see them dramatize what they have been studying. Occasionally, the class may go farther and invite their parents. This is one way of getting the parents to take more interest in the school.

ASSEMBLY PROGRAMS

In some schools it is customary for the assembly programs to be in charge of the pupils. The work in the social studies offers splendid opportunities for assembly programs. It is not difficult for a class to get material for an assembly program from the social studies. Quite frequently, the pupils are able to dramatize the work which they have studied. Current events are often the basis of a good program.

If an assembly program is going to be in charge of a class, the teacher and the pupils should be notified far enough in advance so that they will have plenty of time to plan a good program. As much of the responsibility as possible is given to the pupils. After much careful planning with the teacher, they decide the nature of the program and what each one will do in it. Possibly, committees will be appointed to look after certain parts of the program. The pupils should feel that it is going to be their program and that the whole school is expecting them to do their best. An assembly program is very good for teaching social living.

In some schools, the commencement program is in charge of the pupils. Some of the work of the year may be dramatized. Pupils are sometimes invited to furnish programs for meetings held by their parents and teachers. Much of the material for such programs is commonly taken from the social studies.

DANGERS TO AVOID

Some teachers permit the pupils to spend too much time on dramatization, and not enough time upon the solving of worthwhile problems. Such teachers forget that their main purpose is to teach the social studies and not dramatization. They should employ dramatization only when it aids the pupils in accomplishing their work. If it is necessary to spend much time in practicing for a play, the teacher should clearly understand that practicing for a play is not exactly the same as working out problems in the social studies. Most of the dramatized work should be spontaneous and it should require no extra time.

There is a danger of stressing minor points in dramatization, unless special care is taken by the teacher. Pupils must be taught to select the important points. Portrayals of events should be made as true and as real as possible. Otherwise, pupils will get incorrect impressions and the work will be of little or no value.

3. THE STORY

IMPORTANCE

During the first two or three years in the elementary school, instruction must be chiefly oral. For this reason, the story method of instruction is sometimes used. However, it is not so important as one might think.

A few years ago, the story method was overworked in some schools because teachers did not know how to make good use of it and they did not understand the nature of children. It was erroneously believed that a young child was unable to do much thinking or active work. Today, we know that young children like to be doing something. They take an active interest in looking at pictures, going on short excursions, examining real objects, dramatizing scenes, and in doing various other activities which are on their level.

In the social studies, true stories should generally be told in place of fairy tales. There are so many interesting happenings in nature and in the lives of men that a teacher has little excuse for telling untrue stories. Again, it seems as if children have a habit of remembering the untrue tales which are told. A teacher who has the knack of telling stories should be able to tell a true, interesting story from what he knows or reads. Sometimes a teacher tells a story about a trip he has taken, describing the things which he saw. Examples of stories told by teachers are,—"The Story of a Loaf of Bread," "The Story of a Piece of Coal," "What Byrd Found in Antarctica," and "A Trip to Alaska."

HOW TO TELL A STORY

Whether the pupils get much from a story depends largely upon the way the story is told. Some teachers are very poor storytellers. A good storyteller makes the pupils feel as if they are actually experiencing or seeing what is being described. A teacher should use enough detail to explain what he is saying. Sometimes he may follow a short outline which he has written on the board. He may occasionally ask questions as he tells the story so that the pupils will feel as if they are having an active part in it. He may use pictures, museum materials, maps, graphs, and other objects to make the story more meaningful. Sometimes he draws pictures on the blackboard to explain some point or to arouse the interest. Good well-told stories appeal to the imagination and to the observational powers of children. A teacher should enter enthusiastically into the telling of a story. Enthusiasm is catching and the pupils live the story along with the teacher.

WHEN TO USE THE STORY METHOD

One good way of getting the pupils interested in a unit of work in the lower grades is by telling a story about some phase of it. This method is frequently used by teachers.

In the upper grades, the story method may still be used, but it is not the same type of story that is told to lower grade children. Teachers frequently use the story method when they do not realize they are using it. They may tell their classes about some trip they have taken. Probably a teacher has visited the Supreme Court Building in Washington and has seen the judges handing down decisions. He describes what he saw to his class. Possibly a teacher took a trip during his summer vacation to Mexico or to some distant place. He may give talks to his class describing some of his experiences.

The pupils in the lower grades should be encouraged to tell stories of what they read or see. These stories are simple and short. As pupils grow older and have more experiences, they will tell longer and more complicated stories. In the upper grades, the pupils often give floor talks or reports on what they read, places they have visited, or what they have heard. Such reports are not called stories because the pupils are advanced, yet the stories in the lower grades have many elements which are in common with the reports or floor talks in the upper grades.

PROBLEMS FOR DISCUSSION AND RESEARCH

1. Discuss the steps in teaching a unit by the imaginary journey method.

2. Let us suppose an eighth grade class is studying the Amazon Region. Show how the unit may be taught by using the imaginary journey method.

3. Why should the pupils be encouraged to use dramatization in their work?

4. Explain the various ways of preparing material for dramatization.

5. What use may be made of plays which have been published in magazines and books?

6. Suppose you are teaching a sixth grade class which is asked to put on an assembly program. Outline the nature of the program which might be given by your class.

7. What are some of the possible dangers of dramatization?

8. Describe a scene which the children in the second grade might dramatize when they study about "Our Neighborhood Workers."

9. Discuss the essential factors in the telling of a good story.

10. What are some reasons for using the story method?

11. Write a good, interesting story which might be told with profit to a third or fourth grade class.

REFERENCES

Barton, Thomas, "The Penguin and the Ostrich," The Journal of Geography, XXXVIII, 188-191, May, 1939.

Brainard, Eleanor, "Christ of the Andes," play published by the Pan American Union, Washington, D. C.

Bratton, Dorothy, "Dramatization in the Social Studies," Social Education, IV, 250-258, April, 1940.

Byers, Jean, "And the Stars Heard," The Journal of the National Education Association, XXX, 243-246, November, 1941.

Calloway, Katharine, "Songs and Poems of Many Lands," The Journal of Geography, XXXI, 330-342, November, 1932.

Cherry, Donald, "Pseudobroadcasts," Social Education, II, 481-484, October, 1938.

Cleveland, J. E., "Democracy on the Air," The Grade Teacher, LIX, 51, November, 1941.

Davidson, Sue, "I Pledge Allegiance," The Grade Teacher, LVIII, 40-41, 72, 73, June, 1941.

Dix, John, Training in Democratic Fellowship and Leadership," Social Education, II, 99-102, February, 1938.

Downes, Lillian, "Christmas in Our Community," The Instructor, LI, 54-55, 70, December, 1941.

Doyle, Alice, "The Pilgrim Fathers," The Grade Teacher, LIX, 46, 67, November, 1941.

Griffin, Geraldine, "We Love Our Flag," The Grade Teacher, LIX, 26, November, 1941.

Hahn, Christine, "Cargoes from Abroad," The Journal of Geography, XXXIV, 12-20, January, 1935.

Handel, Hazel, "The Use of Dramatization in Junior High School Geography," The Journal of Geography, XXXVII, 351-357, December, 1938.

Harris, Mildred, "Flag of the Free," The Grade Teacher, LIX, 48-49, 72, November, 1941.

Hart, Isabelle, "The Need for and Nature of Journey Geography," The Journal of Geography, XXX, 170-176, April, 1931.

Horn, Ernest, Methods of Instruction in the Social Studies. New York: Charles Scribner's Sons, 1937.

Chapter XI. Devices for Stimulating the Imagination, 441-480.

James, Linnie, "A Progressive Assembly Program Motivates Junior High School Geography," The Journal of Geography, XXXVII, 369-371, December, 1938.

Lane, Evelyn, "Chicago's Americanism," The Chicago Schools Journal, XXI, 274-275, May-June, 1940.

McWhinnie, Mary, "A South American Assembly Program," The Instructor, L, 38, 78, 79, April, 1941.

Mercer, Phyllis, "Thanksgiving Stories With Class Activities," The Grade Teacher, LIX, 20-21, 65, November, 1941.

Murray, Josephine and Bathurst, Effie, Creative Ways for Children's Programs. New York: Silver Burdett Co., 1938.

Oleson, Lillian, "A Dramatization to Vitalize Geography Teaching," The Journal of Geography, XXXIII, 91-97, March, 1934.

Pearson, Gertrude, "This Is Thanksgiving," The Grade Teacher, LIX, 31, 63, November, 1941.

Reinhard, Dorothy, "Thanksgiving Through the Ages," The Instructor, 46, 76, November, 1941.

———, "The Return of Christopher Columbus," The Instructor, L, 42, 66, October, 1941.

Rice, Rebecca, "Minute Dramatizations," The Instructor, L, 44, October, 1941.

Schlichter, Etta, "Grandpa's Thanksgiving Story"; Price, Nell, "The Jolly Sailor Boy"; Vandevere, J., "A Field and Four Friends," The Instructor, LI, 20-21, 70, November, 1941.

Schwarz, John, Social Study in the Elementary School. New York: Prentice-Hall, 1938. Chapter VI.

Strandberg, A. Edith, "A Creative Assembly," The Chicago Schools Journal, XIX, 127-128, January-February, 1938.

Tozer, Agnes, "Social Science Project," Sierra Educational News, XXXVII, 37, June, 1941.

Wall, Edith, "Why We Have No Large Oak-Hickory Forests in Southern Illinois," The Journal of Geography, XXXVIII, 193-194, May, 1939.

———, "A Thunder Shower," The Journal of Geography, XXXVIII, 191-192, May, 1939.

Washington, Mary, "Gateways of the World," The Journal of Geography, XXVI, 57-65, February, 1927.

Wells, Harriet, "The Bill of Rights," The Grade Teacher, LIX, 41, 72, November, 1941.

Whitney, Ronald, "We Travel by Truck," The Grade Teacher, LIX, 16-17, September, 1941.

Chapter Sixteen: SOME OTHER METHODS

BRIEFLY DISCUSSED

1. THE CONTRACT METHOD

WHAT IT IS

TEACHING BY contracts is a form of individual instruction. A contract contains definite instructions which the pupils are to follow. It has questions and problems to be answered. Specific references are given to books, magazines, pictures, and other study materials. Suggestions may be made about excursions to take and activities to do. Some contract sheets even suggest that the pupils listen to certain radio programs. The contracts are typed, mimeographed, written in longhand, or produced in some other way so that each pupil may have one when he is ready to get to work on it.

HOW USED

There are various ways of using the contract method. Generally the pupils are called together at the beginning of a unit to get them interested in it. At this time the teacher tries to get the pupils to see the scope of the unit and something of what it includes. The method of studying is explained and all needed instructions are given to the pupils. When the teacher feels sure that they are sufficiently interested in the unit and know how to proceed in studying it, the first study sheet or contract is given out. When a pupil completes a contract or study sheet, he has his work checked and is ready to be examined on it. Various methods are used by teachers in checking the work and in examining a pupil. Sometimes some of the pupils aid in checking the work. If a pupil succeeds in having his work accepted and in passing the test, he is given another contract or study sheet. Usually a pupil must do the work on a contract by a certain time. In most schools, the pupils begin a new unit at the same time.

While the pupils are working on their unit, they meet together from time to time as a group to discuss problems which all have in common. In some schools, definite periods are scheduled for the meeting of the class. In other schools, the time of the meeting is determined by the needs of the pupils.

The contract method is better adapted for upper grades and high school pupils than for lower grade pupils. It is only one way of teaching pupils. Pupils would undoubtedly get tired of the plan if they had to use it all the time.

DANGERS TO AVOID IN THE CONTRACT METHOD

Some of the dangers to avoid in using the contract method are the following:

(1) One great danger is that there are likely to be too many questions which emphasize facts and which can be answered by copying certain sentences from a book. Thought questions are often lacking. The assignments are often poorly made and many of the suggested activities are of little value. Isolated facts are frequently stressed and relationships are generally left undeveloped.

(2) Another great danger of the contract method is that the pupils do not learn to work together, unless special care is taken. No class should be conducted solely upon the individual basis. Pupils must learn to cooperate and to work in groups. There must be ample opportunity for pupils to meet and discuss common problems.

(3) Another great danger is that the pupils are likely to do the work on their study sheets in a mechanical manner. It frequently happens that the pupils are given study sheets with little effort being made to interest them in the work. The pupils hurry over their work and remember very little of what they are doing.

(4) If the teacher is not careful, some pupils will waste much time. Certain pupils may think the questions are so easy that

they do not give them much thought while answering them. The slow pupils may be unable to do very good work since they are often thrown too completely upon their own resources. They may continue to work half-heartedly on difficult problems when they should be seeking help from the teacher. They may make many mistakes before being noticed by the teacher.

2. LABORATORY METHOD

Since pupils in studying the social studies need materials with which to do many kinds of activity work, some teachers believe there should be a room where such materials are found. This room is called a laboratory and the teaching that goes on in the room is known as the laboratory method. The well equipped social studies laboratory contains such equipment as textbooks, reference books, encyclopedias, dictionaries, pamphlets, maps, globes, atlases, pictures, museum materials, and models. The room has tables or desks, chairs, blackboards, and bulletin boards. It may also have a radio. There are shelves and cases for books and cabinets for holding materials. Due to lack of money and to crowded conditions, many laboratories are not equipped with all the materials that are needed, but this does not keep the laboratory method from being used. The teacher and pupils should work with the aim of improving the laboratory as time passes.

Since the laboratory is so valuable in teaching the natural sciences, some teachers think that it will be just as valuable in teaching the social studies. This is not necessarily true since scientific observations made in the natural sciences are not the same as the observations made in most of the social studies. If a laboratory is needed in the social studies, it is needed because the work of the pupils can be done better in a laboratory than in an ordinary classroom.

Some teachers do not feel the need of a special laboratory in which to teach the social studies. They claim that they can do good work in a classroom which is reasonably well equipped with books, maps, and other materials useful in teaching. They make use of the library and other sources of help, and bring materials to the classroom when they are needed. It is true that a good teacher is very necessary and that good teaching is far more important than a well equipped laboratory. A good teacher knows how to get results by using the resources he has at hand. He does not go around complaining about the lack of suitable materials for teaching. He makes the best use of what he has and endeavors at the same time to get some of the materials which he thinks will improve his teaching.

Where a laboratory is used, the pupils must have definite assignments so that they will not waste time. The teacher is present to correct any mistakes, to give aid where it is needed, and to see that all the pupils are working efficiently. In a laboratory all the pupils are unlikely to be doing the same work at a given time. Some pupils may be studying books while others are looking up references. A number of pupils may be consulting the dictionaries about the meanings of words, while some others may be examining maps and atlases. Certain pupils may be drawing maps, graphs, and pictures, while others may be making models and different kinds of scenes. Possibly over in the corner of the room a small group of pupils are preparing a committee report or writing a play. In another part of the room, a teacher may be giving assistance to one or more pupils.

A social science laboratory, or any classroom where all pupils are working according to their ability and doing worthwhile work, is certainly a busy place. Some teachers like to use the term "workshop" for such a room. If a workshop is a place where pupils are busily engaged in doing worthwhile work in solving problems, any school should have a number of workshops. In fact, teachers often think of the school as a beehive of industry.

3. SUPERVISED, OR DIRECTED STUDY

WHAT IS IT?

Many teachers feel that the children need help and guidance in studying. They believe that bad habits of study and much wasted time are due to lack of supervision. Pupils should be taught how to work efficiently. The trouble with many poor students is that their teachers take for granted that they know how to study when in fact they know almost nothing about the art of studying.

Supervised or directed study consists chiefly of two parts. The first part is the making of clear and definite assignments. Many pupils idle around when they do not know what to study. Again, if a pupil is not exactly clear about the assignment he will not enter into doing his work whole-heartedly. He will likely become disgusted and say to himself, "Oh, what's the use? I am probably doing it wrong anyway."

Experienced teachers know the value of good assignments. This is the reason why they often spend much time in making them. A pupil with a good start is on the road to solving his problems, but a pupil with a poor start is likely to get lost before he gets very far in his work.

The second part of supervised study is the directing of the study of the pupils. There are several ways of doing this. Some teachers give oral assignments which the pupils are supposed to keep in mind while studying. Other teachers give written instructions to their pupils which they are to follow. The instructions should be clear and simple. Before the written instructions are given, the teacher should make sure that the pupils have had enough experience to interpret them. Written instructions are usually very helpful aids in supervised study, but a few children never seem able to follow them very closely. They sometimes pay little attention to them. This is especially true of certain children in the grades, although it applies to some high school students as well.

THE FUNCTION OF THE TEACHER

Directed study needs more than written instructions. A teacher is often needed to help the pupil understand his problems and to clear up his difficulties. For example, a pupil comes across something that puzzles him. He does not know just what to do. He may happen to guess the right thing to do and succeeds in getting his work done. On the other hand, he may guess wrongly, waste much valuable time, and get discouraged before he finds he is on the incorrect track. The "let down" in morale is more hurtful than many teachers realize. If a teacher were on hand to help the pupil, he could soon learn what to do and he would be able to proceed along the right lines in solving his problems.

It is a question just how much home work should be required of pupils. Some educators believe that they should do most of their work under the supervision of a teacher. Parents usually do not have the time to help their children in studying their problems. Parents are generally untrained in the art of teaching and they are likely to teach the children in the wrong way. Teachers are employed to teach and they should not expect the parents to do their teaching for them. The responsibility of teaching rests upon the teacher, not upon the parents.

Guidance in study is often combined with the recitation period. Sometimes the whole period may be spent in study and at other times only a part of the period may be used for study. There are times when the whole period may be given over to class discussion. During a directed study period, the teacher is on hand to give aid whenever it is needed. It is just as important for the teacher to know when to give aid as it is to know how to give aid. When the pupil is in doubt what to do, he should consult the teacher. By a few simple questions or suggestions, the teacher may show the pupil what to do. Sometimes a pupil cannot find the answer to a question. The teacher may answer it and thus save the pupil much time in trying to find the answer. If the teacher finds that certain pupils do not know how to study, he should demonstrate to them how they might go about their work.

Pupils do much reading in the social studies. They should be taught how to use the library in getting information. Upper grade and high school students should be taught that some books must be read carefully, while other books are to be read hurriedly. They should be shown the difference between the careful reading of a book and the skimming of one. The social studies call for much activity work which should be done under the guidance of a teacher. A suggestion by the teacher to the pupil may open up some new trend of thought. Superior pupils need help just the same as slow students. Some teachers make the mistake of spending most of their time in helping the slow pupils and the average pupils, while the superior pupils are left to shift for themselves.

All good methods make use of supervised or directed study. The problem that many teachers have is to find sufficient time for guiding the study of their pupils. However, they should find time because a pupil cannot study efficiently by himself until he has learned to study. Ways must be found of giving each pupil the individual attention he needs in the early years of school work.

4. THE SOCIALIZED RECITATION

ONE VIEW

The socialized recitation is a plan of socializing the work of the classroom. The idea is to make the class discussions more realistic and natural. It is often used by those teachers who believe that class work should be lively and interesting.

There are generally two views concerning the socialized recitation. One view is that any lesson is socialized if (1) the pupils are actively engaged and are working according to their ability, (2) the pupils raise questions as well as answer them, (3) the pupils raise problems for discussion, (4) the pupils are learning to work independently and to accept responsibility, (5) the pupils feel free to discuss their work and to ask for assistance, and (6) the teacher is on hand as a guide and a leader, and not as a taskmaster whose every word must be followed with no variations. Under this view, the teacher may be anywhere in the room and he may lead the discussion or have some of his pupils lead it.

ANOTHER VIEW

Another view of the socialized recitation is that a lesson is socialized only when the pupils are conducting the recitation and the teacher occupies a less prominent place in the room. The pupils think of themselves as an organization. They appoint their own officers such as president and secretary. Then the work of the class is carried out under the direction of the officers. The teacher is considered as one of the group.

There are other plans of organizing the class. Sometimes the class may act as if it were a city council, a House of Representatives, or a club. At other times, the class may merely appoint one of its members to be the chairman, and certain ones may be appointed to lead discussions on the various topics. The idea is to let the pupils manage as much of the recitation as possible. Since the pupils shoulder much of the responsibility in a socialized recitation, some people might think that the teacher has an easy time. However, he has anything but an easy time if the socialized recitation is carried out successfully. The teacher should always be on the watch to see that everything runs smoothly and wisely. His aid is frequently needed. He must see that the work is well planned and organized.

The teacher should see that the chairman or leader conducts the discussion in a satisfactory manner. It must be remembered that the pupils are not expected to know very much on the subject. The leader is one of the pupils, and he may not know any more than some of the other pupils. He may not always know when inaccurate statements are made. Hence, the teacher must help the leader from time to time with suggestions and questions. It is unwise to expect any pupil to take the place of a teacher and conduct a class in as skilful a way as a teacher might conduct it. A teacher has spent considerable time in preparing himself to teach and in learning the subject. Hence, no class of pupils can get along without a teacher being on hand to give advice and guidance and to keep everything working harmoniously and efficiently.

Some children like to talk, while there are other children who are timid and prefer to keep still. The teacher should see that none of the pupils monopolize the recitation. All pupils should be given a chance to speak. The timid pupils should be encouraged to express their views and the talkative pupils should be taught to respect the opinions of others.

If care is not taken, some of the pupils will raise questions which have no bearing upon the problem being discussed. The leader should keep the pupils upon the topic. Otherwise, the class will waste time and the pupils who want to learn something will become disgusted. There is also danger that the work will be covered unsatisfactorily and the subject matter will be poorly mastered. Classes using the socialized recitation are likely to become dull and uninteresting whenever proper precautions are not taken by the teacher.

When the pupils conduct their own recitation, the chief value is likely to be of a social nature and not in the subject matter learned. If there is much content to be mastered, most teachers believe some other method should generally be used. If a teacher does not believe in the plan, he should not use it. Some pupils never seem to like it and some teachers never succeed in having much success with it.

If skilfully conducted, the socialized lesson develops leadership and initiative. It furnishes an opportunity for pupils to express themselves. It teaches cooperation and the spirit of good fellowship. Thinking is developed and a pupil learns to defend his opinion when questioned by some other pupil.

5. THE PANEL DISCUSSION

If sufficiently encouraged, pupils like to talk and discuss topics of interest to them. Sometimes all the pupils in the class enter into the discussion. At other times, a group of students discuss the problem while the rest of the members listen. In the upper grades and high school, panel discussions are held frequently. The chief factors in a panel discussion are (1) the group of students composing the panel, (2) the topic being discussed, and (3) the listening students.

Generally from four to nine students make up a panel. The discussion may occupy all the class period or only a part of it. The length of the discussion will be determined by a number of factors such as, (1) the importance of the problem being discussed, (2) the knowledge that the members of the panel have about the subject and the interest they take in the discussion, (3) the interest shown by the listeners, (4) the age of the pupils, and (5) the time that the class thinks can profitably be given over for discussion.

The members on a panel prepare themselves as thoroughly as possible on the subject to be discussed. They study all the available references in books, pamphlets, magazines, and newspapers. They consult adults, listen to appropriate radio programs, attend lectures, take excursions to numerous places, and go to various other sources for information.

Certain activities may be done to illustrate a point or to make it clearer. The members of a panel outline the main topics or problems to be discussed. They decide what pupils will be responsible for starting the discussion on different topics. They determine somewhat the order of the topics, but of course they cannot be expected to hold strictly to the order when the discussion takes place.

When the group is ready to give its discussion, the names of the pupils on the panel are announced. An outline of the problem, some of the questions which the group is going to discuss, and a list of references are generally given to the class. The outline and questions will guide the group in its discussion, and they will also aid the other members of the class in following the points which the different speakers make.

The panel discussion should not be allowed to become a debate, because a debate is likely to confuse the question. There may be frequently a difference of opinion and each pupil will give the facts as he has interpreted them. The idea is for the panel members to discuss their topics in a clear manner so that pupils may have enough reliable material to come to some kind of conclusion about the subject.

The last part of the discussion is thrown open to all the pupils. They ask questions of those on the panel. They may take issue with some of the statements made. They discuss some of the questions. Very often the most profitable part of the discussion is near the close when all the pupils have the opportunity of taking an active part in it. At the end, the chairman sums up the points that have been made and gives any conclusion that may have been derived from the discussion.

6. DRILLS AND GAMES

DRILLING ON ESSENTIAL FACTS

There is no question but that pupils should accumulate a certain amount of useful knowledge in school. If they did not do this, there would be little need to employ teachers to teach them. The business of the teacher is to see that the children have placed before them those experiences which they should have in order to bring about the desired kinds of learning. The pupils will study many problems and gather various sorts of information, but they are not expected to remember everything that they read, hear, or see. Minor details are often needed to make a problem clear and meaningful, but they may soon be forgotten. Only the important details should be remembered.

Just what facts should pupils be expected to remember? Educators are not agreed upon this question. Some teachers believe that pupils should learn a good many facts, while others believe that the number is small. Textbooks and other books contain many facts, but the pupils cannot be expected to remember every fact which they read. Teachers agree that pupils should not try to remember a mass of unrelated facts and that only the most important and useful ones should be remembered. However, teachers are not agreed upon what are the most important and useful facts for children to learn.

It is a big problem to decide just what facts should be learned, since there is no common agreement among teachers on this point. For example, certain educators have tried to determine the chief facts of geography and history, but their results are not entirely satisfactory. We still are undecided about such problems as what places a pupil in a certain grade should be able to locate, what dates he should know, and what knowledge he should have about certain problems. It is very difficult to get reliable and valuable data on such problems. The nature of the social studies, the changing world, and the various experiences and viewpoints of teachers make a common agreement almost impossible.

After careful consideration, the teacher must determine the facts upon which he is going to drill. He must think of interesting ways of presenting the material to the pupils. The material should be approached from new viewpoints. The more ways a pupil looks at something and studies it, the more likely he will remember it. Outline maps are found to be useful in having drills in certain phases of the social studies. Making outlines are also good ways of conducting drills and reviews. The question and answer method may also be used to good advantage. The resourceful teacher has many ways of having reviews.

GAMES

Even games occupy an important place in drills and reviews. It is good teaching occasionally to use games, providing they aid the pupils in solving their problems and in accomplishing the objectives which the teacher has in mind. Sometimes the teacher and pupils make a game out of the work which the class is doing.

A few examples of games or parts of games follow. In most cases only enough of a game is given to show the teacher what it is like. After getting the idea, the teacher and pupils may make their own game.

a. What City Am I In and Where Is It?

Question: I am in a city which is at the place where two rivers come together to make a large river. There are many iron and steel mills in the city. Glass and many iron and steel products are made. Coal is mined in the surrounding region. A fort was built here many years ago. It is a gateway city. What city am I in and where is it?

Answer: You are in Pittsburgh, in western Pennsylvania, at the place where the Monongahela and the Allegheny rivers come together to form the Ohio River.

b. A Radio Quiz

The children play games such as the Quiz programs heard over the radio. They write questions and answers on pieces of paper, each piece of paper having one question and the answer. The pieces of paper are folded and put into a box. One of the children acts as the leader. All the children may take part in answering the question, or only a certain number may take part. Sides may be selected, if it is so desired. Each player, in turn, draws out a piece of paper. The leader unfolds the paper and reads the question. The player answers it. Scores are kept to see which child or which side wins. There are different ways of conducting this program. Listen to some good radio programs and you will receive ideas about how to conduct such a game in school.

c. What Is It?

This game is often played after a unit of work has been completed. A pupil describes something he has learned and calls upon another pupil to give the right answer. The pupil giving the right answer becomes the one who asks the next question.

Question: I am thinking of the greatest railroad center in the world. What city is it?

Answer: You are thinking of Chicago.

d. Game of Famous Men

Question: He was a pioneer who made a trail across the Appalachian Highlands to Kentucky. Who was he?
Answer: He was Daniel Boone.

e. Game of Products

Question: I come from a tree which grows in southeastern Brazil. I am used for making a drink. What product am I?
Answer: You are coffee.

f. A Spelling Game

Pupils should learn to spell certain words in their social studies, such as names of famous people and places. The teacher decides what words the pupils should be able to spell. A list of the words is put on the board for the pupils to study. After the pupils have had time to learn their spelling, the game is as follows:

The teacher starts the game by saying: I am thinking of a large seaport in California that begins with "S." He calls upon some pupil to name the city and spell it or write it upon the blackboard. If the pupil spells the word correctly, he becomes the leader. He gives the first letter of a word to be spelled and tells an interesting fact about it.

g. Of What Am I Thinking?

Question: I am thinking of the first person to reach the North Pole. Of whom am I thinking?
Answer: You are thinking of Admiral Robert Peary.
Question: I am thinking of a great event which occurred in 1776. Of what am I thinking?
Answer: You are thinking of the signing of the Declaration of Independence.

h. Game of Abbreviations of States

The abbreviations of ten or fifteen states may be used in this game.

1. *Question:* What state reminds you of an ancient boat?
   Answer: Ark.
2. *Question:* What state reminds you of being sick?
   Answer: Ill.
3. *Question:* What state reminds you of a doctor?
   Answer: Md.

i. A Guessing Game

1. *Question:* What tree reminds a person of being dressed up?
   Answer: Spruce.
2. *Question:* What island is always long?
   Answer: Long Island.

j. Game On Neighborhood Workers and Protectors

The pupils think of neighborhood workers and protectors. One pupil comes to the front of the room and acts the part of a neighborhood worker or a protector. The pupil who guesses correctly the person represented goes to the front of the room and acts the part of another worker or protector.

k. Games of Directions

Pupils learning to tell directions in the lower grades frequently play some of these interesting games:

1. All the pupils rise. Then the teacher gives them directions such as, face north, face east, etc.

2. A pupil is appointed leader. He directs someone to do something which will show that he knows his directions. For example, he may say, "John, turn and face the south." "Susie, put the book on the table near the east window."

3. In the lower grades the children occasionally play the following game:

a. They play they are engines and puff to the west.
b. They play they are birds and fly to the north.
c. They play they are guideposts and point to the south.
d. They play they are boy scouts or girl scouts and march to the east.

e. They play they are bees and buzz to the west.

4. Children like to play this game. A child is chosen to be the leader and he represents the weather man. The rest of the pupils represent the wind. The children stand and face the leader.

When the leader says, "The wind blows from the north," the children turn and bend their bodies toward the south, since the wind blows from the north toward the south. They may make a noise like the wind. If there is room to walk, they may walk toward the south. The leader gives various directions from which the wind blows and the children act accordingly.

To create more interest, the leader occasionally says, "We are in a big storm." Then the children jump up and down and wave their arms. The teacher may also say, "The air is still." The children sit and become still.

l. Short Answers

The teacher and the pupils make a list of questions based on the unit which they have been studying. The answer to each question is short. Questions are given to the pupils from time to time. Examples of such questions are the following:

What is the longest river system in the United States?

What is the capital of Argentina?

Who invented the cotton gin?

Who discovered the Mississippi River?

Which is our largest state?

m. Game of Descriptions

A pupil describes some event, important person, product, place, or animal. The other children try to give the right answer. For example, here is a description given by a fourth grade pupil who was studying the hot deserts: "I carry people on my back. I can go three days or more without water. My skin is thick and I have padded feet so that I will not sink into the sand. Some people call me the ship of the desert. What animal am I?"

Answer: "You are a camel."

n. Game of Flags

The flags of certain countries are displayed. The pupils try to identify the flags.

PROBLEMS FOR DISCUSSION AND RESEARCH

1. Explain the contract method of teaching.
2. Give the advantages and disadvantages of using the contract method of teaching.
3. Read about several plans which make use of the contract method of teaching. Also try to visit schools where some contract plan is being used. Discuss what you learn with the class.
4. What is the laboratory or workshop method of teaching the social studies? Discuss its advantages and disadvantages.
5. Do you think it is essential that the social studies should be taught in laboratories and workshops?
6. Discuss the importance of supervised or directed study.
7. What is the function of the teacher in directed study?
8. Discuss the two views which are commonly held concerning the socialized recitation.
9. What are the strong points of having the pupils appoint a chairman to conduct their recitations? What are the weak points?
10. Describe various ways of conducting a class discussion.
11. Which do you prefer, a panel discussion or a discussion where all the pupils take part?
12. Explain four good ways of conducting a review.
13. What is the value of games?
14. Describe some games of considerable value in the teaching of the social studies which are not given in this chapter.
15. Talk to teachers and pupils and visit a number of schools. Learn if it is a common practice for the teacher to make use of games in teaching the social studies.

REFERENCES

Bining, Arthur and Bining, David, *Teaching the Social Studies in the Secondary Schools.* New York: McGraw-Hill Book Co., 1941. Chapters VI, VII, and VIII.

Blanchard, W. C., "Geographic Games and Tests," the Social Studies, XXXII, 255-259, October, 1941; 315-320, November, 1941; 349-353, December, 1941; XXXIII, 13-18, January, 1942; 58-63, February, 1942.

Blanchard, W. C., "A Geographic Museum," The Journal of Geography, XL, 117, March, 1941.

Bohlman, Edna, "The Teaching of Current Events," The Social Studies, XXVI, 91-96, February, 1935.

Broeing, Angela, "The Laboratory Plan of Teaching Geography," The Journal of Geography, XXVI, 99-104, March, 1927.

Brown, Ralph Adams, "The Town Meeting Comes to the Classroom," Social Education, V, 516-519, November, 1941.

Brownell, William, "What Has Happened to Supervised Study?" Educational Method, XVII, 373-377.

Casto, E. Ray and Beard, Garnet, "The A B C's of the A B C Countries," The Journal of Geography, XXXVIII, 112-114, March, 1939.

Ellwood, Robert, "Current Events by Panel Discussion," Social Education, III, 381-384, September, 1939.

———, An Evaluation of the Unit-Directed Study Procedure. Normal: Illinois State Normal University, 1939.

———, "Evaluation of the Unit-Directed Study," Social Education, IV, 266-272, April, 1940.

Frederick, Robert and Sheats, Paul, Citizenship Education Through the Social Studies. New York: Row, Peterson and Co., 1936. Chapter IX.

Habberton, William, "Socialization of Education," Social Education, I, 336-339, May, 1937.

Hodgkins, George, A Guide to Newer Methods in Teaching the Social Studies. Washington: National Council for the Social Studies, 1937, 15-22, 27-38.

Jessop, Grace, "Study Guides," The Journal of Geography, XXXVII, 243-245, September, 1938.

Lacey, Joy, Teaching the Social Studies in the Elementary School. Minneapolis: Burgess Publishing Co., 1941. Chapter IV, Trends in Curriculum Construction, 24-42; Chapter V, Learning Sequence of Curriculum Content, 43-51.

Lathrop, H. O., "An Experiment with the Contract Method in High School Commercial Geography," The Journal of Geography, XXVIII, 29-39, January, 1929.

Mayer-Oakes, G. H., "The Dalton Plan in a Small High School," Education, LVII, 244-248, December, 1936.

Miller, George, editor, Activities in Geography. Bloomington: McKnight and McKnight, 1937.

Muchow, Clifford, "Problems of America on the Air," School Activities, XIII, 21-22, September, 1941.

Reeder, Edwin, "Directing Children's Study of Geography," Educational Method, XVII, 386-390, May, 1938.

Riley, Noma, "Review and Recall," Social Education, V, 199-201, March, 1941.

Royals, Bertha, "Effective Citizenship is Fostered in Social Studies Workshops," Chicago Schools Journal, XXII, 120-125, January-March, 1941.

Schauer, Virginia, "A Study Guide For the Textile Districts of the British Isles," The Journal of Geography, XXXVII, 156-163, April, 1938.

Selke, Arthur, "The Riddle as a Geographic Teaching Device," The Journal of Geography, XXXVI, 283-284, October, 1937.

Symonds, Clare, "Panel Discussions Foster Sustained Group Attention," The Journal of Geography, XL, 221-225, September, 1941.

Tyron, Florence, Directing Pupils' Study in the Social Studies, Eighth Yearbook, National Council for the Social Studies, 1937, 75-108.

Ware, Amy, "The World's Fiber Problems: A Laboratory Exercise," The Journal of Geography, 168-169, April, 1938.

Wesley, Edgar, Teaching the Social Studies. New York: D. C. Heath and Co., 1937. Chapter XXXI.

Chapter Seventeen: THE CURRICULUM OF
THE SOCIAL STUDIES

WHY A CURRICULUM IS NEEDED

SOME TEACHERS think of a curriculum as being the course of study which gives the subject matter which a school is to follow. Others think of it in broader terms. To them it includes all the activities which are carried on under the direction of the school.

If we go back to the time when there were very few people upon the earth, we find that primitive society was very simple. In those days, many of the things which a person needed to know were handed down from father to son and from mother to daughter. For example, a son was taught how to hunt animals and how to make certain kinds of tools. A daughter was shown how to do the work which was commonly done by the women in their homes.

As the years passed, people gradually accumulated knowledge and skills. The new knowledge and skills in one generation were added to those of all the preceding generations. As time passed, it became impossible for one person to have a detailed knowledge of everything. Writing came into use so that events could be recorded. Parents could no longer hand down to their sons and daughters all the knowledge and skills which they should have. Society became too complex for this. Children had to be trained by others than their parents. Schools came into existence where children could be taught certain desirable things.

Today, the curriculum of a modern school is far more complex than the curriculum of a school in colonial times, and the curriculum of a colonial school was more complex than the curriculum of a school during the time of Ancient Greece or Ancient Rome. The curriculum gradually accumulates desirable materials as time passes. We think of the curriculum as containing the fundamental parts of civilization which society wishes to keep. It is our social heritage from the past. It contains information, skills, attitudes, viewpoints, techniques, and other desirable elements which society thinks should be passed on to the youths of our land.

KEEPING THE CURRICULUM REVISED

Since we are living in a changing world, we would not expect the elements in a curriculum to stay put and never change. The curriculum grows and changes along with society, since it is society that eventually determines what is in the curriculum. The curriculum that is used today should not be exactly the one that was used yesterday and it should not be the one that will be used tomorrow. Teachers have the responsibility of seeing that the curriculum is kept in step with the times. This means that the curriculum should have frequent revisions.

Some teachers have the idea that in order to be modern and progressive, a new curriculum should be entirely rewritten every three or four years. They believe that the old curriculum should be thrown overboard and a new one made to take its place. It is true that a new curriculum should be entirely rewritten when the old one is so completely unrelated to modern educational thought, that revising it would not bring about the necessary changes nearly so well as rewriting the whole course from a new viewpoint. However, most teachers do not believe that it is necessary to write an entirely new curriculum every three or four years. They believe that after a curriculum has been made, providing it is a good one, it should usually be used for a reasonable number of years, with frequent revisions keeping it up to date. Great changes do not generally occur all at once, but they gradually come about over a period of time. In making a curriculum, educators should keep in mind that many of the events of today are only of passing importance. Curriculum makers should have a broad, long-range view in place of a narrow, short-term view. They should realize that the curriculum is only one of the many factors that influence the development of the child.

Teachers become accustomed to a course of study and it is

not wise to make new ones too frequently. It takes time for teachers to get acquainted with a course of study and to work out plans and to collect materials for teaching it successfully. Teachers should feel free to do their best work and they should be enthusiastic over what they are doing; but who can enter into his work in a whole-hearted manner if he has his methods of teaching disrupted constantly by new courses of study?

THE PROBLEM OF SELECTING MATERIALS

It is no easy matter to determine what materials to include in a curriculum. For a great many years, people have been collecting information about society and have been passing it on to succeeding generations. There is a mass of material which might be selected for a curriculum, but only a small part of it can be included. There is not time for the pupils to study everything that is worth knowing. Hence, those who are responsible for making the selection should use as much wisdom and common sense as possible. Even after the materials have been selected and the curriculum is completed, it is difficult to prove that the curriculum is superior to some other one which has just been completed by another group of people. There are so many good things that must be left out of any curriculum, that it is practically impossible to prove with much degree of satisfaction that one good curriculum is superior to any other good curriculum.

Some educators often mislead themselves by believing that children see relationships which they really do not see. It is rather easy for a person who has spent much thought and time in making a course of study to believe that pupils will see how the material in the course of study is related to present-day conditions. Teachers sometimes think that certain relationships must be developed regardless of whether the pupils are old enough to understand them. In such cases, pupils generally memorize words about relationships without realizing that they actually exist. It should be understood that young pupils are unable to do abstract thinking. So why expect them to do things which a little thinking tells a person they cannot do?

Teachers sometimes think they are progressive by requiring pupils to do much reading and to go to considerable effort to get information on all sides of a question. Sometimes the more material a pupil brings in, the more progressive a teacher thinks he is. The teacher may be correct in his thinking, but in some cases he is wrong. There is a point beyond which pupils should not go to obtain information or to read additional references. Whenever the information or reading matter fails to make a worthwhile contribution to the study of the problem, the work is of little value. Confusion, in place of illumination, will likely result.

Let us suppose the pupils are studying about the part that the automobile plays in transportation. To get a clear idea of the contribution of the automobile to transportation, it is unnecessary for them to treat in detail every possible angle of the problem, although some teachers seem to have this idea. For example, knowing something about the mechanism of the automobile may interest a few pupils, but it is folly to expect all pupils to be interested in this. Requiring children to study such material would cause most of them to lose interest in the problem. If the teacher is not careful, the children will become lost in a mass of complex detail which contributes very little to the understanding of the problem.

KNOWLEDGE IS POWER

There was probably a period in history when an intelligent person could have stored in his mind most of the existing knowledge of that day. After writing came into existence, there was undoubtedly a time when a few books could have held most of the existing knowledge which was considered to be important. Those times have passed long ago. It takes many books to record the existing knowledge of today. No living teacher is able to teach all the knowledge which his pupils should have in the years to come. Neither is any teacher sure of what problems his pupils will face in the future. About the only thing that the teacher really knows concerning these matters is that his pupils will have many problems in the future, and the more knowledge they can bring to bear upon these problems, the more likely they will be to solve them satisfactorily. Knowledge is power in that it helps people to accomplish certain things.

Since the vision of teachers is limited, they must do their very best to select the right materials for teaching. They should endeavor to instil in the hearts and minds of their pupils a desire to learn. They should give their pupils practice in solving problems so that they will have scientific and useful principles which they may use in the solution of any problem that may arise in later years. Teachers must not consider the brain as a storehouse for a mass of unrelated facts which can be recalled when needed. Unrelated facts are likely to be forgot. Those facts that are usually remembered are generally learned in meaningful situations and they are frequently used. Teachers should endeavor to select those materials in the social studies that will give pupils the experiences they need in solving worthwhile problems.

The materials that are taught in the social studies are taken mainly from geography, history, civics, economics, and sociology. All of these subjects deal with human relations. Geography tells us something about the ways that human relations are affected by the natural environment, while history is the story of human relations in the past and how they are related to present events. Civics is a study of human relations in government, while economics shows us how business, industry, and the earning of a living are connected with human relations. Sociology teaches the connection between human relations and social groups.

FACTORS IN SELECTING MATERIALS

Teachers and others should keep in mind a number of factors when they start to select the materials for the curriculum. They should clearly formulate the objectives for teaching the social studies and these objectives must have enough definiteness to have meaning. The curriculum should reflect the most recent knowledge in the field. Since curriculum makers cannot afford to speculate on what is going to happen in the world, it is clear that the printed materials in the curriculum will always be a little behind actual happenings. However, the course should be so written that teachers may keep the work of their pupils attuned with the times.

In writing a course of study, the training and experiences of the teachers who are to use it should be considered. Poorly trained teachers need more help than average trained teachers, and average trained teachers need more help than highly trained teachers. Likewise, wide-awake and experienced teachers need less assistance than unprogressive and inexperienced teachers.

The material in a course of study and that which is taught must be accurate. Careful thought and training are needed to determine the accuracy of the material. This is one reason why teachers should know the subject matter of the social studies. Teachers with little knowledge cannot be expected to know accurate from inaccurate statements.

A study of the material in a course of study should be useful to pupils for solving present-day problems. It should also prove to be useful in solving future problems. It is rather difficult to know exactly how useful any material is or will be. Teachers help to make up their minds on this problem (1) by consulting the opinions of experts in the field, (2) by examining newspapers, magazines, and other current materials, (3) by examining books, and (4) by carrying on other kinds of research work.

The ease of learning the material should also be carefully considered before it goes into the curriculum. The ability of the pupils must be kept in mind and the material must be on their level. Some material is too difficult for certain grades. The material must be connected with the past experiences of the pupils. Too much abstract material should be avoided. In selecting materials for a curriculum, each grade should be considered in relation to all the other grades. The course should be so planned that certain units naturally belong to a given grade. Teachers should cooperate with one another in the same school system by following the course of study so that the units in one grade will not be repeated in another grade.

The time element is also important in deciding what materials to select for a curriculum. A wide and varied program in the social studies may be carried out in those schools which have ample time for teaching the social studies. There are many schools which do not give sufficient time to teaching the social studies. In such schools, the program of the social studies is necessarily curtailed. There is so very much material that might be taught, and there is so little time to teach it, that the curriculum makers and teachers have a difficult problem of deciding what to teach. After doing their utmost in selecting materials to be taught, they can only hope that the future will show that they used good judgment.

WHO SHOULD MAKE OR REVISE
THE CURRICULUM?

It is a question just how many people should be engaged in making or revising the curriculum. The persons who are on the curriculum committee should be given enough time from their regular school work in order to do a good job. Teachers who serve on such an important committee are likely not to give very much thought to the various problems that arise, if the making of a curriculum is extra work and if they meet after school or on their own time. Making a good curriculum is expensive of time and effort.

Some of the people who should be on a curriculum committee or should be represented are classroom teachers, principals, experts in the subject matter of the social studies, educational experts, and frontier thinkers. In the past, there have been too many curriculums in which classroom teachers had no active part in their making. Classroom teachers help to make the curriculum more practical and they will take more interest in using a course of study which they have helped to make. Subject matter experts are necessary because they have a well-rounded knowledge of the content of the social studies. Frontier thinkers are usually one step ahead of ordinary thinkers and their advice should be sought, but at the same time it should be remembered that some of their ideas might be too far ahead of the times or they might be impractical.

METHODS USED BY CURRICULUM MAKERS

Let us suppose the members of a curriculum committee are ready to begin work in revising the curriculum. Just how will they proceed? Different plans may be followed. There is no one best plan which should be followed by every curriculum committee. Each committee decides what plan to follow after its members have had ample opportunity for discussion. There are certain procedures which committees usually follow regardless of what plans are being used. The most important of these procedures are the following:

1. Courses of study for other school systems are consulted. If they are recent and are approved by educational experts,

much valuable help and many suggestions are obtained from them. There is no good reason why use should not be made of other courses of study. There are some problems which are common to all schools, since one school has the same general objectives in education as any other school.

2. Magazine articles, books, and other printed material are examined to learn what has been written about the curriculum in the social studies.

3. Reports which have been written by various committees on teaching the social studies are read and discussed.

4. Experts in education, experts in the social studies, teachers, selected groups of people, and other interested persons are asked to appear before the committee to give advice and help on the many problems involved in making the curriculum.

5. A study of the resources of the community is made with a view of determining how they can best be used by the pupils.

6. Textbooks are examined to learn what certain writers think children should study. Most textbooks are written by teachers and specialists who have had experience in teaching children and who believe they know the subject matter which children should study.

7. Other school systems are visited to inspect the work which is being done and to learn what teachers in the field are actually thinking and doing. The experience of other teachers is often found to be very inspiring and helpful.

8. Newspapers, magazines, and other current materials are examined, radio programs are analyzed, meetings are attended, and people are interviewed to learn what the American people are thinking and discussing.

9. The committee makes a list of the objectives of the social studies.

10. The committee makes an ideal program for the different grades and revises the curriculum in view of this new program.

ORGANIZING THE MATERIALS

1. Vertical Articulation and Horizontal Articulation

The organizing of the materials in the curriculum requires considerable thought and care. A long range view of the work for all the grades must be taken. The work should gradually advance from year to year and each unit should contribute to the growth of the child. This is another way of saying that the pupils should make steady progress. The units for a certain year in the social studies should be related to one another and the work of one year should help to prepare for the work of the following year. This is sometimes called vertical integration or vertical articulation. The work of the social studies should be related to the other kinds of work in the curriculum which the children are studying. All the subjects should work together to educate the children. This is frequently called horizontal integration or horizontal articulation.

2. Use of Community Resources

Efforts should be made to use the local resources whenever possible and profitable. The program should be well balanced by making a careful selection of units. Frequent use should be made of first-hand experiences.

3. Individual Differences

The course of study should pay some attention to individual differences. Suggestions may be made that will keep all children working at their own rate of speed. It is not necessary for a child to do everything that is suggested in the course of study. A certain amount of activity work, other than reading books, may be done. The work of the social studies should raise problems that seem real to the child. The school should be a place where groups of people are actually living and gaining worthwhile experiences. For example, children often obtain a practical knowledge of government by making laws to govern themselves in the schoolrooms and on the playgrounds.

4. Real Problems

The units in the curriculum should center around real problems which can be made interesting to the pupils who are going to study them. The problems should be adapted to the age of the child so that there will be no difficulty of interpreting them.

The program should be flexible. It is impossible for curriculum makers to see very far ahead. They cannot know all the problems which are going to arise in the future. Schools must keep up with the times. They must have curriculums which are flexible enough so that new problems may be studied and old ones discarded.

5. *The Cycle Plan*

One question that confronts curriculum makers is, "What use should be made of the cycle plan?" Where the cycle plan is used, the topics or units are repeated at different grade levels. The chief reason usually given for repeating the work is that the children cannot get very much out of their first study of a unit. They are too young to study the subject very thoroughly. Therefore, the material should be repeated in more advanced grades. For example, much of the geography and history that used to be taught in the first six grades were repeated in the seventh and eighth grades.

One argument against the cycle plan is that children become tired of studying the same topics or units a number of times. The work becomes dull and uninteresting to the children and many of them form a dislike for the subjects they are studying.

It is true that by studying a topic or unit merely once, young children will receive a small amount of information and they will have only a slight acquaintance with the material. Every experienced teacher knows that a small child cannot go very deeply into the subject. Hence, what is the solution to the problem of using the cycle plan? Probably the answer is to use the modified cycle plan. Of course it is necessary to repeat some phases of the subject matter in more advanced grades. When work is repeated, it should be studied in a different way and the repetition of the work should cause the child to advance continuously in the power to use the knowledge which he has already gained. The pupil should have the feeling that he is actually gaining new information.

6. *Teaching History Chronologically*

Another question is, "Should we teach history chronologically or should we teach it with little attention given to chronology?"

Teaching history chronologically may be called the forward way of teaching it. History is a record of the continuous growth of man from the beginning to the present. It is only natural to trace the historical development from long ago to the near at hand, or from yesterday to today. Children should gradually gain a sense of time, but it is a difficult thing to do. Most teachers think this sense of time can be gained better by studying the actions and thoughts of man as he has advanced in civilization. While studying history in this way, the past should be continuously related to the present, because present events have their roots in the past.

7. Teaching History Backwards

Some teachers do not approve of teaching history chronologically. Since the chief reason for studying history is to learn how to interpret and understand the present and to prepare for the future, they think we should teach history by beginning with present problems and proceeding to the past. This is sometimes called teaching history backward, or chronology in reverse. These same teachers claim that the extent of time means very little to a child and that better results will be obtained if he begins to study history through present-day problems. They say that teaching history chronologically stresses history at the expense of the child and that present events are not sufficiently related to past events. In fact, some teachers never reach the present in their class discussions. They only get as far as their textbook happens to go.

One objection that is commonly given against teaching history backward is that the child is likely to miss much of the history which he should study. He will probably develop a poor sense of time. This would be very unfortunate, since the time element is very important in history.

8. Teaching Biography

Just what part should biography play in the teaching of history? Some years ago, the biographical method of teaching history was much used in certain grades. The claim was made that by studying the lives of important men in history, children would learn about the events which took place during the periods in which the famous men lived. It was furthermore thought that children would enjoy their history by studying about great people. Since all people love heroes, it was believed that the pupils would look upon many of the men as heroes. Many teachers even thought that the children would try to emulate the good deeds of their heroes. On the other hand, they thought they would naturally overlook their bad deeds.

As time passed, many teachers began to doubt the wisdom of trying to teach history around the lives of famous men. In the first place, there was no general agreement on what biographies to study or how many. Again, if the biographies were too personal, many of the events of the times were omitted; while if many events were included, the personal element was often lacking. Then there was the question about how much influence biographical studies really have upon the lives of children. Many teachers came to the conclusion that it is not as great as had been claimed. They also believed that big gaps would be left in history if it were taught only by the biographical method. Teachers also noticed that history was likely to be dull and uninteresting in those classes where only the biographical method was taught.

Biographies of great men who have played important parts in history should not be omitted altogether. They still have an important function to perform. Probably the lives of famous men should be grouped around events. Children are bound to learn a certain amount of history by reading about the lives of great men, and a few well selected biographies will help to make the study of history interesting to almost everyone.

INTEGRATION VERSUS SUBJECT ORGANIZATION

1. Fusion and Integration

During recent years such terms as correlation, integration, fusion, concentration, unification, synthesis, and the core curriculum have been used. Just what do these terms mean to the average teacher? If a person reads only one book where these terms are discussed, he may get the idea that they have different meanings and that it is rather easy to give a definition for each term. However, if a person keeps on reading various authorities he will probably change his mind about being able to tell how one term differs from the others. He will likely agree with Dondineau and Dimond, who state in the Eighth Yearbook of the National Council for Social Studies, 1937, that these terms are used interchangeably by various authorities to show the close relationships existing between all subject matter which is taught. So when one teacher speaks of integration, he may have the same idea as another teacher who uses the word fusion, correlation, or any of the other terms which have been mentioned in this paragraph. The main point is that subjects stand to lose their identity when units are being studied by children. For an interesting discussion showing how different writers have used the terms "fusion," "integration," "correlation," and the "core curriculum," read "Clarifying Social Studies Terms," by Park and Stephenson, in Social Education for May, 1940.

Of course there are some teachers who have thought out a difference in the meaning of some of these terms. For example, the claim is often made that fusion does not recognize the boundaries of subjects that make up the social studies, while integration and correlation do recognize the boundaries. In this book, fusion and integration are used interchangeably, since the two terms have practically the same meaning to most teachers.

Johnson, in his charming little book, "An Introduction to the History of the Social Studies," shows that the fusion idea is nothing new. Some people advocated the idea many years ago. There have been educators throughout the ages who have dreamed of doing away with subjects and of having a unified course. However, most teachers have preferred to teach by subjects because they thought this was the most practical way. These teachers usually realized that all subjects are related to one another and that all of them taken together give children the knowledge, habits, ideals, attitudes, and other qualities which tend to make them good citizens. Although these teachers believed in teaching each subject separately, they never hesitated to use materials from any subject in making meaningful the unit which they were teaching.

Shortly after the first World War, the fusion idea began to gain considerable headway and the idea has created considerable discussion ever since. The world has been passing through a period of much unrest and many people are dissatisfied with existing conditions. The big idea has been to bring about improvements in various lines of effort. Teachers have caught the spirit of change and many of them are dissatisfied with the results which they are obtaining. It is the mark of a good teacher never to be entirely satisfied, but to strive to get better results by using some other plan. There is always a better way of doing a piece of work, although we may not know this better way.

During the last two decades, many teachers have been experimenting with teaching a unified course where subjects lose a part or all of their identity. The argument is given that we are teaching children, not subjects; that all subjects are closely related to one another; and that it is impossible to teach very well any one subject by itself. For example, history and geography are so closely related, that it is impossible to teach one without teaching a certain amount of the other.

The advocates of an integrated course or a fusion course claim that by studying a large unit, the pupils become very much interested in it because they can bring in any kind of material that is needed in the solution of the problems that may arise. In working along this line, the pupils study history, geography, civics, or any other subject whenever there is a real need. It is maintained that they study only what they need to know in solving their problems, and not a mass of facts that have no connection with their problems.

The claim is commonly made that in a fusion course, a pupil studies all the facts of history, geography, civics, and the other social studies that he will ever need to know in the grades. He is not made to study facts when he has no need of them. He studies facts in relation to one another and in building up the whole unit. Hence, he is interested in his work and he will likely remember what he is studying. The pupil receives very good training in understanding the social problems of the day and in playing his part as a good citizen.

2. *Teaching Subject Courses*

The Commission of Social Studies in their "Conclusions and Recommendations," 1934, refused to endorse any detailed scheme of organization. Wilson, in the final chapter of his book, "The Fusion of Social Studies in Junior High Schools," 1933, writes that the evidence at that time seemed to favor the teaching of subject courses. Many experienced teachers advocate teaching the various subjects of the social studies separately. They think that better results will be obtained. Some of the arguments for teaching the subjects separately follow:

1. It is not true that in life we study everything from the standpoint of the whole. If a big problem confronts us, we study different phases of it and then after making our study and collecting our data, we put things together and come to a final conclusion. Children should learn to make their own generalizations and not be encouraged to accept those made by specialists. Again, most of the people who advocate an integrated course do not practice what they preach. These same people, in solving an important problem, usually break it into parts before studying it. Even in our universities and training schools, subjects are still taught and most of them have few integrated courses in comparison to the number of courses on subject matter.

2. Pupils are unable to get the best results from their study if fusion units are taken. A fusion unit causes the pupils to branch out into many fields and they are swamped by a mass of material. The work is bound to be shallow, since the pupils have not had much experience in facing the problems of life. A large mass of complex data is collected. The pupils are likely to become confused and lost. Likewise, conclusions are drawn and many of them are probably inaccurate. In many cases, the teacher draws the conclusions for the pupils and poor habits of study are formed. The pupils are too young to handle such complicated masses of material.

3. In a fusion course where the work is taught around large units, there will be much valuable geography that a pupil will never get. Today, we must know the geography of our own country and of the other countries of the world if we are going to solve satisfactorily local, national, and international problems. People in all regions of the earth are interdependent. It is impossible to teach all the geography which pupils should have in a fusion course.

Likewise, in a fusion course, the pupils do not get all the history they should have in preparing themselves to meet successfully the problems of life. Certain values are obtained in the study of history which no fusion course can give. Similar statements may also be made for the other subjects in the social studies.

4. Practically all the values which are claimed for a fusion course may also be obtained by teaching subjects separately.

3. Conclusions

At the present time there is no satisfactory proof that teaching fusion courses is better than the teaching of the traditional subjects in the social studies. Many of the experiments that have been tried were carried out under conditions that might not give the same results a second or a third time. Much that has been written and said on the subject is merely the opinions of the speakers and writers. Enthusiastic teachers often work hard to put an idea across and they sometimes imagine results which never really occur. Some teachers like to depart from the customary way of doing something because they think this is a sign of progress. In the Eighth Yearbook of the National Council for the Social Studies, 1937, Dondineau and Dimond give the results of a study which they made of published materials on correlation involving the social studies. They state that the claims for special values for integration had not been proved up to that time. In fact, some of the studies seemed to favor integration, while others seemed to favor teaching by subjects.

In concluding, it should be stated that the teacher determines to a large extent the final results that pupils obtain in their study of problems and units. An enthusiastic teacher, filled with a knowledge of the subject and having a love for children and an interest in his work, cannot help but get good results no matter whether traditional subjects or a fusion course is taught. Very often it is the teacher and not the course of study that should be blamed for poor teaching.

It should be remembered that all subjects are related to one another. In teaching any one subject, we must not be afraid to use other subjects when it is necessary to make the meaning clearer. All the subjects which are taught help the pupils form the right ideals, habits, attitudes, and understandings which they need if they are going to live together as useful members of society. All educators admit that there is yet much to learn about our methods of teaching. Hence, teachers must be encouraged to experiment with the hope of finding some better method of organizing materials for teaching purposes.

THE PROGRAM OF THE SOCIAL STUDIES

One great question that confronts curriculum makers, as well as all teachers, is "What units or topics should be taught at the different grade levels?" Everyone generally agrees that the main objective of the social studies is to develop the individual into a good and useful citizen who believes in the American way of life. A person who is just beginning his service as a teacher might naturally imagine that there would be common agreement among educators on the program of the social studies which children should follow, since all of us have the same general objectives for teaching the social studies. However, there is no general agreement on the program in the social studies for the different grades above the primary grades. Probably this should be expected, since all teachers in a democracy have a right to think and to express their opinions, and since there is much more good material than any teacher can possibly find the time to teach to the pupils while they are in school.

It is often difficult to prove that one topic or unit should be taught in a certain grade in preference to some other topic or unit. Nevertheless, some teachers think that it would be a progressive step if there were more of an agreement among educators upon the program of the social studies for the different grades.

There is rather common agreement among school people about the program which should be followed in the kindergarten and the primary grades. In these grades the work centers around the interests of the child living in the community. Such topics as the school, the home, the neighborhood, and activities in the community are discussed.

No specific program for the social studies can be given here that will suit the majority of teachers, since no such program exists. After examining a large number of courses of study the following subjects were found to be commonly offered for the given grade levels:

Grades 1, 2, 3. The school, the home, the neighborhood, activities in the neighborhood, obtaining the necessities of life, simple facts about citizenship, American heroes and holidays.

Grade 4. Early American History, Indians, Home Geography, World Geography.

Grade 5. Early American History, Citizenship, Current Events, Geography of the United States and Continental Geography.

Grade 6. Recent American History or European Background of American History, State History, Continental Geography.

Grade 7. United States History, Regional and Economic Geography.

Grade 8. United States History, Civics, Study of the Community, Regional and Economic Geography of the United States and of the World.

Grade 9. Civics, Ancient and Medieval History.

Grade 10. World History, Modern European History.

Grade 11. United States History, Economics, Sociology, Industrial and Commercial Geography.

Grade 12. Problems of Democracy, United States History, Economics or Sociology, Civics or Government, Geography.

Probably the outline of courses which has just been mentioned is not very valuable, since it is general. If it succeeds in making the reader think a little more on the subject, then the author will feel that his outline has not been made in vain.

PROBLEMS FOR DISCUSSION AND RESEARCH

1. When we speak about the curriculum of a school, what do we mean? Examine a curriculum for the social studies before you give your answer.

2. Show how the curriculum has grown.

3. Why should a curriculum usually be revised in place of being totally made over?

4. Discuss the problem of selecting materials for the curriculum.

5. Explain the statement "Knowledge is Power."

6. Show how the social studies deal with human relations.

7. Discuss some of the factors that should be considered in selecting materials for the curriculum.

8. What people should make or revise the curriculum?

9. What are vertical articulation and horizontal articulation?

10. What mention should be made of community resources in the curriculum?

11. What should the curriculum do about individual differences?

12. Discuss the cycle plan of teaching the social studies.

13. Give the arguments for teaching history chronologically.

14. Give the arguments for teaching history backwards.

15. What use should be made of biographies?

16. Discuss integration or fusion versus subject matter organization. Give reasons for and against integration or fusion. Give arguments for and against subject matter organization.

17. What are the steps or procedures which are generally taken by committees in revising the curriculum?

18. Examine one or more curriculums for the social studies. Tell what materials are taught in the different grades.

REFERENCES

Baldwin, J. W., *A Survey of the Present Status and Current Trends in the Social Studies Curriculum in Texas Schools.* Austin: The University of Texas, 1941.

———, "The Dilemma of Social Studies Curriculum Committees," Social Education, IV, 242-246, April, 1940.

Barton, Thomas, "Primary Geography," The Journal of Geography, XXXIX, 243-246, September, 1940.

Bathurst, Effie, *Curriculum Content in Conservation for Elementary Schools,* Bulletin, 1939, No. 14. Washington: Superintendent of Documents.

Bining, Arthur and Bining, David, *Teaching the Social Studies in the Secondary Schools.* New York: McGraw-Hill Book Co., 1941.
    Chapter X. The Materials of Instruction, 184-201.

Bining, Arthur, Mohr, Walter, and McFeeley, Richard, *Organizing the Social Studies in Secondary Schools.* New York: McGraw-Hill Book Co., 1941. Chapters I, XIV, XV, XVI.

Bollinger, Clyde, "A Plan for the Correlation and Articulation of Geography, History, and Civics in the Junior High School," The Journal of Geography, XXXI, 245-252, September, 1932.

Bryan, Pauline, "The Unification of an Eighth Grade," High School Journal, XXIII, 366-372, December, 1940.

Burgess, H. O., "Integration Principles," Social Education, II, 21-24, January, 1938.

Burnham, Archer, "Basic Generalizations in Fourth Grade Geography," The Journal of Geography, XXXIX, 110-117, March, 1940.

———, "A Basic Reference List of Geographic Terms for Fourth Grade Geography," The Journal of Geography, XXXVIII, 283-288, October, 1939.

———, "Place Names in Fourth Grade Geography," The Journal of Geography, XXXVIII, 117-120, March, 1939.

Bruner, Herbert and others, *What Our Schools are Teaching.* New York: Bureau of Publications, Teachers College, 1941.

Chapter IV. Analysis of Selected Courses of Study in Social Studies, 112-148.

Chapter VI. Some Suggestions and Conclusions Emerging from this Study, 195-210.

Appendix I. Criteria for Evaluating Teaching and Learning Materials and Practices.

Crane, Katharine, "Teaching American Biography," Social Education, I, 421-434, September, 1937.

Falk, Ethel, "In Defense of Planning," Social Education, I, 495-498, October, 1937.

Forsythe, Marion, "Home Geography and Its Relation to the Elementary Course in Geography," The Journal of Geography, XXXII, 14-20, January, 1933.

Hahn, H. H., "The Teaching of Home Geography," The Journal of Geography, XXXVIII, 1-8, January, 1939.

Harper, C. A., "History as a Social Study," Education, LVII, 290-293, January, 1937.

Heffernan, Helen, An Experiencing Curriculum in the Social Studies, Twelfth Yearbook, National Council for the Social Studies, 1941, 57-77.

Hooper, Laura, "Children's Interests and the School Curriculum," American Childhood, XXII, 12-13, 57, May, 1937.

Hopkins, L. Thomas, "Making the Curriculum Functional," Teachers College Record, XLIII, 129-136, November, 1941.

Houston, Cole, "Objectives in High School Social Studies," The Social Studies, XXXI, 356-359, December, 1940.

Jensen, Alma, "On Trial—A Regional Program in Minnesota," Social Education, III, 554-561, November, 1939.

Johnson, Henry, Teaching of History. New York: The Macmillan Co., 1940. Chapters 4-8, 10, 15, 17.

Johnson, The Reverend George, "The Activity Curriculum in the Light of Catholic Principles," Catholic Educational Review, 65-72, February, 1941.

Kelty, Mary, The Selection and Adaptation of Subject Matter in the Social Studies, Twelfth Yearbook, National Council for the Social Studies, 1941, 78-100.

———, "Content for the Middle Grades," Social Education, I, 183-189, March, 1937.

———, "Middle Grade Sequences," Social Education, II, 549-558, November, 1938.

———, Learning and Teaching History in the Middle Grades. Boston: Ginn and Co., 1936, 10-19.

Kidger, Horace, "Organization for Curriculum Revision," The Social Studies, XXVII, 233-236, April, 1936.

Knowlton, Daniel, "Social Studies in the Intermediate Grades," Social Education, I, 409-414, September, 1937.

———, "Should the Social Studies Be Integrated?" School and Society, XV, 625-630, May 18, 1940.

Kopf, Helen, "One Cycle or Two Cycle Geography," The Journal of Geography, XXXI, 193-198, May, 1932.

Kronenberg, Henry, "Social Studies in the New Curriculum," Social Education, I, 344-350, May, 1937.

———, "Separate Subjects, Integration, and Problems," Social Education, II, 108-116, February, 1938.

———, editor, Programs and Units in the Social Studies. Washington: The National Council for the Social Studies, 1941.

Moffatt, M. P., "Student Reports in the Social Studies," The Social Studies, XXXII, 271-273, October, 1941.

Moran, Grace, "Pre-Geography Learnings Resulting from Community Life Studies," The Journal of Geography, XXXIV, 196-201, May, 1935.

Mudge, E. Leigh, "Humanizing Our National Heroes," Education, LVIII, 18-22, September, 1937.

National Council for the Social Studies, Sixth Yearbook, 1936. Anderson, H. and Hill, H., "The Correlation of Social Studies and Other Subjects," 171-197.

National Council for the Social Studies, Eighth Yearbook, 1937. Dondineau, Arthur and Dimond, Stanley, "Correlation Involving the Social Studies," 109-135.

National Society for the Study of Education, the Thirty-Second Yearbook, The Teaching of Geography. Bloomington: Public School Publishing Co., 1933.
    Sections II, III, and IV, pp. 73-314.
    Section VI, 431-539.

Nolan, M. Olive, "Correlation of Geography, History, Civics, and Economics," The Journal of Geography, XXVII, 76-81, February, 1928.

Park, Joe and Stephenson, O. W., "Clarifying Social Studies Terms," Social Education, IV, 311-317, May, 1940.

Parker, Edith, "Principles Underlying the Construction of a Geography Curriculum," The Journal of Geography, XXXII, 136-138, April, 1933.

Pease, Marion, "English Errors in Social Studies," High Points, XXIII, 50-52, February, 1941.

Pingrey, J. L., "A Junior High School Social Studies Curriculum," The Social Studies, XXVIII, 81-84, February, 1937.

Rennes, Mayme, "Geography in Poetry," The Journal of Geography, XXVIII, 292-298, October, 1929.

Research Bulletin of the National Education Association, XV, November, 1937. Chapters II and III.

Ridgley, Douglas, "Geography in the Elementary School as Revealed in Textbooks," The Journal of Geography, XXXIV, 237-243, September, 1935.

Robinson, T. H., "Unity in the Social Studies," Social Education, III, 631-635, December, 1939.

Rothwell, Ethel, "Some of the Outcomes of the Study of Foods," The Journal of Geography, XXXVII, 232-237, September, 1938.

Schuck, Myrna, "Curriculum Enrichment for Rapid Learners," Social Education, III, 173-177, March, 1939.

Schutte, T. H., *Teaching the Social Studies on the Secondary School Level.* New York: Prentice-Hall, 1938. Chapter V.

Schwarz, John, *Social Study in the Elementary School.* New York: Prentice-Hall, 1938. Chapter V.

Smith, Texie, "Making the Social Studies an Adventure in Individualized Teaching," The Social Studies, XXXII, 247-250, October, 1941.

Stadtlander, Elizabeth, "Geography as the Core in Unit of Thought Teaching," The Journal of Geography, XL, 19-23, January, 1941.

The Social Studies Curriculum, Fourteenth Yearbook of the Department of Superintendence of the National Education Association, 1936.

Part II. The Social Studies Curriculum, 51-280.

Part XIV. Continuous Curriculum Revision, 344-364.

Troelstrup, A. W., "Curriculum Materials on Housing," Social Education, III, 486-491, October, 1939.

Washburne, Carleton, "The Case for Subjects in the Curriculum," The Journal of the National Education Association, XXVI, 5, January, 1937.

Wasson, Roy, "Measuring Primary Grade Children's Understanding of Home and Family Relationships," The Elementary School Journal, XLI, 108-117, October, 1940.

Weisberg, B., "Should We Have an Integrated Social Science Course in Our Schools?" The Social Studies, XXXI, 59-61, February, 1940.

Wesley, Edgar, *Teaching the Social Studies.* New York: D. C. Heath and Co., 1937. Part Three.

——, The Nature and Functions of the Social Studies in the Elementary School, *Twelfth Yearbook, National Council for the Social Studies,* 1941, 47-56.

Whitney, Ronald, "Science Fairs for Correlation of Subject Matter," School Science and Mathematics, XLI, 447-448, May, 1941.

Wilson, Howard, *The Fusion of Social Studies in Junior High Schools.* Cambridge: Harvard University Press, 1933.

Wolfe, Alice, "Social Science in a Junior High School Core Curriculum," Social Education, V, 280-283, April, 1941.

Wood, Hugh B., "Modern Problems in the Curriculum," Social Education, IV, 90-93, February, 1940.

Young, William and Heyl, Helen, An Approach to a Social Studies Program in the Elementary Schools. Albany: University of the State of New York, 1939.

Chapter Eighteen: TESTING IN THE

SOCIAL STUDIES

HISTORY OF TESTING

TESTING IS almost as old as the human race. In those days of long ago, when writing was unknown and teaching was done by the parents, oral questions were frequently used by the father and mother to see if their children were learning the necessary things of life. Even after schools were started, the oral quiz was found to be very useful. During colonial times and in the early years of our republic, oral questions were usually used in place of written questions. We read about children being asked questions by their teachers and by prominent people in their neighborhood. Even a teacher was usually given an oral test by the school directors before he was employed to teach in a school. In those days, paper and writing materials were scarce; so it was only natural for most of the questions to be oral.

As schools became more numerous and as pencils, ink and writing paper became more common, written tests gradually grew in importance. Today, the written test is commonly used in all schools where children are old enough to write. The written test has largely taken the place of the oral test.

ORAL TESTS

The oral test may be used with much profit in a small class, but it is not adapted for testing a large class if the questions involve much thinking. For example, let us suppose a teacher has a class of thirty pupils and he is going to give them an oral test which involves considerable thinking on the part of the pupils. If each pupil is asked only one question during the period, this means that the teacher should have thirty good questions, because each pupil should be given a different question. However, no pupil can be said to have been given a fair test on a piece of work if he is given only one question to answer. There is always a possibility that a good student will get a question that he cannot answer, while a poor student may get a question that he can answer. To test fairly, each pupil usually should be asked several questions. This means that the teacher should think of a large number of good questions.

Again, if each pupil is given two minutes to answer a question orally, it would take a class of thirty pupils sixty minutes to complete the oral test. If each pupil is given two questions to answer, it would take two hours to hold the test. Of course, some pupils might need more time to answer their questions, others might need less time, but a question that involves thinking does take a certain amount of time. If a period for testing is too long, the pupils grow restless and inattentive. What often happens in an oral test is that a teacher gives questions to the pupils at such a rapid rate that they never have much time for thinking.

The oral test may be used where pupils are asked questions which involve little thinking and where the answers are given quickly and briefly. Oral questions often stimulate the pupils to work more diligently. They may guide them in their work by raising questions to study and by opening new lines of thought.

WHY GIVE TESTS?

Many pupils dislike to take tests because they have been led to think that the main function of a test is to decide the mark which they get in a subject. Modern educators no longer claim that this should be the chief function of tests, although some teachers do not know this. Tests should benefit both pupils and teachers. In those schools where tests are wisely used, pupils look upon them as an aid in doing their work.

Tests aid the pupils by showing them whether or not they are learning those things which they think they are learning. A pupil often thinks he clearly understands a problem and a test may prove that he is right. It gives him a certain amount of satisfaction to be able to prove that he has accomplished certain goals. On the other hand, a test may prove that the pupil does not understand the problem. If this is the case, he analyzes his method of attack to learn where improvements may be made.

If conducted in the right way, a test stimulates a pupil to do better work and to work more diligently. It causes him to review his work from time to time. A pupil is able to compare his rank with that of his classmates. If he learns that he ranks much lower than most of the other members of the class, he should be encouraged to see if he cannot work a little more efficiently to raise his mark. On the other hand, if he ranks high he should be encouraged to continue the fine work which he is doing. A teacher should be very careful to see that the pupils do not become discouraged when they learn that they rank low in their work. A little praise given at the right time will cause anyone to have more faith in himself.

Tests are often given at the end of a unit or at certain places to help pupils organize their work and to fix in mind some of the important things which they should remember. They act somewhat as a reminder to pupils that it is time for them to stop and take stock of what they have been doing.

Tests benefit the teacher in a number of ways. They show the teacher what the pupils are actually accomplishing. If the pupils indicate by their tests that they are learning to solve problems, the teacher has the right to feel that he is using good methods of teaching. On the other hand, the teacher should change his methods of teaching if the tests show that pupils are doing poor work or are not progressing at a fair rate of speed. Too many teachers blame the pupils for failing in a test when the blame should fall upon themselves. If a series of tests shows that the pupils are not making the right progress, a teacher should immediately begin to try to learn the reasons for the poor work of the pupils. If normal pupils who attend school regularly fail in their work, the fault lies with the teacher and those who are in charge of the school, not with the pupils. There should be no failures among such children. Teachers are employed to teach children. Teaching means more than hearing lessons and drawing a salary. Many teachers seem to have the mistaken idea that children somehow will learn to form good habits of study and to solve problems without receiving much aid or guidance from them. Those teachers who fail to profit by their mistakes and who are unable to change their methods to bring about more desirable results should look for some other position than that of teaching the social studies.

A test often shows the teacher that the pupils are doing poor thinking. It may help to locate certain errors that the children are making. The pupils may be confused about certain terms and the knowledge they have of them may be shown to be inaccurate. A test gives the teacher an excellent opportunity of helping pupils form right ideas and of spurring them on to do good thinking.

A test is often given by a teacher at the beginning of a unit to learn what the pupils know about the new work which they are going to study. Such a test shows the teacher what topics to stress. There is no need of teaching topics that the pupils already know. Sometimes a test shows it would be a waste of time for most of the pupils to study the unit. At other times, a test may show that the pupils have very little knowledge of the new unit.

A teacher sometimes gives tests to learn how his pupils rank (1) among one another, (2) with the members of similar classes in other rooms, and (3) with similar classes in other schools.

Certain dangers sometimes arise when tests are misused and when the teacher and pupils do not fully understand the value of tests. Some of these dangers are cheating, cramming, nervousness, and poor habits of study. There is no need for such dangers to occur and they are not likely to occur in a room where tests are correctly used. Pupils should become accustomed to being tested, because when they leave school they will learn that they must undergo many tests in facing the problems of life. Life is made up of test after test. The person who is able to pass them successfully is the one who is succeeding. It is only when a person fails to meet his tests successfully that he is on the decline.

In judging the pupil, many other factors, besides tests or examinations, should be considered. The daily work and the judgment of the teacher are very important. A pupil should form the habit of working steadily and not just before a test is given. If an experienced teacher has been with a pupil for a number of months, he should be able to form a rather accurate opinion of the quality of work which the pupil is doing.

KINDS OF TESTS

There are different ways of classifying tests. Broadly speaking, tests may be grouped as (1) essay tests and (2) objective tests. Essay questions generally require rather detailed descriptions and lengthy answers, while objective questions usually require only checks or very short answers. Essay questions are more difficult to mark accurately than objective questions. Another name for the objective type of tests is the new type examination.

Tests may be classed as standardized and non-standardized tests. A standardized test is one that has been given to a large number of pupils in different parts of the country. From the scores which the pupils made, certain standards have been set up which may be used to make comparisons when other pupils take the test. The ordinary tests which teachers make for use in their schoolrooms are not standardized because they have not been tried out in many places.

Tests may also be classed as intelligence tests, achievement tests, and diagnostic tests. Intelligence tests are used to test general intelligence and are composed of many different items. However, we are not sure just what intelligence tests actually measure. Achievement tests are used to show the progress of pupils in the work which they are studying. Final examinations are usually achievement tests. Diagnostic tests are used to obtain various kinds of information about individual pupils so that the instruction may be adapted to their needs. There is sometimes no difference between an achievement test and a diagnostic test. However, many tests are used chiefly for diagnostic purposes.

ESSAY TESTS

Many teachers prefer to use both essay tests and objective tests. Both groups of tests occupy important places in teaching. Each type of test is especially valuable for measuring those qualities which the other test does not measure so well. The essay test is especially valuable for measuring the ability of a pupil to reason, to develop a line of thought in writing, to organize materials, to describe events and places, to express himself clearly and accurately, and to show his appreciation and attitude toward the people of other lands. It is usually not so good for the recall of specific information as the objective test. Some arguments against essay tests are (1) they are time consuming, (2) they cover less ground than the new type objective tests, (3) the questions are often indefinite, and (4) their marking is difficult and frequently inaccurate, since teachers do not agree on the interpretations of the answers.

Essay tests may often be improved. Many teachers do not realize that it takes time to make good essay tests. Some teachers hurriedly construct questions without giving much thought to the objectives which they are testing and to the answers which they are expecting the pupils to make. An essay question should be clear and meaningful to the pupils. It should be definite enough so that the pupils will feel sure they are proceeding along the right lines in answering it. Before making the test, the teacher should determine what objectives he wishes to examine. When marking a paper, he should not try to judge it for very many things at a single reading. If the teacher has several important purposes in mind, it is highly desirable for him to read each paper more than once.

Without giving the question much thought, many teachers might think that there would be no difference in the preparation of the pupils for taking either an essay test or an objective test. However, when a test is announced in the upper grades or high school, the pupils often ask what kind of test it will be. Some students study differently for different kinds of tests. If the test is of the essay type, the pupils will likely give more attention to organizing the material and to forming conclusions than to the memorizing of details. On the other hand, if the test is to be of the objective type, the pupils will likely try to memorize facts and details. Some of them may even try to memorize the words of the book. Since there seems to be a difference in the way many pupils prepare for the two kinds of tests, some teachers think it is a good plan to give both types of tests at one time. Then the pupils will be sure to prepare for the test in the best possible manner.

OBJECTIVE TESTS

There are many reasons why objective tests came into use. As progress was made in teaching, it was only natural that we should improve our methods of testing. As we keep on making progress, we will continue to improve our testing methods.

One of the main reasons for introducing objective tests was that many teachers and pupils were dissatisfied with essay tests. Teachers often found it to be difficult to give satisfactory explanations to a pupil about the marking of the questions. The pupils often thought that their papers were marked unfairly. In many cases, they were probably correct in thinking as they did, but the teachers were not to blame. The teachers did not intend to mark the papers unfairly, but various factors tended to make the exact marking of essay questions a difficult task.

Let us suppose that five teachers are grading the same set of essay questions. In place of each paper receiving a single mark, it will likely receive five different marks. Each teacher uses his judgment in marking the papers and his judgment is somewhat different from that of the other teachers. Again, many personal factors influence the grading of essay questions. As the examiner grows tired, he is likely to change the standards of grading. If he feels well and happy, he may grade a set of papers differently than if he feels sick and gloomy. Sometimes a teacher thinks of the pupil who wrote the answers he is grading. If he thinks favorably of the pupil, he may tend to mark the answers higher than if he thinks unfavorably of him. Many teachers are unconsciously influenced in their marking of papers by their feelings toward the pupils. Hence, we often speak about the grading of essay tests as being subjective.

It is also true that some teachers mark higher than other teachers in a school system. The pupils who receive high marks from a teacher who marks high may not be doing any better work than the pupils in a room who receive low marks from a low-marking teacher. The children usually know the high markers and the low markers. Essay tests are likely to cause the difference between the marks of the high-marking teachers and the low-marking teachers to be greater than if objective tests are used.

Objective tests have certain advantages over essay tests. The answers are definite, since there is only one right answer to each question. This means that any teacher marking a paper will give the same mark as any other teacher. He will also be able to mark a paper quickly. A greater range of information may be tested during a stated time. Most questions require very short answers such as a check, a single word, the underlining of some word or group of words, or the filling in of a blank. Many questions may be answered in a short period of time, since there is so little writing to do.

Teachers should keep in mind certain facts when they use objective tests. In the first place, much time is required to construct a good set of objective questions, usually much more time than a large number of teachers are willing to spend. In the second place, it is easier to make questions which measure the recall of information, in place of making questions which measure appreciations, attitudes, skills, personality, character, and the ability of reasoning and interpreting facts and of using necessary materials. Pupils with good memories are often able to put down many correct answers even though they do not understand what they write. In the third place, objective tests usually do not require much organization of facts and they generally do not furnish an opportunity for pupils to develop a certain line of thought. In the fourth place, objective tests may encourage guessing.

A problem which confronts the teacher who makes his own objective tests is how to get the tests before the pupils. Essay tests may usually be written upon the blackboard because they do not take up much space. Since a set of objective tests has many questions, it is frequently impractical to write the tests upon the board. There is generally not enough blackboard space that can be seen from all parts of the room. It is also usually a poor plan to read the questions to the pupils, since the pupils may have difficulty in hearing and understanding them. The best way of getting the tests before the pupils is to reproduce them on paper by means of some kind of a duplicating machine.

QUALITIES OF GOOD TESTS

A good test should measure what it is supposed to measure. This is called validity. For example, if the test is to measure the ability of pupils to locate places and to recognize dates, there should be ample opportunity for the pupils to do these activities.

A good test should possess reliability. This means that if the pupils in a class should take the test a second time, they would be ranked practically the same as they were the first time they took the test; providing conditions have not changed very much. A good test should possess objectivity. This means that any number of people are able to score it and get the same results, since all scorers have the same answers in mind.

A good test should be clear and meaningful to the pupils and it should arouse their interests and cause them to develop good habits of study. It should not be too difficult nor too easy for those who take it. Neither should it be too long nor too short. It should examine enough of the material so that the knowledge of the pupils will be fairly tested and the teacher will be able to determine something about their reasoning abilities. A good test skilfully conducted should cause closer relationships to exist between the teacher and the pupils.

TYPES OF TESTS

Every teacher should know some of the common types of tests and how to construct them. It is usually advisable for the teacher to make his own tests on the units which the pupils study. In teaching a unit, the teacher has certain objectives in mind which he wants the pupils to obtain. Tests show if his pupils have obtained these objectives. It is often impossible for a teacher to buy tests that cover satisfactorily the work he has been teaching. Again, many teachers can make more suitable tests for their work than some outside person who has no direct contact with the children who are to be tested. Therefore, the teacher makes most of the tests which are used in his classes.

Some of the more common types of objective tests are (1) the true-false test, (2) the completion test, (3) the matching test, (4) the arrangement test, and (5) the multiple choice test. Examples of these tests follow.

TRUE-FALSE TEST

Probably the true-false test is the best known of the objective tests. Pupils are asked to mark in a certain way whether a statement is true or false. They are to think carefully before making up their minds about a statement. Some people object to this type of test because untrue statements are put before pupils as if they were true. They think that the pupils will likely have the untrue statements impressed upon their minds in such a manner that confused thinking may result in later life. There is probably nothing to this belief. However, to make sure that nothing like this happens, the teacher and pupils should always go over the questions after the papers have been corrected and returned.

Another criticism of the true-false test is that it encourages guessing more than most other kinds of tests. Of course a pupil has a fifty-fifty chance of getting the statements right. To overcome the danger of guessing, a large number of statements should be given.

Examples of true-false statements follow:

Test I

DIRECTIONS: Some of the following statements are true, others are false. Think carefully as you read each statement. Underline the word "true" if the statement is true, underline the word "false" if the statement is false.

True   False   1. Alaska is larger than Texas.

True   False   2. The United States has fewer people than the continent of South America.

True   False   3. Washington was the first president of the United States.

True   False   4. A person must be at least 21 years old to be able to vote for the president of the United States.

True   False   5. The Mississippi River was discovered by Balboa.

Test II

The yes-no type of question is practically the same as the true-false type, except that the question is answered by yes or no. For example:

Read each question carefully. Write yes if the answer is yes, write no if the answer is no.

..........1. Is Chicago the largest city on Lake Michigan?

..........2. Is there an election for president of the United States every four years?

.........3. Did McCormick invent the sewing machine?

.........4. Has any president of the United States ever been elected for a third term?

.........5. Does the United States rank first in the mining of coal?

COMPLETION TEST

The completion test is much used for testing information and thinking. Blanks are to be completed with the correct words. It takes time to make a good completion test, although some teachers do not realize this. Teachers should not copy sentences from textbooks, omitting certain words for the blank spaces, because this will tend to cause pupils to try to memorize certain sentences in their book. The completion test should call for specific information which well-informed pupils should be able to give.

Examples of completion tests follow:

Test I

In the following sentences the blanks stand for missing words. Read each sentence carefully and try to fill in the blanks correctly. The name of a person, the name of a place, a date, or other information should be put in each blank.

1. The cotton gin was invented in ....
2. The Pacific Ocean was discovered by ....
3. The capital of the United States is .... It is on the .... River.
4. The president of the United States is elected every .... years.
5. The four cities in the United States having the most people are ...., ..., ..., and ....

Test II

Read each question carefully. Write the correct answer in the blank at the end of the sentence.

1. What country mines the most iron ore? ....
2. What is the leading port in the United States? ....

3. What is the name of the continent around the South Pole?
. . . .

4. With what colony was Captain John Smith associated?
. . . .

5. What great event took place on July 4, 1776? . . . .

MATCHING TEST

The matching test is very good for testing the understanding of relationships, as well as for specific information. It is well adapted for reviews. It consists of two columns of items. The items in one column are to be identified or matched with the descriptive items in the other column. There should usually be no more than eight or ten items in a column. The second column should have a larger number of items than the first column so that some of the answers may not be obtained by the process of elimination. Generally speaking, matching tests are easy to make and to correct.

Examples of matching tests follow:

Test I

Two columns of items are given. The dates in the first column tell when five of the events in the second column happened. Place the number of the date in the first column before the event to which it belongs in the second column.

1. 1492   . . . . The first World War began.
2. 1607   . . . . The Revolutionary War ended.
3. 1914   . . . . The Erie Canal was completed.
4. 1789   . . . . The cotton gin was invented.
5. 1825   . . . . Columbus discovered North America.
         . . . . George Washington became president.
         . . . . Jamestown was settled.

Test II

The items in the first column tell something about some of the items in the second column. Place the number of each item in the first column before the item in the second column to which it belongs.

1. Largest city in the United States. . . . . .Atlantic City
2. A great iron and steel center   . . . . .Akron
3. Center of the motion picture in-
dustry   . . . . .Salt Lake City
4. A great resort city   . . . . .Pittsburgh
5. A great rubber manufacturing
city   . . . . .Boston
                                    . . . . .New York City
                                    . . . . .Los Angeles

ARRANGEMENT TEST

Tests may be used to learn if pupils are able to arrange certain events or places according to some scheme. Events may be arranged according to time. Places may be arranged according to size or location in certain regions. Other arrangement schemes may be used.

Examples of arrangement tests follow:

Test I

Five events are given in the first column. Think carefully and arrange them in the second column in the order in which they happened, beginning with the earliest event.

Events	Order of Happening
1. First successful airplane flight in America	1. . . . .
2. Invention of the cotton gin	2. . . . .
3. Invention of the steamboat	3. . . . .
4. Invention of the telephone	4. . . . .
5. Invention of the telegraph	5. . . . .

Test II

Five countries are listed in the first column. Arrange the countries in the second column according to their areas, beginning with the largest.

Countries	According to Areas from the Largest to the Smallest
1. Panama	1. ....
2. Brazil	2. ....
3. Mexico	3. ....
4. United States	4. ....
5. Canada	5. ....

Test III

Arrange the following regions in order of their distances from the equator, beginning with the region nearest the equator.

Regions	Order of Distance from the Equator
1. Mexico	1. ....
2. United States	2. ....
3. Northern Brazil	3. ....
4. Alaska	4. ....
5. Southern Canada	5. ....

MULTIPLE CHOICE TEST

Some teachers believe that the multiple choice tests are the most valuable tests in the social studies. It is claimed that they measure information, relationships, attitudes, and certain other elements. Two simple kinds of multiple choice tests are (1) the correct answer and (2) the best reason. In the correct answer test, the pupil selects the correct answer from four or more possible answers, only one of which is correct.

Test I

Only one correct answer is given in each of the following statements. Place a check before the correct answer in each statement.

1. Cincinnati is on
   (1) Lake Michigan

(2) the Mississippi River

(3) the Ohio River

(4) the Missouri River

(5) Lake Erie

2. In 1850, if a person wanted to travel from New Orleans to St. Louis in the shortest possible time, he would have got passage on

(1) an airplane

(2) a steamboat

(3) a train

(4) a stagecoach

(5) a bus

3. The first capital of the United States was

(1) Philadelphia

(2) New York City

(3) Washington

(4) Baltimore

(5) Boston

Test II

In the best reason test, the pupil selects the best reason from four or more reasons, all of which are correct. Examples of the best reason test follow.

Check the best reason which is given for each of the following statements:

1. Chicago is a great city because

(1) of its location near the southern bend of Lake Michigan.

(2) it is within easy shipping distance of coal fields and iron ore fields.

(3) it has good railroad transportation.

(4) it has a fine climate.

(5) it has energetic people.

2. The Louisiana Territory was purchased from France because

(1) it had many resources which would make our country greater and stronger.

(2) of the love for expansion of the American people.

(3) there was danger that France would sell the land to

some other country, and the interior people of the
United States wanted to get control of New Orleans,
which was in the territory.

(4) the American people wanted it since it was rich in
fur-bearing animals and it would make fine land to
settle.

OTHER TYPES OF TESTS

Other tests are given on the use of maps, pictures, graphs,
books, and similar materials. Pupils should be tested on their
ability to get information from all these materials. Outline maps
are especially good for measuring the ability of pupils to understand location. A simple way of giving a test on the location of
places is to give the children an outline map. As the teacher
names the places, they are located on the map. Many kinds of
relationships may also be developed by using maps. The resourceful teacher can think of many ways of testing the class.

A FINAL WORD

During recent years, great improvement has been made in
testing, but there is still room for much more improvement. Attempts have been made to measure something more than mere
information, and much real gain has been made. It is very difficult
to measure such elements as skills, attitudes, habits of study,
critical thinking, the ability to work independently, the ability
to work in groups, honesty, morality, character, good citizenship,
judgment, and self-control. Probably some teachers make greater
claims for their tests than the results seem to justify.

In measuring the work of the pupils and the progress they are
making, many factors should be considered. However, the teacher
can never have all the evidence which is actually needed to determine whether a pupil will be a successful citizen in a future
changing society. Such evidence is bound to be limited. The
teacher should not be discouraged. He should try to place before
each pupil many worthwhile and wholesome experiences, which
will help him to live a useful and enjoyable life now and in the
future.

Written and oral tests probably never will be able to measure satisfactorily all the traits of a pupil. For example, a written or an oral test may show that a pupil knows (1) he should look up the meaning of new words in a dictionary, (2) he should cooperate with his neighbors, (3) he should not cheat, (4) he should study his work diligently, and (5) he should be a good citizen in the school. Knowing such things does not always mean that a pupil will do them. Many pupils know better than to act the way they do, yet they go ahead anyway.

The teacher should not rely only upon written and oral tests for judging his pupils. Among other things he should observe (1) the actions of the pupils on and off the school grounds, (2) the interest of the pupils in their work and their attitude towards one another, (3) the work done by the pupils, and (4) the willingness of the pupils to assume responsibility and to work independently. The judgment of the teacher is of value in evaluating those traits which tests do not measure.

AVOIDING COMMON ERRORS

There are a large number of common errors which many people make in the social studies, even though they have a fairly good education. Probably the chief reason for such errors is that their teachers took too much for granted. Many teachers make the common mistake of thinking that since the meaning of a term is clear to them, it is bound to be clear to their pupils. They also often go on the erroneous supposition that just because a pupil recites very well it is a good sign that he clearly understands what he is saying. Teachers should endeavor to make sure that pupils really understand the fundamental facts and not take too much for granted.

A short test based on mistakes which people commonly make in geography is given here. The correct answers are given at the left of the statements. Enough questions are listed to show the teacher the possibilities of making similar tests.

Yes	1.	Is a cyclone different from a tornado?
No	2.	Is a mountain always higher than a hill?
Yes	3.	Does a branch of a river flow towards the main stream?
No	4.	Is a river system the same as a drainage basin?

Yes   5. If a person goes upstream is he traveling against the current?

No   6. Are all plains on the earth almost as level as the top of a table?

No   7. Is a peninsula a body of land surrounded by water only on three sides?

No   8. Is the beginning of a river its mouth and is the end of a river its source?

No   9. Do the words "climate," "weather," "rainfall," and "temperature" mean practically the same?

Yes 10. Is a mountain peak different from a mountain range?

No 11. Do the words "products," "industries," and "occupations" mean practically the same?

No 12. Is any large piece of floating ice in the ocean an iceberg?

No 13. Is it usually correct to say up north and down south?

Yes 14. Are deserts frequently found on the leeward sides of mountains?

No 15. Is a country the same as a continent?

No 16. Do few rivers flow north because they would be flowing up hill?

No 17. Is a parallel the same as latitude?

No 18. Is longitude the same as a meridian?

Yes 19. Do all deserts receive rain at some time?

No 20. Is it always correct to say that the farther we go southward the warmer it becomes?

No 21. Are all very hot places found within a few miles of the equator?

No 22. Is the sun directly overhead at the equator during every day of the year?

No 23. Are all very cold places found within a few miles of the poles?

No 24. Is our cold weather due to the fact that the sun is farthest from the earth in winter?

No 25. Do most Eskimos live in snow houses and do they live in a land where the sun never shines for six months at a time?

Yes 26. Does snow sometimes fall at certain places near the equator?

Yes   27. Are some places in the Torrid Zone very cold?

No   28. Is all the land in the North Polar Region always covered with ice and snow?

Yes   29. If a person travels from 30 degrees north latitude to 10 degrees south latitude is he going southward?

Yes   30. Does green vegetation grow in places in the North Polar Region in summer?

Many common errors are made by children in history and civics. A brief test is given here to show the teacher the possibilities of making similar tests. The correct answers are given to the left of each question.

No   1. Is the President of the United States elected by the direct votes of the people?

Yes   2. Does the Secretary of State succeed to the presidency of the United States in case of the death of both the President and the Vice-President?

No   3. Are the judges of the Supreme Court elected by the people?

No   4. May a naturalized citizen become President of the United States?

Yes   5. Does the United States have laws which limit the number of immigrants which can come to our country?

Yes   6. Are members of the House of Representatives elected for a term of two years and are members of the Senate elected for a term of six years?

Yes   7. Is a senator a congressman?

Yes   8. May a person become a member of Congress who was born in a foreign country?

Yes   9. Is it possible for a woman to become President of the United States?

No   10. Is being nominated for an office the same as being elected to it?

No   11. Did Eli Whitney discover the cotton gin?

No   12. Does explore mean the same as discover?

Yes   13. May every state have two senators in Congress?

Yes   14. May a President serve for more than two terms?

No   15. Is the Declaration of Independence the same as the Constitution of the United States?

PROBLEMS FOR DISCUSSION AND RESEARCH

1. Make a list of the ways in which tests benefit teachers.
2. Make a list of the ways in which tests benefit pupils.
3. What are the advantages and disadvantages of using oral tests?
4. What are the advantages and disadvantages of using essay tests?
5. List the advantages and disadvantages of using objective tests.
6. List the qualities of a good test.
7. Name the chief types of objective tests. Illustrate each type.
8. What are some of the mistakes that teachers frequently make in respect to tests?
9. Should children be permitted to help the teacher correct tests?
10. What should be done with the papers after they have been corrected by the teacher?
11. Could a good teacher get along without giving tests?
12. Examine a course of study and learn what units are taught in a given grade. Make a study of one of the units. Make a series of tests which may be given to the pupils after they finish a study of the unit.
13. Suppose you are a teacher in the sixth grade. How would you use tests? When would you use tests? Where would you get tests to use? Would it be wise to let the pupils help you make tests?
14. Make a list of the common errors in history which adults frequently make.
15. Make a list of the common errors in geography which adults frequently make.
16. Make a list of the common errors in civics which adults frequently make.

REFERENCES

Anderson, Howard, "Increased Efficiency in Grading Examinations," Social Education, III, 30-32, January, 1939.

———, "Testing in the Social Studies," Education, LIX, 545-549. May, 1938.

Association of Social Studies Teachers of New York City, A Teaching Guide for the Social Studies. New York: College Entrance Book Co., 1941, 163-172.

Baker, Emily, "Diagnosing Children's Ability to Use Maps," The Journal of Geography, XXXVII, 227-231, September, 1938.

Bining, Arthur, and Bining, David, Teaching the Social Studies in the Secondary Schools. New York: McGraw-Hill Book Co., 1941.

Chapter XVII. Tests and Measurements, 313-337.

330   TEACHING THE SOCIAL STUDIES

Branom, M. E. and Branom, F. K., *The Teaching of Geography*. Boston: Ginn and Co., 1921.
Part VI. Tests and Scales, 265-288.

Cain, Maud, "A Study of Thirteen Standard Geography Tests," The Journal of Geography, XXXIV, 252-256, September, 1935.

Collins, A. W., "Pupil Comprehension of Place Location Data in High School United States History," The Journal of Geography, XXXVIII, 325-329, November, 1939.

Frederick, Robert and Sheats, Paul, *Citizenship Education Through The Social Studies*. New York: Row, Peterson and Co., 1936.
Chapter X. Testing in the Social Studies, 225-250.

Galford, Mary, "Socialized Geography Tests," The Journal of Geography, XL, 259-261, October, 1941.

Hamalainen, A. E., "Evaluation in the Social Studies," The Social Studies, 250-252, October, 1937.

Jessop, Grace, "A Map for Diagnostic Purposes," The Journal of Geography, XXXVII, 112-115, March, 1938.

Johnson, Henry, *Teaching of History*. New York: The Macmillan Co., 1940. Chapter XVIII. The Examination, 362-390.

Kelly, Truman and Krey, A. C., *Tests and Measurements in the Social Studies*. New York: Charles Scribner's Sons, 1934.

Kronenberg, Henry, The Influence of Objective Testing on Methods of Teaching. *Fifth Yearbook, National Council for the Social Studies,* 1935, 196-204.

Lacey, Joy, *Teaching the Social Studies in the Elementary School*. Minneapolis: Burgess Publishing Co., 1941. Chapter VIII, 79-86.

Lefever, D. Welty, "What Every Classroom Teacher Should Know About Testing," Education, LVIII, 520-522, May, 1938.

Lord, F. E., "Diagnosing Study Difficulties in Elementary Geography," Educational Method, XVII, 273-277, March, 1938.

Mikesell, Ruth, "Geographic Tests: A Tool of Guidance," School Science and Mathematics, XLI, 517-520, June, 1941.

Moore, Clyde and Wilcox, Lillian, *The Teaching of Geography*. New York: American Book Co., 1932.
Chapter XVII. The Use of Standardized and Informal Tests, 227-240.

National Society for the Study of Education, the Thirty-Second Yearbook, *The Teaching of Geography*. Bloomington: Public School Publishing Co., 1933.
Chapter XXI. Testing in the Field of Geography, 333-344.

Parker, Edith, "The Technique of Error Diagnosis in Geographic Instruction," Educational Method, XVII, 269-272, March, 1938.

Pressey, Luella, "Fundamental Vocabulary in Elementary School Geography," The Journal of Geography, XXXIII, 78-81, February, 1933.

Research Bulletin of the National Education Association, XV, November, 1937, Chapter VII. Standard Tests in the Social Studies, 232-237.

Schutte, T. H., *Teaching the Social Studies on the Secondary School Level.* New York: Prentice-Hall, 1938.
Chapter IX. Testing, Measuring, and Examining, 466-562.

Schwarz, John, *Social Study in the Elementary School.* New York: Prentice-Hall, 1938.
Chapter XI. How to Test for Results, 183-203.

Shoen, Harriet, "Work Exercises and Test Items, A Contrast of Purpose," Social Education, II, 333-340, May, 1938.

Smith, Harry, "The Use of Standardized Tests," The Journal of Geography, XXXVI, 93-98, March, 1937.

Svec, M. Melvina, "A Method of Testing," The Journal of Geography, XXXII, 295-297, October, 1933.

Taba, Hilda, General Principles and New Practices in Evaluation, *Twelfth Yearbook, National Council for the Social Studies,* 1941, 215-229.

* *The Social Studies Curriculum,* Fourteenth Yearbook of the Department of Superintendence. Washington: National Education Association, 1936.
Chapter XIII. Evaluating the Outcomes of the Social Studies Curriculum, 312-343.

Uttley, Marguerite, "Fourth Grade Geography Test," The Journal of Geography, XXXIX, 269-273, October, 1940.

Wesley, Edgar, *Teaching the Social Studies.* New York: D. C. Heath and Co., 1937, Chapter XXXIII, 569-603.

Wrightstone, J. Wayne, Measuring and Evaluating in a Specific Social Studies Situation, *Twelfth Yearbook, National Council for the Social Studies,* 1941, 230-243.

———, "Recent Trends in Social Tests," Social Education, I, 246-250, April, 1937.

———, "Are Essay Examinations Obsolete?" Social Education, XXVIII, 401-406, September, 1937.

———, "What Do You Know About Testing?" Social Education, II, 385-386, September, 1938.

———, "Let's Measure Our Social Studies," Indiana Teacher, LXXXV, 187-207, February, 1941.

———, Testing in the Social Studies, *Eighth Yearbook, National Council for the Social Studies,* 1937, 207-239.

INDEX